Does It Follow?

A First Course in Logic

Patrick Kenny

Kendall Hunt
publishing company

Cover image © Shutterstock, Inc.

Kendall Hunt
publishing company

www.kendallhunt.com
Send all inquiries to:
4050 Westmark Drive
Dubuque, IA 52004-1840

Copyright © 2018 by Patrick Kenny

ISBN 978-1-5249-4931-0

Published in the United States of America

Contents

Preface

To the Instructor

My goal in this book is simple: to guide first-time students of formal logic through the fundamentals of the discipline. There are different kinds of first-time logic students, of course, and I have tried to keep each one in mind. Some students will be taking a logic course to satisfy a requirement in their computer science program, for example, and so will already have some skill in thinking abstractly. Such students will embrace the rigor contained in the book, and begin to understand the affinity computer science has with logic and philosophy. Other students will already be thinking of pursuing more advanced courses in philosophy and logic, and the book provides all the necessary foundational materials for such a pathway. Still other students will be taking a logic course merely to satisfy a general education requirement. These students will be thankful for the informal and user-friendly manner in which difficult concepts and methods are described, and will hopefully be empowered to apply what they learn in logic to issues they encounter in other disciplines. I have also kept in mind the fact that taking a logic class has been the gateway to philosophy for more than a few of my students. In general, my intention is that anyone who absorbs the concepts and methods found in the book will have secured for themselves a solid logical foundation for whatever pathway they are on.

I love teaching logic. My general take is that it's all about communicating to students how, once we appreciate the importance of reasoning in our lives, or in our studies, we can roll up our sleeves and try to understand the general features of how to reason *well*. As an introductory text, this book does not give students or readers the *whole* story of course, but hopefully it will provide a decent flavor of the discipline. I have, of course, learned a lot about how to teach the subject from the excellent textbooks that I have used over the years: Howard Pospesel's *Introduction to Logic: Propositional Logic*, Patrick Hurley's *A Concise Introduction to Logic*, Stan Baronett's *Logic*, and P. D. Magnus's *For All X*.[1] Each of these texts takes a different pedagogical approach to the subject. This book represents my own approach: as a book on formal logic, it is rigorous when it needs to be; but, as an introductory text, it is patient and encouraging in all the right places. Such, at least, was my purpose in writing the book.

Here is a brief overview of what is covered in the pages that follow:

- Chapter 1 introduces the basics of the discipline of logic: what motivates the study of reasoning, and how we can go about doing it. As is appropriate in an introductory text, I make explicit how the subject matter can be narrowed down into something manageable. The student is left in no doubt: we are focusing on *sentences in the logical sense*, and *deductive arguments* composed of these kinds of sentences; the main concern will be *deductive validity*—checking for validity will be the specific way of approaching the question of the book's title: *Does it follow?*
- Chapter 2 gets going on logical form. I introduce the language of Sentential Logic (SL), and students learn how to capture the logical form of sentences and arguments with this new formal language. Each truth-functional sentence operator is covered in some detail, and there are lots of in-text examples, as well as exercises, that gently guide the student through the translation process.
- Chapters 3 and 4 cover truth tables. Ultimately, of course, truth tables provide us with a way of checking an SL argument for validity, though students also encounter many of the other tasks for which truth tables are appropriate: categorizing an individual sentence as a tautology, contradiction, or contingent sentence;

---

[1]For full bibliographic details for these texts, see the Bibliography.

checking pairs of sentences for logical equivalence; checking sets of sentences for logical consistency. I have also included a section on the brief truth-table method for checking an argument for validity.

- In Chapter 5, students learn how to construct proofs within a natural deduction system. The system I use is based on that found in the aforementioned Pospesel and Magnus texts, in which each sentence operator of SL is ascribed an Introduction inference rule and an Elimination inference rule. I have found that students appreciate the simplicity of this approach to proofs. Chapter 6 covers some derived inference rules for the natural deduction system and also introduces students to some substitution rules.

- Chapter 7 introduces students to Predicate Logic (PL), which is explicitly characterized as an extension of SL. Here, students learn how to ramp up their translation skills so as to capture the logical form of sentences and arguments in this new formal language. The quantifiers receive extensive treatment, and sections on multiple quantifiers and identity are included.

- In Chapter 8, after getting some practice with translating arguments into the language of PL, students are guided through the construction of proofs in this language. Five new inference rules are added to the natural deduction system we developed for SL: an Introduction and Elimination rule for each of the quantifiers, plus one substitution rule: Quantifier Exchange. The chapter does not cover proofs involving nested quantifiers or identity. The counterexample method of checking a PL argument for invalidity is also covered, though I have decided to exclude discussion of what is sometimes called the finite universe method, which involves the construction of models or interpretations.

Each chapter—indeed, each section of each chapter—contains many practice questions, with which students can familiarize themselves with the concepts and methods covered. Each exercise set begins with questions that invite the student to complete his/her answer in the book. Other questions require students to work on a separate sheet of paper.

Finally, thank you for choosing to assign my book for your logic class. Please feel free to share any feedback you might have. You can email me at kennyp@sunyocc.edu.

To the Student

Welcome to the discipline of logic! Thanks for dropping in on the preface. I will outline just three points that will serve as a heads-up on what you will encounter in this book:

- First, here is an initial definition of the subject matter: logic is the study of reasoning and how to systematically differentiate between good reasoning and bad reasoning.

- Second, this focus on reasoning means that logic has been a traditional part of the discipline of philosophy. (Your instructor is probably from your institution's philosophy department). If you leaf quickly through the chapters, however, you will see lots of symbols that suggest a different academic discipline: mathematics. This might make you want to get started on logic right away . . . or it may fill you with dread! Either way, such symbols are unavoidable. Reasoning, it turns out, is like a lot of things: to more fully understand it, we need to work with abstractions. Think about the sciences here, for example: physics, as the science of the physical world, uses the tools of mathematics; likewise, logic, understood as the science of reason, uses mathematics-like tools.

- Third, and related to this second point, is that logic, like philosophy and mathematics, is something you *do*. (In fact, I have heard logic described as a contact sport!) And, to get *good* at doing anything, you usually need to *practice* doing that something. Because of this, I have included lots of practice exercises in the pages that follow. Of course, you will likely end up working through a lot of these exercises because your instructor assigns them as homework. However, you should also do your best to tackle *all* the exercises in your own time. Try to avoid some of the typical excuses for *not* doing the exercise sets. For example, many students make the mistake of thinking they can learn everything in college passively—just by sitting back and absorbing information. This is absolutely *not* the approach to take in logic. Students also sometimes avoid the necessary practice in logic because they think that they are pretty rational already;

they ask, "What can a class in logic teach me?!" Well, maybe you are pretty rational—that's great!—but people can always do better, and logic provides us with the tools to *reason* better—and that can only be a good thing, right?

And that's it for the preface, as far as you, the student, are concerned. At this point, make your way to Chapter 1 and away you go! I hope you enjoy the subject of logic.

(Did I mention that you ought to do the practice exercises?)

Acknowledgments

I would like to thank my colleagues in the Social Sciences and Philosophy Department at Onondaga Community College for their support over the years. Thanks, in particular, to my philosophy colleague, Dr. David Bzdak, who read drafts of each chapter of the book and provided me with a lot of valuable feedback. Any errors that remain in the text are my responsibility.

I would also like to extend gratitude to the president of Onondaga Community College, Dr. Casey Crabill, for approving my application for sabbatical leave to complete this project.

Some people at Kendall Hunt Publishing also deserve mention, in particular Brenda Rolwes and Brandon Bourke. This book would not have been completed without their patience and guidance.

Last, and most, I must acknowledge the love and support of my wife, Megan, and my sons, Ronan and Tiernan, without whom I would not even have been able to embark on this project. I dedicate the project's end result—this book—to them.

Chapter 1

Logic: The Fundamental Concepts

1.1 Reasoning, and How to Study It

Logic is one of the traditional subject areas of philosophy. To get a sense of what logic is all about, then, it is useful to look at how it relates to the discipline of philosophy.

The English word "philosophy" comes from the ancient Greek words for "love of wisdom." A philosopher, therefore, values wisdom and whatever enables us to become wise. One cannot become wise, of course, without *knowing* some things. So, a philosopher is interested in gaining knowledge of the world. But what does it mean to gain knowledge of the world? Philosophers disagree (a lot!) about this, but most think that knowledge at least involves getting at the truth about things, or forming true beliefs about the world. And, in order to increase our chances of arriving at the truth, philosophers insist that we ought to use *reason*. So, if we *(a)* want to form true beliefs about the world, and *(b)* think that using reason will help us get there, then it will likely be worth our while to *study* reasoning. In particular, we should do our best to understand the difference between *good* reasoning and *bad* reasoning. And this, essentially, is what the discipline of logic is all about: it is that branch of philosophy that systematically studies reasoning, in an attempt to more fully appreciate the difference between good and bad reasoning.

> **LOGIC** is the systematic study of reasoning; it is the attempt to understand the difference between good reasoning and bad reasoning.

Here is an analogy that might help you appreciate the role that logic plays in philosophy. Let's say you want to get to the city of Buffalo, New York. You are, of course, aware that driving a car is a good way to get there. However, you need to know how to drive a car; that is, you need a specific set of skills that will enable you to get to your destination. To further guarantee that driving a car will get you to Buffalo, you might even set about learning how a car works: you look under the hood, you see that there is an engine with lots of different parts that work together, and you take the time to learn how this engine functions. If the car were to break down on the way to Buffalo, you would then be in a position to fix the problem and continue on your way. Think, then, of acquiring logical skills as analogous to learning how to drive a car and learning how a car's engine works. In philosophy, we're not (usually) heading to Buffalo; rather, the destination is the truth. This means that in logic we develop the skills that enable us to arrive at the truth as reliably as possible.

Let's say a little more about what it means to reason. Consider the following simple scenario:

A mother tells her son Bobby to stop hitting his little brother. Bobby asks "why?" And the mother responds with "because I said so!"

What might Bobby make of this? Here is one way his thought process might go:

Mommy says I should stop hitting my brother; I ought to do everything my mommy says; so, I should stop hitting my brother.

Here, Bobby formulates a belief about what course of action he should take, based on some other information he had: the fact that mommy says he ought to do it, and also the fact that he ought to do everything that mommy says. Of course, children are often dissatisfied with the response "because I said so!" So, let's say that little Bobby in the above scenario continues to ask "why?", as in "why should I do what you tell me to do?" Maybe Bobby's mother will respond with something like "it's wrong to hit your brother." Cue another "why?" Mommy then will probably say, "It's wrong to hurt other people," or perhaps "would you like it if he did that to you?" Bobby ends up thinking as follows:

Mommy said I should stop hitting my brother. It is wrong to hit other people. I would not like it if he hit me. Therefore, I should stop hitting my brother.

In each of these scenarios, Bobby is basically looking for *reasons*. Then, *based on these reasons*, he formulates a belief on what his course of action should be. This is typical of reasoning in general: it involves going **FROM** something **TO** something else; that is, **FROM** some beliefs or information that we already have, or that we are given, **TO** some new information, or some new belief. We can call this movement from something to something else an **inference**. When we infer something, we "make" an inference, or "draw" an inference. Let's try to illustrate this:

Reasoning:

Here is another example of reasoning:

All Buffalo Bills fans are loyal to their team. Alice is a Buffalo Bills fan. Therefore, Alice is loyal to her team.

There is clearly an inference being made here. The person uttering these sentences is reasoning **FROM** the claim that all Buffalo Bills fans are loyal to their team and the claim that Alice is a Buffalo Bills fan, **TO** the claim that Alice is loyal to her team.

It is not difficult to come up with more examples of reasoning. Think about all the inferences you make on a typical day:

- The alarm goes off and you have to decide whether to press snooze.
- You're out of milk for breakfast, and you have to decide whether to take a super-quick trip to the store or just do without milk.
- You see a link to an item of news in your Facebook feed and you have to figure out if the claims made are true or not.
- You're late on an assignment, but you believe that you can get an extension because, well, you had a really bad cold.
- You decide to look for a recycling bin because you reason that if everyone recycled then the environment would be in better shape.
- You have to figure out if you ought to get the flu shot, so you look at the evidence that supports this and also at those claims that suggest that you should not get the shot.
- You have to get to work: Should you take route A or route B?

- You need a new phone: Should you get an iPhone or an Android? All your friends have an iPhone, but Androids are typically cheaper.
- . . .

Reasoning is something we do all the time! Either consciously or subconsciously, our minds are inference engines! Making inferences is not *all* we do, of course, but it is certainly an important part of our everyday lives.

And notice that reasoning is different from having the facts, or having beliefs about what the facts are. One can grasp a fact, or form a belief about something, in an instant. Reasoning, on the other hand, takes some time: the mind "moves" from one thing to something else, and this "movement" takes place over a period of time. This period of time may be a split second, or a few minutes. In fact, reasoning can take days, months, or even years! *Studying* reasoning involves studying what happens during this time interval.

To understand *how* the discipline of logic approaches the study of reason, it can be useful to appreciate some other ways one might do this. Reasoning can be viewed from a number of different perspectives:

From an ***anthropological*** point of view. Consider an anthropologist who is interested in understanding how tribe X in the Amazon rainforest comes to have its beliefs about the world. She may immerse herself in the culture for some time, for example, and record what the individuals in the tribe do, i.e. how they reason, when making judgments about the world around them.

From a ***historical*** point of view. For example, a historian might try to understand how an individual or government arrived at a particular decision at such-and-such a time. Why, for example, did Napoleon invade Russia in 1812? How did he arrive at the belief that this was a good idea? What reasons did he give?

From a ***psychological*** point of view. We have all developed habits of mind, and one of the things a psychologist is concerned with is explaining how this happened. For example, a psychologist might try to understand a person's behavior, worldview, and reasoning process in terms of his/her traumatic childhood experiences. Consider also the field of neuropsychology: here, practitioners can look at a person's brain in an fMRI machine, for example, and see what parts become active when the person reasons about different things.

From a ***sociological*** point of view. A sociologist tries to understand the extent to which our beliefs and actions are influenced by social forces. We tend to form beliefs about what is morally right or wrong based on what members of our peer group believe, for example. The sociologist tries to provide a systematic account of exactly how influential the structure of society is in the formation of these beliefs.

This is not meant to be an exhaustive list, but it does give us an appreciation of the fact that there are many important and fascinating ways of studying reasoning. However, the focus of these disciplines is different from what we do in logic in one very important respect. The key difference is that the anthropologist, the historian, the psychologist, and the sociologist are interested in understanding reasoning as it ***actually*** occurs; that is, in these academic fields, the main goal is to understand what happens (or happened) when a person or a culture reasons (or reasoned) to a particular belief. In logic, on the other hand, we are interested in how reasoning ***ought to*** occur: we want to develop a way to understand the difference between good reasoning and bad reasoning.

Here is another way to characterize the distinction. Remember how we just described reasoning as something that takes place over a period of time? Anthropology, history, psychology, and sociology seek to ***describe*** what occurs over this period of time; that is, they may be characterized as ***descriptive*** in their approach. Logic, however, may be viewed as a ***normative*** discipline: it seeks to understand how reasoning ***ought to,*** or ***should,*** occur. Given that reasoning occurs over a period of time, there is an opportunity for it to misfire. The discipline of logic tries to identify any such misfiring, while also developing ways of preventing reasoning mistakes.

One other important point: there is an ***objective*** difference between good reasoning and bad reasoning. That is, I don't get to decide that all of my reasoning is good reasoning simply because it is me who is doing it! And you don't get to decide that all of your reasoning is good either! Some things *are* subjective like this, of course—I am the authority on what my favorite flavor of ice-cream is, for example—but reasoning is not one of these things. To more fully appreciate this objectivity, let's take an example from mathematics, a field closely related to logic. If I ask you to add 3 to 2, you would correctly answer "5." The sentence "2 + 3 = 5" is true no matter what anyone thinks about it. Of course, different cultures might use different words or different symbols to express this truth, but two things added to three things will, objectively speaking, always get you five things. Even if there is no one around to think through the addition, it is *still* the case that $2 + 3 = 5$. A hundred million years ago, for example, two dinosaurs hanging out with three more dinosaurs resulted in five dinosaurs! And to think that the sentence "$2 + 3 = 5$" is false is somehow to misunderstand what is going on; it is objectively wrong to believe this. Mathematics consists of objective truths.

Logic is understood to be like mathematics in this respect. To see why, let's look at another simple example of reasoning:

All elephants are mammals. Cuddles is an elephant. Therefore, Cuddles is a mammal.

In this piece of reasoning, the claim that Cuddles is a mammal *follows from* the other two claims, right? If all elephants are mammals, and if Cuddles is an elephant, then there is just no way out of it: Cuddles is a mammal! This is a good piece of reasoning. And the fact that this is a good piece of reasoning is independent of what anyone happens to think about it. If, for example, someone comes along and says that the first two sentences logically entail that Cuddles is *not* a mammal, then that person is objectively mistaken. We may, of course have got our facts wrong: perhaps Cuddles is not an elephant, for example. Nevertheless, it is *still* objectively the case that the first two sentences of the above passage logically entail the last sentence of the passage. Logic is a discipline that judges the worth of instances of reasoning, and there are objective truths about what is or is not a good piece of reasoning. Consequently, logic, like mathematics, consists of objective truths.

In this last paragraph, of course, we have been getting a bit ahead of ourselves. It is important, however, that we appreciate this point about the objectivity of logic. Rest assured that a more thorough treatment of what goes on in the above example is on its way! We will begin in the next section.

Exercise Set 1.1

Q1. Describe *three* instances of reasoning that you did in the past week. In each case, indicate whether you think it is an instance of good reasoning or bad reasoning. Briefly explain your answer.

Reasoning instance #1

Good or bad reasoning?

Reasoning instance #2

Good or bad reasoning?

Reasoning instance #3

Good or bad reasoning?

Q2. Describe *three* instances of other people reasoning that you encountered in the past week, either in person, online, or wherever. In each case, indicate whether you think it is an instance of good reasoning or bad reasoning. Briefly explain your answer.

Reasoning instance #1

Good or bad reasoning?

Reasoning instance #2

Good or bad reasoning?

Reasoning instance #3

Good or bad reasoning?

1.2 Sentences in the Logical Sense

To really get going with our study of reasoning, we will have to agree on a way of talking about it. We will also have to make sure that we understand the scope of our inquiry. This means that we will need to define some technical terms. Let's begin with a basic unit of language, the *sentence*. If we can speak, read, or write English, then we know what it takes to construct, or recognize, a grammatical English sentence. In logic, we pay special attention to sentences that make assertions, and we will call these *sentences in the logical sense*, or simply *logical sentences*.[1] An important aspect of any assertion is that it is either true or false, so we build this into our definition:

> A **SENTENCE IN THE LOGICAL SENSE** is an assertion about the world that is either true or false.

As just hinted at, not all grammatical sentences of English make assertions about the world, and so will not count as sentences in the logical sense:

Order sentences
For example, if I say to you "close the door," I am not saying anything about the way the world is. I have used the English language correctly, that is, my grammar is fine, but I am not making an assertion.

Questions
For example, if I ask you "is it raining?" I am not in that moment making an assertion about the weather. Your response to my question will likely make an assertion, but the question itself does not do so.

Exclamations
For example, my response to my team winning the Super Bowl might be "wow!" or "holy crap!" Again, grammatically speaking, these sentences are fine, but they do not make any assertion.

Here is a handy way of checking if a sentence is a sentence in the logical sense: put the phrase "it is true that" before the sentence and see if what you end up with makes sense. Consider the sentence "today is Thursday," for example. To say "it is true that today is Thursday" makes perfect sense; so the sentence "today is Thursday" is a sentence in the logical sense. (Of course, it might *not* be Thursday, but both true and false sentences are considered sentences in the logical sense). What about the sentence "come over for dinner sometime"? Well, consider the following: "It is true that come over for dinner sometime"? This doesn't make any sense, grammatically speaking. Consequently, the sentence "come over for dinner sometime" is not a sentence in the logical sense.

Our first step, then, when isolating our subject matter in logic, is to make sure that we concentrate on sentences in the logical sense:

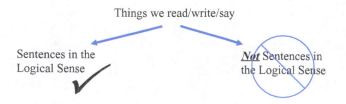

Why do we focus on sentences in the logical sense? Well, we are interested in studying reasoning, and as we have seen, reasoning is all about moving from something (facts, or beliefs about what the facts are) to something else (another fact, or another belief about what the facts are). Logic is particularly interested in whether the

---

[1]Logicians also speak of *propositions* here. The idea is that sentences of English *express* propositions, with these propositions being the focus of logic.

latter *follows from* the former. We can best understand this as trying to figure out when an *assertion* about the world follows from *other assertions* about the world.

Our definition of a sentence in the logical sense incorporates the possibility of a sentence being true and the possibility of a sentence being false. Another way of putting this is to say that every logical sentence has one of two **truth-values**: either it has the truth-value of "true" or it has the truth-value of "false." However, you might be asking if every assertion is in fact either true or false. Isn't it possible for an assertion to fall somewhere in between truth and falsity? For example, the sentence "Bob is happy" clearly qualifies as a sentence in the logical sense as defined earlier, but would it ever be appropriate to assign "full" truth or "full" falsity to the sentence? Or perhaps it doesn't make sense to ascribe *any* truth-value to some logical sentences. What about the sentence "it will rain in Syracuse, New York on March 20th, 2117"? Is this sentence true *right here and now*, or false *right here and now*? In general, is it appropriate to assign a truth-value to assertions about the future?

These are good questions. And, in philosophy, pretty much any claim is open to questioning. However, it is usually not a good idea to question everything at the same time! So, as this is an *introductory* text in the discipline of logic, we are going to make some assumptions that for the time being will go unchallenged, even though it may make sense in other contexts to question them. Our first assumption about logical sentences is as follows:

The Principle of Bivalence
Every sentence in the logical sense is either true or false.

This principle says that one of the two truth-values gets to be assigned to each and every logical sentence. Different systems of logic in which this principle is denied have been developed over the years. We might, for example, introduce a third truth-value to cover cases in which it is not clear that assigning either truth or falsity to a sentence makes sense. Or maybe there is an entire spectrum of truth-values between true and false. However, as mentioned, such considerations, though fascinating, are beyond the scope of this text.[2]

Here is another assumption about logical sentences that we will be making:

The Principle of Non-contradiction
No sentence in the logical sense is both true and false.

This principle says that the two truth-values, i.e. truth and falsity, are mutually exclusive. This is an intuitively plausible principle, and is one of the so-called *classical laws of thought*. Some potential counterexamples can be proposed, however. The logical sentence "it is raining," for example, can surely be both true and false, you might think: it might be raining in one place and time and not raining in another place and time. In uttering the sentence "it is raining," however, you are likely making the assertion that it is raining *here and now*—so to utter the sentence in two different locations is really to make two different assertions. And we can take the Principle of Non-contradiction to apply to the assertions that a sentence is being used to make, and not to the utterance in English. Such considerations might not remove all of your concerns, though, and the principle can still be challenged.[3] Again, however, we are setting any objections to the principle aside here. Both the Principle of Bivalence and the Principle of Non-contradiction will be assumed true for the remainder of the book.

---

[2]If you are interested in these ideas, a good place to start is with the "Many-Valued Logic" entry in the *Stanford Encyclopedia of Philosophy*.
[3]The view that there are true contradictions is called *Dialetheism*. One prominent proponent of this view is the Australian philosopher, Graham Priest.

Exercise Set 1.2

Which of the following sentences are sentences in the logical sense?

1. Today is Thursday.
2. Syracuse is the capital city of the United States.
3. I love fluffy puppies.
4. Roughly 66 million years ago, a dinosaur named "Fluffy" stepped on a butterfly named "Flappy."
5. Stop talking so loudly.
6. It is either raining or not raining.
7. Why do fools fall in love?
8. Ghosts do not exist.
9. All red fire trucks are blue.
10. Ouch—stop it!
11. I wish today was Friday.
12. Vote for Juan!
13. I am going to vote for Juan.
14. Where is Ahmed?
15. There are nine planets orbiting the sun.
16. Eeeeew—mint ice-cream!
17. All birds can fly.
18. I could have been a rock star.
19. I am possibly a poached egg.
20. Euthanasia is morally permissible.

1.3 Arguments

Sometimes we encounter logical sentences in isolation, but often we bunch sentences together to indicate that there is some sort of relationship between them. A *narrative*, for example, consists of sentences that are arranged to form a coherent story. An *explanation* is a set of sentences that attempts to explain some phenomenon or other. At other times, a set of sentences is supposed to show that some other sentence is true. In this kind of scenario, we have an *argument*: one sentence is being *supported by*, or *inferred from*, some other sentences. The supporting sentences are called *premises*. The sentence they are meant to support is called the *conclusion*. Here is the technical definition of an argument:

> An **ARGUMENT** is a sequence of logical sentences. One of the sentences is the conclusion. The rest of the sentences are the premises.

This is how the concept of an argument is understood in logic. In an everyday setting, the word "argument" is sometimes used to mean a disagreement, or a quarrel, between two or more people. However, in logic, we do not include this connotation. We do not even require that two people be involved. An argument is simply a particular way of putting logical sentences together; it is an attempt to conclude one logical sentence (i.e., the conclusion) on the basis of some other logical sentences (i.e., the premises). Every argument has just one conclusion, though it can have any number of premises.

An argument may be thought of as a unit of reasoning. Each of the reasoning examples we described at the start of this chapter is an argument. To be an argument, one sentence in a sequence of sentences must be in some way identified as the conclusion, and it should be clear that this conclusion is supposed to follow from some identified premises. Consider the following example:

Since all elephants are mammals, and all mammals have some hair, we can conclude that all elephants have some hair.

The phrase "we can conclude that" makes it clear here that there is some attempt to *show*, or *establish*, that all elephants have hair. This kind of phrase is called a *conclusion indicator*: when you see these words, you can generally infer that what comes directly afterward is the conclusion of an argument. Many other words and phrases serve as conclusion indicators in English. Here are some of the more common ones:

Some Conclusion Indicators

Therefore, . . .	Hence . . .
So, . . .	It follows that . . .
Thus, . . .	We can conclude that . . .
Consequently, . . .	This entails that . . .
Ergo . . . (Latin for "therefore")	This shows that . . .

Conclusion indicators are like signposts in that they inform us that a conclusion is on the way. However, they are not part of the conclusion itself.

No matter how you identify the conclusion, the fact that there *is* one is a guarantee that there is a piece of reasoning present, and that at least some other sentences in the neighborhood of this conclusion are premises upon which it is supposedly established. In the above example, it is clear what is being cited as evidence for the conclusion: the claim that all elephants are mammals, and the claim that all mammals have hair. In this case, the word "since" serves to indicate that the sentence or sentences that follow are going to serve as premises in an argument; that is, it is a *premise indicator*. Other words and phrases perform a similar task. Here are some of those:

Some Premise Indicators

Since . . .	If we assume that . . .
Because . . .	Given that . . .
Due to the fact that . . .	Considering that . . .
If we assume that . . .	If we consider that . . .
For the following reasons: . . .	

Like conclusion indicators, premise indicators are like signposts: they serve to indicate that what follows is a premise, but they are not part of the premise itself.

It is natural to think of the conclusion as the last sentence of an argument: it is the sentence you *arrive at* after appealing to some other sentences. This is reflected in how arguments are conventionally presented. Here is the above argument re-written according to this convention:

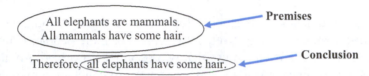

Here, everything above the horizontal line is understood to be a premise. The sentence below the horizontal line—everything after the "therefore"—is understood to be the conclusion.

Identifying the premises and the conclusion of an argument is not always as straightforward as in the above example. Consider the following argument:

All mice have tails. So, Squeakers has a tail, because Squeaker is a mouse.

The conclusion in this argument is the assertion right after the conclusion indicator "so," that is, "Squeakers has a tail." The assertion after the word "because" serves as a premise, as does the first sentence of the passage. We can present the argument as follows:

All mice have tails.
Squeaker is a mouse.
_____

Therefore, Squeakers has a tail.

The presence of conclusion indicators and premise indicators is very helpful in identifying the different parts of an argument. However, it is possible to have an argument that has neither premise indicators nor a conclusion indicator. Here is an example of this:

You should get an iPhone. Apple products are the best and they have come down in price recently.

There are no explicit words or phrases here that tell us which sentence is the conclusion, or which sentences are the premises. A close reading of the passage, however, reveals that there is an attempt to establish one of these claims on the basis of the other claims. In other words, there is an argument: you should get an iPhone *because* apple products are the best and they have come down in price recently. Or, in the conventional format:

Apple products are the best.
Apple products have come down in price recently.
_____

Therefore, you should buy an iPhone.

Arguments versus Explanations

Consider the following passage:

My car has just broken down. It must be because I left the lights on all night.

Clearly, there is some sort of relationship between these two sentences; however, it is not an *inferential* one: there is no attempt to *establish* either of these sentences based on the truth of the other sentence. Instead, we are told that the two sentences are true and that the truth of one of them *explains* the truth of the other one. In other words, we have a phenomenon, i.e. the broken-down car, and this is accounted for by some other phenomenon, i.e. the lights being left on all night. The passage, in a sense, is an attempt to "work backward" to try to *give an account of why* something is the case. Arguments, on the other hand, "work forward" and try to *show* that something is the case.

The distinction here can be a tricky one to grasp. The problem stems from the fact that both arguments and explanations can be offered as responses to "why?" questions. Notice that the word "because," even though it is listed above as a premise indicator, can also indicate that there is an attempt to explain something. Here is another example that might help clear things up:

Bob says that women are inferior to men. Sheila asks why he thinks this, and Bob replies as follows: "I was raised in a household and a culture that believed that women were inferior to men."

Has Bob responded appropriately to Sheila's question? In one sense, yes: Bob offers an *explanation* for why he thinks that women are inferior to men. It might not be a good or complete explanation for why Bob believes what he does, but it is an appropriate kind of response to Sheila's "why?" question. In another sense, however, Bob's response to Sheila is wholly inadequate: he hasn't offered any *reasons* for why we should think that women are inferior to men. That is, he hasn't provided her with an *argument* for his belief. If Bob were to provide an argument, it might include such statements as "most women are physically weaker than men," or "women are more emotional than men." Of course, neither of these statements provides *good* support for Bob's claim that women are inferior to men, but I hope you can see how, by appealing to them, Bob would be at least attempting to provide an argument. These statements comprise a different kind of response to Sheila's original "why?" question.

Logic, then, focuses on sentences in the logical sense, and on those sets of logical sentences that constitute arguments:

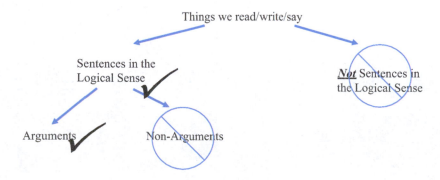

In the next section, we will move on to *evaluating* arguments.

Exercise Set 1.3

Q1. Each of the following passages contains an argument. In each case, identify the premises and the conclusion. Ignore whether the argument is a good or a bad one. Write your answers in the space provided. The first one is done for you.

1. The weatherman said that it was going to snow today. Since he is never wrong, we can conclude that it will snow today.

> **Premises:** 1. The weatherman said that it was going to snow today.
> 2. He is never wrong.
>
> **Conclusion:** It will snow today.

2. All dogs can bark. Furthermore, all dogs can swim. Rover is a dog. Therefore, Rover can both bark and swim.

> **Premises:**
>
> **Conclusion:**

3. You really ought to watch the TV show *The Wire*. It's a show set in Baltimore, and you love everything about Baltimore.

> **Premises:**
>
> **Conclusion:**

4. People and societies often have different views on moral issues. Thus, we can conclude that there is no objective truth in morality.

> **Premises:**
>
> **Conclusion:**

5. Scientists often have different opinions about how the world works. So, we can conclude that there is no objective truth about how the world works.

> **Premises:**
>
> **Conclusion:**

6. Strangers are just friends you haven't yet met. People are nice wherever you go.

> **Premises:**
>
> **Conclusion:**

7. It's going to be a really nice day tomorrow. The sky is very red, and this is a sign of nice weather ahead.

> **Premises:**
>
> **Conclusion:**

8. Every Friday we go to Dunkin Donuts. Today is Friday, so I expect we will go to Dunkin Donuts today.

> **Premises:**
>
> **Conclusion:**

9. Ottawa must be the capital city of Canada. It's not Montreal and it's not Toronto.

> **Premises:**
>
> **Conclusion:**

10. If it's not raining tomorrow, then we will have a picnic. If we have a picnic, then I will probably eat too many sandwiches. Consequently, if it's not raining tomorrow, I will probably eat too many sandwiches.

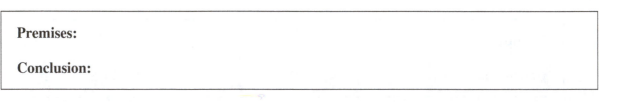

> **Premises:**
>
> **Conclusion:**

11. Astronomers say that there are now only eight planets in the solar system. Until recently, they said there were nine planets in the solar system. Clearly, then, astronomers have no idea how to count.

> **Premises:**
>
> **Conclusion:**

12. Assuming that Bob can spell his name and that Beatrice can spell her name, we can conclude that all people whose name starts with 'B' can spell their name.

> **Premises:**
>
> **Conclusion:**

13. Some people say that a tomato is a fruit. But nobody puts tomatoes in a fruit salad. This entails that a tomato is not a fruit.

> **Premises:**
>
> **Conclusion:**

14. Everyone should be nicer to animals. Animals can feel pain just like us, and the less pain there is in the world the better!

> **Premises:**
>
> **Conclusion:**

15. The area of a circle is πr^2. The volume of a sphere is $4/3\pi r^3$. The volume of a cylinder is $\pi r^2 h$. All of this goes to show that π is a very important number in geometry.

> **Premises:**
>
> **Conclusion:**

Q2. For each of the following passages, determine if there is an argument present. If you think there is an argument, make sure to identify the premises and the conclusion of the argument. If you think there is no argument, explain why you think this. The first one is done for you.

1. In my opinion, the Boston Red Sox are the best team in baseball.
    Answer: this is not an argument. It contains just one sentence.

2. All good things come to an end.

3. The Lakers are going to win on Sunday. They are playing at home, and have a perfect home record this season so far.

4. People are weird. At the mall today, I met a person wearing two completely different shoes. And then I passed a car on the highway with the roof down—in 20-degree weather!

5. "Apple products are the best," said Adam. "No, you're wrong," said Beatrice, "Microsoft products are the best."

6. Be careful when crossing the road. People drive really fast around here.

7. Most people think that the earth is getting warmer. But some people disagree.

8. All dogs are mammals, and all mammals are hairy. Doesn't it follow that all dogs are hairy?

9. Those who cannot remember the past are doomed to repeat it. (George Santayana)

10. I got sunburned today. I must have forgotten to put on my sunscreen. (Patrick Kenny)

11. Lower taxes mean that I get to keep more of my paycheck. And the government is promising that lower taxes are on the way. Thus, I will shortly be keeping more of my paycheck.

12. Everyone I know is going to the party. I guess I should go too.

13. It is always wrong to tell a lie. James just lied to Maria about how much money he has in his wallet. Hence, James just did something wrong.

14. The universe had to have a beginning, but it couldn't just come from nothing. Consequently, there has to be some entity outside the universe that created the universe.

15. Young people today are so rude! Back in my day, kids had respect for their parents. And they weren't walking around with their heads stuck in a phone!

1.4 Evaluating Arguments

We have defined logic as the systematic attempt to understand the difference between good and bad reasoning. If we take an argument to be a piece of reasoning, then logic becomes an investigation into the difference between good and bad *arguments*. So, what *is* the difference between a good and a bad argument? It turns out that there are two different ways to judge the worth of an argument. Consider the following, for example:

> All horses have four legs.
> Barack Obama is a horse.
> _____
> Therefore, Barack Obama has four legs.

Is this a good argument or a bad argument? Well, in one sense this is a good argument: the premises and the conclusion "fit together," so to speak. That is, if all horses have four legs and if Barack Obama is a horse, then the conclusion just has to be true—Barack Obama has four legs. In another sense, of course, this is *not* a very good argument: granted, all horses have four legs, but Barack Obama is not a horse! The second premise is obviously false, and surely any argument that contains falsehood cannot be a wholly good argument.

If there are different ways in which an argument can be good or bad, then we need to be more precise. Here is a basic distinction that will help us to do this:

Two ways of evaluating an argument:

A. *Examine the logical* **relationship between** *the premises and the conclusion*
Here, all we are interested in is the strength of the connection between the premises and the conclusion. We are *not* interested in whether the premises are true. We are *not* interested in whether the conclusion is true. We are just asking: To what extent does the conclusion *logically follow* from the premises? The above argument is a good one in this sense: the truth of the premises *guarantees* the truth of the conclusion.

B. *Ascertain the* **truth-values** *of the premises and the conclusion*
Here, we are concerned with the truth-value of the individual sentences of the argument. The above argument is a bad one in this sense: the second premise and the conclusion are false.

It can be difficult to keep this distinction in mind when evaluating arguments, but it is extremely important that we do so. We'll try to keep things simple for now, and focus on arguments in which the truth-value of the sentences involved is not an issue. Here is another argument to consider:

> Adam P. is a fisherman.
> All fishermen have caught at least one fish.
> _____
> Therefore, Adam P. has caught at least one fish.

Who is Adam P.? We have no idea! Is he really a fisherman? Who knows?! Have all fishermen caught at least one fish? Probably, but maybe there are a few unfortunate fishermen out there who have never had a bite. Has Adam P. caught at least one fish? Again, we are completely in the dark here! We are just not in a good position to ascertain the truth-value of any of the sentences in this argument. However, I can *still* evaluate the argument in the first of the two ways described above; that is, I can check to see how strong the logical relationship is between the premises and the conclusion. In this case, we have a "watertight" logical relationship: the conclusion follows from the premises necessarily. Consequently, this is a good argument in this respect.

Notice, then, that a lack of background information does not mean that we have to remain silent on the merits of an argument. We can say something informative about an argument in the complete absence of knowledge of the facts. In particular, we will always be able to ask, and answer, questions like "given the premises, how sure can we be about the conclusion?" or "to what extent does the truth of the premises guarantee the truth of the conclusion?" These questions pertain to the relationship between the premises and the conclusion, and our ability to answer them does not depend on any knowledge we have about the truth, or falsity, of the premises and the conclusion of the argument. In short, this way of evaluating an argument requires us to explore a "what-if" scenario: *If* the premises are true, does the conclusion follow? If the conclusion *does* follow, then we have a good argument. If the conclusion does *not* follow, then the argument is not so good. The first kind of argument, i.e. one in which the truth of the premises guarantees the truth of the conclusion, is called a ***valid argument***. This is a hugely important concept to grasp. Let's talk some more about it.

Validity

As just indicated, the concept of validity pertains to the relationship between the premises and the conclusion of an argument. A valid argument is one in which that relationship is logically "watertight." Here then is a good first definition of validity:

> A **VALID ARGUMENT** is one in which the truth of the premises guarantees the truth of the conclusion.

The best way to make sure that we understand this important concept is to work through some more examples. Let's try this one:

> Most students at College X are rich.
> Ahmed is a student at College X.
> _____
> Therefore, Ahmed is rich.

As in the previous example, we don't have much background information here: I don't know where College X is, I don't know who Ahmed is, and I don't know if he is rich. However, I can still examine the relationship between the premises and the conclusion. This time, the truth of the premises does *not* guarantee the truth of the conclusion. Even if Ahmed is a student at College X, the first premise leaves open the possibility that he is one of those students who is not rich. The argument, therefore, is invalid.

Notice what we are doing when we evaluate an argument for validity: we are *assuming* that the premises are true and then checking to see if, based on this assumption, the conclusion *has* to be true. In the above example, I don't have sufficient background information to ascertain the *actual* truth-value of the premises, but I can *pretend* that they are true and then see if the conclusion is also true in that pretend world. And it turned out that pretending that the premises are true does not guarantee that the conclusion is true in that pretend world. That is, it is possible for the conclusion of the argument to be false *if* the premises are true. In a valid argument, it is *not* possible for the conclusion to be false if the premises are true. Let's turn this way of looking at things into another definition of the concept of validity:

> A **VALID ARGUMENT** is one in which it is impossible for the conclusion to be false if the premises are true.

These two definitions of validity amount to the same thing: an argument in which the truth of the premises guarantees the truth of the conclusion is one in which it is impossible for the conclusion to be false if the premises are true. This latter definition, however, is more suggestive of a method of checking an argument for validity. We will call this the ***Counterexample Method:***

The Counterexample Method of Checking for Validity

Step 1:   Assume the premises are true.
Step 2:   Try to describe a scenario in which, given your assumption in **Step 1**, the conclusion is false. There are two possible outcomes here:

    a. You *can* describe such a scenario. This description is a ***counterexample*** to the argument, and it shows that the argument is invalid.

    b. You *cannot* describe such a scenario, i.e. no counterexample to the argument is possible. This shows that the argument is valid.

In our most recent example, when we assumed the premises were true we *could* imagine a scenario in which the conclusion was false. We hinted at a description of such a scenario, i.e. a counterexample to the argument:

Most students attending College X are rich, and Ahmed attends College X. However, Ahmed is one of those students attending College X who is not rich.

A counterexample is like a complete story in which all the premises are true and the conclusion is false. If such a story is possible, then the argument is invalid. In our earlier example involving Adam P. the fisherman, there is no counterexample available. That is, I cannot describe a coherent story in which the premises are true and the conclusion is false. Any story in which the premises were true just had to have the conclusion true as well.

Let's use the counterexample method on another argument:

No dogs live in Antarctica.
Lily is a dog.

Therefore, Lily does not live in Antarctica.

Step 1 asks us to assume the premises to be true. I don't know if any dogs live in Antarctica, but let's assume that the first premise is true. And maybe Lily isn't a dog, but let's assume she is. OK, so we now have no dogs living in Antarctica, and Lily being a dog. **Step 2** asks us to try to describe a scenario in which, given my assumptions in **Step 1**, the conclusion is false. However, no matter how hard I try, I cannot do this: my pretend scenario with no dogs living in Antarctica and Lily being a dog *rules out* the possibility that Lily lives in Antarctica. There is no counterexample available, and so the argument is valid.

It can also be helpful to draw a counterexample to an argument. Take a look at this argument, for example:

All orcs are elves.
Some elves wear t-shirts.

Therefore, some orcs wear t-shirts.

Can I describe a scenario in which the premises are true and the conclusion is false? Yes: such a scenario is represented by the following:

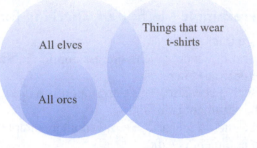

In this diagram, both premises are true: all of the orcs are contained inside the set of elves, and the set of elves overlaps with the set of things that wear t-shirts. However, the conclusion is false: there is no overlap between the set of elves and the set of things that wear t-shirts. Consequently, the diagram serves as a counterexample to the argument.

There is an important proviso to the counterexample method that should be mentioned. If I cannot describe a scenario in which the premises are true and the conclusion is false, does this mean that such a scenario is impossible? Well, that depends. Perhaps I haven't tried hard enough to imagine such a scenario. Or maybe my imagination is curtailed in some way. Consequently, using the counterexample method to show that an argument is valid is somewhat limited. On the other hand, if I *do* manage to describe a counterexample, i.e. a scenario in which the premises are true and the conclusion is false, then I can conclude with certainty that the argument is invalid.

We should also say something about **possibility**. When checking for validity, we are asked to imagine and describe a possible scenario in which the premises are true and the conclusion is false. But, when is something possible and when is it not possible? (Perhaps you have been told that *anything* is possible, in which case, all arguments will turn out to be invalid!) Let's get a little clearer on this. Consider the following sentences:

- LeBron James scored 100 points in an NBA basketball game.
- LeBron James is 35 years old, and it is not the case that LeBron James is 35 years old.
- LeBron James went to the planet Mars in 2016.

All these sentences are false. However, we can still ask if they are *possibly* true. Let's take a look:

- In 1962, Wilt Chamberlain scored 100 points in an NBA game. So, clearly the first sentence is possibly true, even if the scenario it describes remains unlikely to occur.
- The second sentence basically asserts that it is both true and not true that LeBron James is 35 years old. This directly conflicts with the Principle of Non-contradiction mentioned earlier, which stated that no sentence in the logical sense is both true and false. Thus, this sentence is not possibly true. In general, as far as logicians are concerned, those sentences that describe a contradiction or that entail a contradiction are not possibly true. (We will have a lot more to say about such sentences later).
- The third sentence is a bit trickier. As far as we know, no person has ever been to Mars. And, as things stand, we do not currently have the resources to send a person to Mars. What would it take for the sentence to be true? Well, consider the following scenario: NASA is keeping some of its technology hidden from us and has been sending people to Mars (and perhaps to other planets) for a while now. Only very rich people can afford the trip, and in 2016 LeBron James paid $10 million for the privilege of taking a trip to Mars. This is a pretty far-out scenario: it conflicts with our current beliefs about NASA's capabilities, and it also arguably conflicts with what most of us understand to be the laws of physics (to travel to Mars, James would have to be exposed to a lot of harmful radiation, etc.). We might, therefore, be tempted to describe this sentence as not even possibly true. However, the sentence does *not* contradict itself in the way that the second sentence does—and this, for logicians, is sufficient to render the sentence possibly true.

Here's another way to appreciate what's going on in this third example. Ask yourself: Could you write a story, or make a movie, in which the sentence is true? Think of the trailer for such a movie: "In a world in which NASA has been hiding technology from us, rich people have been travelling to Mars for the last few years . . ." Whatever about the merits of this idea as a movie project, this clearly describes a possible scenario. It is at least as possible as one in which brave underdogs use some invisible "force" to defeat an evil empire in a galaxy far away!

When checking an argument for validity, then, we are to understand possibility in very broad terms. For present purposes, the limits of possibility coincide with the limits of our imagination: if we can imagine it, then it is possible, and if we cannot imagine it, then it is not possible. We *can* imagine a scenario in which LeBron James scores 100 points in an NBA game, and we *can* imagine a scenario in which LeBron James went to the planet Mars in 2016. However, we *cannot* imagine a scenario in which LeBron James both is and is not 35 years old.

A related point is that validity is an all-or-nothing, black-and-white, affair. If the conclusion of an argument necessarily follows from its premises, then that argument is valid. If the conclusion of an argument does not necessarily follow from its premises, then that argument is invalid. There is no such thing as a "mostly valid" argument, for example. No matter how unlikely it is that the premises are true and the conclusion is false, if that scenario is possible, then the argument in question is invalid. Consider the following argument, for example:

Either Helen or Madeleine can lift a 300-pound weight.
Helen is 5 years old.
Madeleine is 30 years old.

_____

Therefore, Madeleine can lift a 300-pound weight.

Is this a valid argument? Can we come up with a counterexample, i.e. a scenario in which all of these premises are true and the conclusion is false? Well, yes: Helen is an unusual child—she was genetically engineered to be super-strong, and her parents have insisted on an 8-hour weightlifting regimen every day; meanwhile, Madeleine is an average 30-year-old human who cannot lift 300 pounds. In this unlikely, yet possible, scenario, assuming that the first premise is also true, we have all true premises and a false conclusion. Consequently, the argument is invalid.

Exercise Set 1.4

Use the Counterexample Method to check each of the following arguments for **VALIDITY.** If you judge that the argument is invalid, make sure to describe, or draw, a counterexample to the argument. Write your answers in the space provided. The first one is done for you.

---

1. Either Max or Nathan or Oliver committed the crime.
Max did not commit the crime.

_____

Therefore, Nathan committed the crime.

This argument is **INVALID**.
Counterexample: The second premise rules out the possibility that Max committed the crime. This, together with the first premise, still leaves it open that either Nathan or Oliver committed the crime. So, it is possible for the conclusion to be false even if we assume that the premises are true—which means that the argument is invalid.

---

2. If Adam goes to the party, then so will Angela.
If Angela goes to the party, then so will Bob.

_____

Therefore, if Adam goes to the party, then so will Bob.

This argument is _____.

---

3. The planet Gorgothon has living organisms.

_____

Therefore, there are at least two planets that have living organisms.

This argument is _____.

---

4. The book on the table has a total of 300 pages.
The book on the shelf has a total of 400 pages.

_____

Therefore, the book on the shelf has more pages than the book on the table.

This argument is _____.

5. The book on the table has more than 300 pages.
The book on the shelf has more than 400 pages.
_____
Therefore, the book on the shelf has more pages than the book on the table.

This argument is _____.

6. Alice is sitting in a tree.
Bob is sitting in a tree.
_____
Therefore, Alice and Bob are sitting in a tree.

This argument is _____.

7. Everyone at the game is wearing a watch.
Tom is not at the game.
_____
Therefore, Tom is not wearing a watch.

This argument is _____.

8. 99.9% of the people at the game are wearing a watch.
Tom is at the game.
_____
Therefore, Tom is wearing a watch.

This argument is _____.

9.	All of John's cardigans are red. This is a red cardigan. ——————————— Therefore, this is not John's cardigan. This argument is _____.

10.	All of John's cardigans are red. This is a blue cardigan. ——————————— Therefore, this is not John's cardigan. This argument is _____.

11.	If Tim and Bob go to the movies, then no one will mow the lawn. Tim goes to the movies. ——————————— Therefore, no one will mow the lawn. This argument is _____.

12.	Some lawyers are logicians. Some logicians are cuddly. ——————————— Therefore, some lawyers are cuddly. This argument is _____.

13.
Either Xavier, Thomas, or Cassandra got married yesterday.
Cassandra didn't get married yesterday.
Thomas didn't get married yesterday.
_____
Therefore, Xavier got married yesterday.

This argument is _____.

14.
If my birthday present is a bicycle, then it has two wheels.
My birthday present has two wheels.
_____
Therefore, my birthday present is a bicycle.

This argument is _____.

15.
If my birthday present is a bicycle, then it has two wheels.
My birthday present does not have two wheels.
_____
Therefore, my birthday present is not a bicycle.

This argument is _____.

16.
Point X is north of point Y.
Point Y is north of point Z.
Point Z is north of Texas.
_____
Therefore, point X is north of Texas.

This argument is _____.

17.	Point X is west of point Y. Point Y is west of point Z. Point Z is west of Texas. ——————————— Therefore, point X is west of Texas. This argument is _____.

18.	Planet 9 is 150 million miles from its sun. Planet 99 is 250 million miles from its sun. ——————————— Therefore, planet 51 is between 150 million and 250 million miles from its sun. This argument is _____.

19.	If everyone jumped off a cliff, then little Johnny would jump off a cliff too. If everyone started smoking, then little Johnny would start smoking too. If everyone started doing drugs, then little Johnny would start doing drugs too. ——————————— Therefore, if everyone started drinking blueberry juice, then little Johnny would start drinking blueberry juice as well. This argument is _____.

20.	Political party A is better than political party B. ——————————— Therefore, everyone will vote for political party A. This argument is _____.

1.5 Validity and Truth; Soundness

At this point, it should be clear that the concept of validity is quite different from the concept of truth:

> **VALIDITY** pertains to how the individual sentences in an argument *relate to each other*: an argument is valid whenever the truth of its premises guarantees the truth of its conclusion. It is never appropriate to describe the individual sentences of an argument as "valid" or "invalid." In an everyday context, perhaps, we might congratulate someone on making a valid point when he/she utters just one sentence; but in our technical understanding of validity, the concept applies only to argument, which is a *collection* of sentences.

> **TRUTH** is a property that some sentences, *all by themselves*, have. Each individual sentence of an argument, whether it is a premise or the conclusion, has a truth-value: it is either true or false. It is never appropriate to refer to an argument as "true" or "false;" an argument is just not the kind of thing that has a truth-value.

The examples we have looked at so far make it relatively easy to separate the truth of an argument's sentences from the validity of the argument. Sometimes, however, it can be more challenging to separate these two aspects of an argument. Consider the following example:

Some men are tall.
Some men are doctors.

———————————

Therefore, some men are tall doctors.

All these sentences are true, so we might be tempted to give a thumbs-up to this argument. However, it is an invalid argument! The fact that some men are tall and the fact that some men are doctors do not entail that there has to be some overlap between the set of tall men and the set of men who are doctors. Here is an illustration of a possible counterexample to the argument:

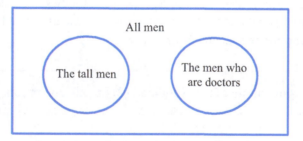

Yes, the argument's premises are true, and its conclusion is true. And having true sentences is great! However, the argument does not succeed in its primary task: providing a logically watertight connection between its premises and its conclusion.

Let's consider another example:

All zebras are fish.
All fish have two heads.

———————————

Therefore, all zebras have two heads.

In this case, all the premises are false, and the conclusion is false. However, this does not mean we should give the argument an automatic thumbs-down! The argument is, in fact, valid: there is no counterexample available. In one sense, then, this argument, which is full of falsehoods, is a *better* argument than the one we just looked at that was full of true sentences. When encountering an argument, then, how shall we approach the issue of truth? Answer: check the argument for validity first. This, as we have seen, means ignoring the *actual* truth-value of the premises and the conclusion. If the argument turns out to be invalid, then it doesn't matter if the premises of the argument are true or if the conclusion is true—we know that the argument fails in its main task, i.e. the premises do not establish the conclusion. If the argument turns out to be valid, *then* we can move on and check to see if its premises are actually true.

Let's try out this approach on the following argument:

All murder is morally wrong.
Abortion is murder.

_____

Therefore, abortion is morally wrong.

Many people have strong views on the issue of abortion, of course, and this has the potential to make evaluating arguments like this rather tricky. Let's follow the above suggestion, however, and check for validity first: Is there a possible scenario in which the premises are true, but the conclusion is false? No: if we assume that all murder is morally wrong, and if we also assume that abortion is an example of murder, then we are forced to conclude that abortion is morally wrong. Consequently, the argument is valid. Now, if you lie on the pro-choice side of the abortion-rights issue, this might sound troubling: here is a valid argument that concludes that abortion is morally wrong! However, the fact that an argument is valid does not force us to accept the conclusion of that argument. When we judge that an argument is valid, we do not say anything about whether the premises are actually true; all we are saying is that *if* the premises are true, then the conclusion is true. And often this is a big "if!" In this example, yes, the conclusion logically follows from the premises, but what about the premises themselves? There is still some doubt here. The first premise is relatively uncontroversial—murder is indeed morally wrong. However, people disagree (a lot!) when it comes to the second premise. And often until this disagreement is resolved, we cannot be said to have *proven* that abortion is murder. That is, we cannot insist that anyone accept the conclusion of the argument.

Our evaluation of the argument is not complete until we more fully engage with the premises by themselves and see if they are true or false. In the above argument, after seeing that it is valid, there now begins an extended conversation on whether the second premise is true or false. Note, though, that we have still made some progress in evaluating the argument, regardless of what our moral commitments are. Checking an argument for validity does not involve taking a position on the actual truth-values of the premises: no matter how strongly you feel about the subject of abortion, we can just set this aside and check to see if the conclusion follows from the premises. Once we see that the conclusion does indeed follow from the premises, *then* we can go back and see if the premises are true or false.

This brings us to another important concept: ***Soundness***:

A **SOUND** argument is an argument that **(1)** is valid and **(2)** has all true premises.

Soundness is the gold standard of arguments: if an argument is sound, then we really <u>are</u> forced to accept the conclusion of the argument. A valid argument has the following property: if the premises are true, then the conclusion must be true; so, if the premises are *in fact* true, then the conclusion is *in fact* true as well.

An argument is not sound if it is invalid, or if at least one of its premises is false, or both. Consequently, all invalid arguments are automatically unsound. If an argument is judged to be valid, however, then it is appropriate to check the premises to see if they are true or false. This suggests the following method for evaluating an argument:

How to evaluate an argument

Step 1:   Check for validity
   If the argument is invalid, then your evaluation of the argument is complete.
   If the argument is valid, then move on to **Step 2**.

Step 2:   Check to see if the argument's premises are true
   If all the argument's premises are true, then the argument is sound.
   If at least one of the argument's premises is false, then the argument is valid, but unsound.

Step 2 here can be very difficult: people often disagree a lot on what the facts are! Sometimes our everyday experiences will tell us if something is true or false, and sometimes a quick Google search will suffice. However, often we will need some specialized knowledge from the sciences, or philosophy, or history, etc. In the above argument, for example, we might need to explore what it means for an entity to be a person before we can say for sure that abortion is murder. So, is this particular argument sound? The best answer to give here is that we simply don't yet have enough information to give a definite "yes" or "no."

Step 1, on the other hand, does not depend on what the facts are; neither common knowledge nor Google can help us out. But, no matter how contentious an issue might be, we can still check for validity. And the good news is that, in logic, we focus primarily on validity. The logician's job is to figure out what follows what, and this can be done without paying too much attention to whether or not the premises of an argument, or the conclusion of an argument, are actually true.

Let's use this method of argument evaluation on a new example:

All mountains in the Himalayas are over 25,000 feet high.
Mount Everest is a mountain in the Himalayas.
_____

Therefore, Mount Everest is over 25,000 feet high.

Step 1 asks us to check for validity. So, is there a possible scenario in which the premises of this argument are true and the conclusion is false? No: there is no counterexample available, so the argument is valid. **Step 2** asks us to check if the premises are true. Most of us will know that the second premise is true, though a quick search on the Internet will confirm it for us, if necessary. Most of us are probably not sure about the first premise, however—but, again, it's Google to the rescue! It turns out that while many mountains in the Himalayas are over 25,000 feet high, not all of them are. So, one of the argument's premises is false: this means that the argument is valid, but not sound.

The next exercise set asks you to check for both validity and soundness. This is to make sure that you fully appreciate the distinction between these two important concepts. However, as just mentioned, the focus going forward will be validity. The following, then, illustrates the scope of our inquiry in this book:

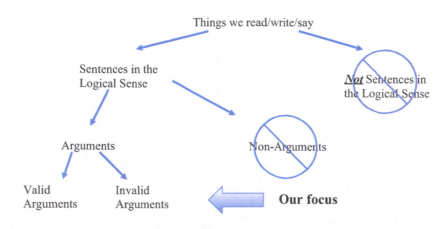

In the next few chapters, we will be developing different ways of checking an argument for validity.

Exercise Set 1.5

For each of the following arguments, do both *(a)* and *(b)*:

(a) Use the Counterexample Method to check each of the following arguments for validity. If you judge that the argument is invalid, make sure to describe, or draw, a counterexample to the argument.

(b) Based on what you ascertained about the argument in (a), check the argument for soundness. You can use the Internet to do any necessary research.

Write your answers in the space provided. The first one is done for you.

1.	The biggest city in each country is the capital city of that country. Ottawa is the biggest city in Canada. ―――――――――― Therefore, Ottawa is the capital city of Canada. The argument is **VALID**. There is no counterexample available: if the premises are true, then the conclusion must be true. The argument is **NOT SOUND.** The second premise is false.
2.	If Ireland is larger than Canada, then Ireland is larger than Mexico. Ireland is larger than Canada. ―――――――――― Therefore, Ireland is larger than Mexico. The argument is _____ The argument is _____
3.	Some days are cloudy. Some days are rainy. ―――――――――― Therefore, some days are cloudy and rainy. The argument is _____ The argument is _____

4. If Thomas Jefferson wrote the Declaration of Independence, then he must be the most important Founding Father of the United States.
Thomas Jefferson did not write the Declaration of Independence.
_____
Therefore, Thomas Jefferson is not the most important Founding father of the United States.

The argument is _____

The argument is _____

5. My car is God.
My car exists.
_____
Therefore, God exists.

The argument is _____

The argument is _____

6. All persons in the Solar System have hair.
_____
Therefore, all persons have hair.

The argument is _____

The argument is _____

7. All people who believe in God live moral lives.
Jane lives a moral life.
_____
Therefore, Jane believes in God.

The argument is _____

The argument is _____

8.	All squares are rectangles. All rectangles have four sides. <hr> Therefore, all squares have four sides. The argument is _____ The argument is _____
9.	Mars is the fourth planet from the sun. Venus is the third planet from the sun. <hr> Therefore, Venus is closer to the sun than Mars is. The argument is _____ The argument is _____
10.	In the year 1275, Christopher Columbus discovered Europe. In the year 1307, Christopher Columbus died. <hr> Therefore, Christopher Columbus died after he discovered America. The argument is _____ The argument is _____
11.	Taylor Swift's songs are more successful than Justin Bieber's songs. Justin Bieber's songs are more successful than Katy Perry's songs. <hr> Therefore, Katy Perry's songs are less successful than Taylor Swift's songs. The argument is _____ The argument is _____

12.	All dogs with waggy tails are mammals. _____ Therefore, all dogs are mammals. The argument is _____ The argument is _____
13.	If quantum gravity is real, then we will be able to create time machines soon. Quantum gravity is not real. _____ Therefore, we will not be able to create time machines soon. The argument is _____ The argument is _____
14.	In some human cultures, infanticide is morally permissible. In some human cultures, cannibalism is morally permissible. _____ Therefore, there are no universal principles governing what is morally permissible. The argument is _____ The argument is _____
15.	A progressive tax system is necessary for the health of the economy. The economy is not very healthy right now. _____ Therefore, we must not have a progressive tax system. The argument is _____ The argument is _____

16. All scientists believe that the earth orbits the sun.
_____

Therefore, the earth orbits the sun.

The argument is _____

The argument is _____

---

17. Androids dream of electric sheep.
Electric sheep are typically blue.
_____

Therefore, at least some of an android's dreams are blue.

The argument is _____

The argument is _____

---

18. Kilimanjaro is the highest mountain in Africa.
Africa is the biggest continent on Earth.
_____

Therefore, Kilimanjaro is the highest mountain in the biggest continent on Earth.

The argument is _____

The argument is _____

---

19. If materialism is false, then it must be the case that the mind is composed of at least two distinct kinds of stuff.
If the mind is composed of two distinct kinds of stuff, then I must have a soul.
If I have a soul, then everyone has a soul.
_____

Therefore, if materialism is false, then everyone has a soul.

The argument is _____

The argument is _____

20.	All dogs are mammals. All mammals have hair. ——————————— Therefore, all dogs have hair. The argument is ———————————— The argument is ————————————

Q2. Write out an argument that fits each of the following criteria. Try your best to come up with an original argument!

1. A valid argument with all true premises and a true conclusion.
2. A valid argument with all false premises and a false conclusion.
3. A valid argument with one false premise, one true premise, and a false conclusion.
4. A valid argument with all false premises and a true conclusion.
5. A valid argument with one false premise, one true premise, and a true conclusion.
6. An invalid argument with all true premises and a true conclusion.

Addendum: Deductive versus Inductive Arguments

Validity is an all-or-nothing affair: if the premises of an argument guarantee the truth of the argument's conclusion, then the argument is valid. Anything short of this guarantee results in an invalid argument. Arguments that are evaluated according to this very high standard are called *Deductive Arguments*:

> A **DEDUCTIVE ARGUMENT** is one in which it is asserted that the conclusion is guaranteed to be true if the premises are true.

All the arguments we have looked at so far, including those in the exercise sets, have been deductive arguments. It is not always appropriate to evaluate an argument according to such high standards, however. Consider the following argument, for example:

The sun rose this morning.
The sun rose yesterday morning.
The sun rose the morning before yesterday.
The sun has risen every morning of my life.
_____

Therefore, the sun will rise tomorrow morning.

This is an invalid argument because we can imagine a scenario, however unlikely this scenario might be, in which all of the premises are true and the conclusion is false. Note, though, that the premises provide lots of evidence for the conclusion. So, the fact that the argument is invalid does not automatically mean that the argument is completely worthless. Sometimes an argument is not offered as a proof of its conclusion, and it can be a good argument as long as it offers some good evidence for the conclusion—that is, if the premises make the conclusion *probably* true. The above argument is like this. Such an argument is called an *Inductive Argument*:

> An *INDUCTIVE ARGUMENT* is one in which it is asserted that the conclusion has a high probability of being true if the premises are true.

Many inductive arguments involve generalizations like in the example above: we have direct evidence of many instances of something occurring and we generalize to all cases, or to all future cases, based on this. And many such generalizations seem quite reasonable: in the above example, the premises go a long way toward establishing the truth of the conclusion. Logicians call such an argument *inductively strong*.

Here is another argument for us to consider:

It rained on Halloween last year.
It did not rain on Halloween the year before last.
_____

Therefore, it will rain on Halloween this year.

This is an inductive argument: based on some past experiences, it draws an inference about something in the future that has yet to be experienced. The argument does not give us good reasons to think that it will rain on Halloween this year; at best, given the premises, there's a 50-50 chance. It is an *inductively weak* argument.

One final example:

The first swan I observed was white.
The second swan I observed was white.
All swans I have observed up to this point have been white.

———————————

Therefore, all swans are black.

Again, this is an inductive argument. However, the argument does a really bad job of providing evidence for the conclusion; it is an inductively very weak argument.

The point is that not all invalid arguments are created equally: some invalid arguments can provide us with good reasons for thinking their conclusions are true, for example, while others can provide us with only a moderate amount of evidence. Evaluating inductive arguments, therefore, is more difficult than evaluating deductive arguments. With deductive arguments, as we have seen, it's all very black and white: either an argument is valid or invalid, and there are no gray areas. That is, an argument's premises either provide 100% support for its conclusion, or they do not provide 100% support for its conclusion. With inductive arguments, however, there can be lots of gray: the premises might provide 99.9% support for the conclusion, or maybe just 99.8% support, or 99.7% support, and so on. That is, the question of *how much* support the premises provide needs to be answered. In an inductive argument we ask the following: given the premises, how *probable* is it that the conclusion is true. And to answer this question, we may need to import from mathematics everything we know about probability!

The good news is that, moving forward in this book, we will be focusing exclusively on deductive arguments: it will *always* be appropriate to evaluate every argument according to the very high standard of deductive validity. For this reason, we will never need to specify that any argument we are evaluating is a deductive argument, and we will simply speak of straight-up **validity** or **invalidity**. It is, however, important to realize that (a) not *all* arguments are deductive arguments and (b) a non-deductive argument can still be a good argument. With this point made, let us proceed.

Chapter 2

Logical Form

2.1 Form and Content

Consider the following word problem you might encounter in grade-school math class:

New York City is 311 miles away. Philadelphia is 289 miles away. How much further away is New York than Philadelphia?

This is pretty straightforward: $311 - 289 = 22$. No problem! Here's another one:

Jack shot a deer that weighed 311 pounds. Tom shot a deer that weighed 289 pounds. How much more than Tom's deer did Jack's deer weigh?

Well, this turns out to be the same problem: $311 - 289 = 22$. Here's one more:

Alice has 311 Lego pieces. Bob has 289 Lego pieces. How many more Lego pieces than Bob does Alice have?

Yet again we have the same formulation: $311 - 289 = 22$. In one sense, these are very different problems: one is concerned with Jack, Tom, and some deer; another is concerned with two cities in the United States; and yet another is concerned with Alice, Bob, and some Lego pieces. In another sense, however, all three cases present us with one and the same problem: that is, the math to be done is the same in each case. We can put the point like this: the **CONTENT**, i.e. *what* each problem is talking about, is different in each case, whereas the **FORM**, i.e. the *structure* of each problem, is the same; and we can *capture* this structure with some mathematical symbols. Furthermore, from the point of view of solving the problems correctly, it is the form that counts: once we move away from the specifics of the content, we can quite easily solve the problem by focusing solely on the form.

A similar distinction between form and content can be applied to arguments. Consider the following argument, for example:

All men are mortal.

Socrates is a man.

―――――――――――

Therefore, Socrates is mortal.

Clearly, this is a valid argument: if the premises are true, then the conclusion must be true. Now, consider another argument:

All giraffes are tall.
Bob is a giraffe.

―――――――――――

Therefore, Bob is tall.

Once more, this is a valid argument. In one sense, of course, these are very different arguments: one is talking about Socrates, being a man and being immortal; the other is talking about Bob, giraffes, and being tall.

Consequently, the arguments have different **CONTENT**. In another sense, however, these two arguments are identical: they have the same **FORM**, or structure. Right now, we don't have the tools to capture the form of an argument, but the following goes at least some way toward representing the form of each argument:

All A's are B's
X is an A

_____

Therefore, X is a B

There is no mention of Socrates, mortality, Bob, or giraffes here, but I hope you can see how, without including these content details, this representation still successfully captures what is going on in each of the above arguments.

Which of these—form or content—do we appeal to when evaluating these arguments for validity? So far in this book, we have used the content of an argument to check for validity. The Counterexample Method, as discussed in Chapter 1, asks us to try to imagine a scenario in which all of an argument's premises are true but in which the conclusion is false. For the first argument, we can see that any scenario in which all men are mortal and Socrates is a man must also be a scenario in which Socrates is mortal. For the second argument, we can see that any scenario in which all giraffes are tall and Bob is a giraffe must also be a scenario in which Bob is tall. Using the Counterexample Method in both of these cases, then, we appeal to the content of each argument: in order to imagine the required scenarios, we need to engage with what the argument is talking about.

But recall that the Counterexample Method is only as good as our imagination: if I cannot imagine a counterexample, then it might be because my imagination is limited in some way. In addition, any prejudices we might have concerning the content of an argument can prevent us from engaging fairly with that content. So, let's also look at the form, or structure, of each argument. If the above representation of the original arguments adequately captures the structure of the arguments, then successfully evaluating this *representation* for validity, would mean successfully evaluating the *arguments* for validity. And there certainly is something valid going on in the representation: if all A's are B's, and if X is an A, then yes, we are guaranteed that X is a B. This tells us something very important: ***the validity of an argument does not necessarily pertain to the content of that argument***. And this suggests that we can judge whether an argument is valid without engaging with the content of the argument.

To further appreciate this point, note that *any* argument that can be represented in the above way will be valid. Consider this one:

All flapdoodles are blingblongs.
Timbob is a flapdoodle.

_____

Therefore, Timbob is a blingblong.

The content here is nonsensical: What the heck is a flapdoodle? What's a blingblong? And who is Timbob? However, the argument's structure is identical to the above two arguments. We have judged this structure to be valid. Consequently, this argument is valid.

All of this suggests that we fine-tune our understanding of validity. In Chapter 1, we defined a valid argument as one in which it is impossible for the premises to be true and the conclusion false. This definition successfully captures the idea that in a valid argument the truth of the premises must guarantee the truth of the conclusion. And if it is possible to evaluate the form of an argument while retaining this core aspect of the concept of validity, then we can define validity as follows:

A ***VALID*** argument is one that has a valid argument form.

From now on, then, let's understand the validity of an argument as pertaining to the logical form of that argument. And if this is how we are to proceed, then to really make progress on understanding the difference between valid and invalid arguments, we need to invest some time in developing the skills for *capturing* the logical form of arguments. This is what we will be doing for the remainder of this chapter.

2.2 Sentential Logic: A Formal Language

In Chapter 1, we defined an argument as a sequence of sentences, one of which is the conclusion, the rest of which are premises. This means that capturing the logical form of an argument will involve capturing the logical form of sentences. But, how do we get at the logical form of sentences? To answer this, let's first observe that most of the sentences in this book are written in the English language. English is what is referred to as a *natural* language: it has evolved naturally down through the centuries without anyone sitting down to draw up its grammar rules. (There *are* grammar rules in English, of course, but native English speakers learn to communicate successfully in the language without ever thinking explicitly about these rules). Like English, most of the languages spoken in the world today are natural languages—Chinese, Arabic, Spanish, and so on—and the primary purpose of these languages is the communication of content. What we need is a way of capturing the form of sentences; perhaps a non-natural, i.e. *artificial*, language will do the job? The primary purpose of an artificial language can also be the communication of content, however; Esperanto, for example, is an artificial language created in 1887 with a view to breaking down the language barriers that exist between speakers of different natural languages. So, the fact that a language is artificial does not, all by itself, mean that this language will help us articulate the logical form of sentences.

Some artificial languages do not focus on the transmission of content, however. One obvious example, perhaps—considering the examples we opened the chapter with—is mathematics. Think of the sentence "2 + 2 = 4." What is being communicated about the world here? Something like "two of anything together with another two of those things will give you four of those things." *What* things? Well, the sentence doesn't specify this—it could be trees, chairs, planets, invisible magic unicorns, or *anything*. The sentence "2 + 2 = 4" is simply not in the business of communicating such content. Instead, it is trying to capture something very general that is applicable to *many* different contexts. What the sentence is capturing is *form*—mathematics is a *formal* language: most of the content, or meaning, of a sentence is set aside, so that we can focus on the deeper structure of the sentence.[1]

Over the centuries, logicians have developed a number of formal *logical* languages that set aside the content of sentences and arguments in order to focus on the structural aspects of these sentences and arguments. In this book, you will be introduced to two of these formal logical languages. This chapter, and the two chapters that follow it, covers is called **Sentential Logic (SL)**. In Chapters 7 and 8, we will encounter **Predicate Logic (PL)**, which is an extension of Sentential Logic.

Sentential Logic (SL)

As suggested by its name, the language of Sentential Logic pertains to sentences, i.e. sentences in the logical sense. It will enable us to capture the logical form of sentences, and, subsequently, the logical form of arguments. When encountering a sentence that is articulated in English, we will speak of *symbolizing* this sentence in SL, or *translating* this sentence into SL.

Every language, whether natural, artificial, or formal, has a **vocabulary** and **rules of grammar**. A language's vocabulary consists of the symbols that are used to construct sentences of that language. A language's grammar rules tell us how to properly use the vocabulary in that language. We will cover both SL's vocabulary and its rules of grammar in this chapter. We begin by presenting its vocabulary. We will develop a sense of SL's rules of grammar as we work through its vocabulary; a formal statement of this grammar can wait until later in the chapter.

Sentential Logic's Vocabulary:
Atomic Sentences: A, B, C, . . . Z. (Subscripts are also allowed, e.g., A_1, M_{47}, etc.)
Sentence Operators: $\bullet$, $\vee$, $\sim$, $\supset$, $\equiv$
Grouping symbols: ( )

---

[1] Two other examples might help here. Computer programming languages, like Java and C++, are formal languages: computers don't really grasp the meaning, or content, of anything, but they can follow general instructions that are written in these languages. We can also understand musical notation as a formal language. To appreciate any meaning, or content, that music has, one ought to play, or listen to, the music; a written musical score, on the other hand, is a formal representation of the notes being played.

And that is the entirety of SL's grammar! The question now is: How are we going to use these symbols to capture the logical form of sentences and arguments? Well, let's get to work!

We begin by considering the following simple sentence of English:

Today is Thursday.

The first thing to notice about this English sentence is that it is a sentence in the logical sense: it makes an assertion about the world that is either true or false. Also note that this sentence cannot be analyzed, or broken down, into other sentences. That is, taking any part of the sentence in isolation will result in sentence fragments, and not a complete sentence. For example, "Today is," or "is Thursday," all by themselves, do not make assertions. This brings us to the idea of an *atomic sentence*:

An **ATOMIC SENTENCE** is a logical sentence that cannot be broken down into component logical sentences.

An atomic sentence is the smallest unit of sentences, so to speak. The concept is analogous to the concept of an atom in physics and chemistry, which was once understood to be the smallest unit of matter.[2]

SL treats atomic sentences in a very straightforward manner, by simply assigning an upper-case English letter to each one. Any of the letters from 'A' through 'Z' can be used; and we can help ourselves to more than just 26 options by allowing for subscripts as well. So, for example, each of the following can be used to translate an atomic sentence of English into SL: 'A,' 'B,' 'P,' 'Z,' 'J_1,' and 'T_{247}.' Returning to the above sentence of English, then, let's just pick an upper-case letter. We can use any letter, but it can be helpful to choose one that is prominent in the original sentence. So, let's choose 'T'. And that's it: the logical form in SL of the above sentence is as follows:

T

Let's congratulate ourselves—this is our first translation from English into SL!

Not all sentences of English are atomic sentences. Consider the following sentence, for example:

Today is Thursday and it is raining.

This is clearly a sentence in the logical sense, but notice that it consists of two smaller logical sentences:

Today is Thursday.
It is raining.

Each of these is an atomic sentence. The original sentence is what's called a *compound sentence*:

A **COMPOUND SENTENCE** is a logical sentence that can be broken down into component atomic logical sentences.

All compound sentences are composed of two or more atomic sentences. Once again, we can appeal to chemistry for an analogy: compound sentences are composed of atomic sentences just like molecules are composed of atoms. In a sense, therefore, compound sentences are the molecules of SL.

---

[2]Of course, early in the twentieth century it was discovered that atoms are composed of even smaller bits of matter; that is, atoms are not really *atomic*! The analogy will hold, however: later in the book, we will be taking a look at the parts of atomic sentences. For the time being, however, atomic sentences will be understood to have no parts.

In SL, the logical form of an atomic sentence is simply whatever capital letter you choose to represent that atomic sentence. However, capturing the logical form of a compound sentence requires more than simply identifying the atomic sentences involved and assigning an upper-case letter to each of them. Notice that, when we analyze the above sentence, and label each atomic sentence with an upper-case letter, there is still a part of the original sentence unaccounted for:

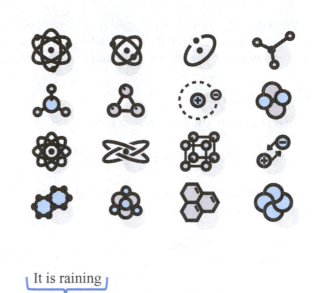

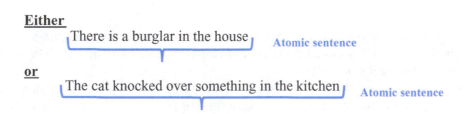

Today is Thursday **and** It is raining

Atomic sentence   Atomic sentence

The word "and" is not part of either atomic sentence; instead, it serves to connect the atomic sentences in a particular way. In this instance, the claim in the compound sentence is that both of the atomic sentences are true: today is Thursday AND it is raining. Here is a different example:

Either there is a burglar in the house or the cat knocked over something in the kitchen.

Again, we can analyze the compound sentence into its component atomic sentences:

Either
There is a burglar in the house   Atomic sentence

or
The cat knocked over something in the kitchen   Atomic sentence

Something different is left over in this case: the words "either" and "or." Again, these terms are not part of the atomic sentences; they serve to connect the atomic sentences, though in a way that's different from the word "and" in the previous sentence. There is no claim that *both* of these atomic sentences are the case; rather, the claim is that *at least one* of these sentences is the case.

The "and" in the first example, and the "either . . . or . . ." in the most recent example are called ***sentence operators***.[3] These are not part of any atomic sentence; rather, they "operate upon" atomic sentences in different ways. A compound sentence, then, is not just a random arrangement of atomic sentences; it is an organized whole in which atomic sentences are bound together in a particular way by sentence operators. So, if our first step in capturing the logical form of sentences was to identify and symbolize the atomic sentences involved, then a second step now suggests itself: identify and symbolize any sentence operators that the sentence may have. You might think that, in English, there would be lots of different sentence operators; as it turns out, however,

---

[3]Sentence operators are also referred to as ***sentence connectives***.

we can do very well by using just *five* different operators. Each of these sentence operators has its own symbol in SL—they are listed in SL's vocabulary given earlier. We will now introduce the first three sentence operators. The remaining two sentence operators will be introduced later in the chapter.

Conjunctions

Consider, again, the following sentence:

Today is Thursday and it is raining.

As noted earlier, this is a compound sentence, with two atomic sentences. Let's assign an upper-case letter to each of these atomic sentences:

T: Today is Thursday.
R: It is raining.

When we assign upper-case letters to atomic sentences like this, we are providing what logicians call a **symbolization key** for the sentence. This is an all-important first step when performing any translation from English into SL. (And remember, the upper-case letters symbolize *entire* atomic sentences, and not just individual words of these sentences. It would be incorrect to think of 'T' as representing "Thursday," for example, or of 'R' as representing "raining.") Using these letters, and including the operator word that is left over, we are left with the following semi-translated sentence:

T and R[4]

The only part of the sentence yet to be symbolized is the word "and." In SL, we symbolize this with a dot: '•'. The result is the following complete translation of the sentence into SL:

T • R[5]

Typically, this is read as simply "T and R." Such "dot sentences" are called **conjunctions**. Everything to the left of the dot (in this case 'T') is called the **left-hand conjunct**; everything to the right of the dot (in this case 'R') is called the **right-hand conjunct**.

Any English sentence in which there is an explicit commitment to the truth of two component sentences can always be translated as a conjunction. Clearly, using the word "and" works in this way, but other words can serve the same purpose. Consider, for example, this sentence:

Today is Thursday but it is raining.

The person uttering these words is, unless she is lying, committed to both of the component atomic sentences being true: today is Thursday, and it is raining. Logicians say that this sentence has the same *logical commitments* as the previous sentence: they are both committed to the claim that today is Thursday, and also to the claim that it is raining. Consequently, like the earlier sentence, it is translated as a conjunction:

T • R

Other English words function in the same way as "and" and "but":

Today is Thursday; also it is raining.

---

[4]This sentence is half Sentential Logic and half English. I have heard such a sentence described as a sentence of *Loglish*!
[5]Two other symbols have been used to translate the English word "and": the '&' (ampersand) and the '∧' (carat). In this book, however, we will stick with the '•.'

Today is Thursday; however, it is raining.
Today is Thursday; fortunately, it is raining.
Today is Thursday; unfortunately, it is raining.

Each of these sentences gets translated as the same conjunction:

T • R

Focusing on the logical commitments of a sentence like this obviously misses out on some subtleties of the English language. This need not overly concern us in the current context, however. Other disciplines take similar liberties. Physicists, for example, will often present an idealized model of a phenomenon that, while leaving out some details, allows for a more straightforward understanding of the phenomenon in question. And mathematics has made lots of progress by appealing to perfect circles, perfectly straight lines, perfect right angles, and so on—even though none of these things actually exist in nature. In the right context, then, setting aside real-world aspects is perfectly appropriate.

One other point before moving on. When assigning an upper-case letter to each atomic sentence, we must be explicit about what the letter stands for, even if there are contractions involved in the original sentence of English. For example, consider the following sentence:

José is tall and so is Ahmed.

The English language is taking a shortcut here: instead of explicitly asserting that Ahmed is tall, there is just the claim that he shares some property with José. We do not take these shortcuts in SL, however, and articulate the symbolization key as follows:

J: José is tall.
A: Ahmed is tall.

The resultant sentence of SL is

J • A

As we move through the gears in SL, it will be important to be on the lookout for how the English language takes shortcuts like this!

V Disjunctions

Here is another sentence for us to consider:

Either I will go to the fair or I will go to the mall.

This is a compound sentence, with two atomic sentences. Here is a symbolization key:

F: I will go to the fair.
M: I will go to the mall.

This enables us to articulate the following semi-translated version of the sentence:

Either F or M

The only parts of the sentence now unaccounted for are the words "either" and "or." Clearly, the person speaking these words is not committed to both going to the fair *and* going to the mall. Consequently, the sentence is not a conjunction. We need a new sentence operator. Traditionally, logicians have used the wedge, i.e. '∨,' to symbolize "either-or" sentences. This gives us the following complete translation of the above sentence into SL:

F ∨ M

Typically, this is read as "either F or M," or just "F or M." Such "wedge sentences" are called ***disjunctions***. Everything to the left of the wedge (in this case 'F') is called the ***left-hand disjunct***; everything to the right of the wedge (in this case 'M') is called the ***right-hand disjunct***. "Either-or" sentences, and all sentences that can be paraphrased as "either-or" sentences, can always be translated as disjunctions.

Here is another example:

Either the Republican candidate or the Democratic candidate will get elected.

Clearly, this is a disjunction, though we need to be careful when assigning atomic sentence letters, because this is one of those cases where English is taking a shortcut:

R: The Republican candidate will get elected.
D: The Democratic candidate will get elected.

We end up with the following sentence of SL:

R ∨ D

∿ Negations

Consider the following sentence:

It is not raining.

It might appear as if there is just one atomic sentence here, but we need to be careful! The atomic sentence in this case is the affirmative claim that it is raining:

R: It is raining.

What is left unaccounted for, then, is the English word "not," which negates this atomic sentence. In semi-translated form, then, we get the following:

Not-R

The "not" here gets its own logical symbol: '~,' i.e. a tilde. The result is the following compound sentence of SL:

~R[6]

Typically, this is read as "not R," or "it is not the case that R." Such sentences are called ***negations***. In English, the "not" can appear anywhere in a sentence; in SL, however, the '~' is always at the front of a sentence. And, in general, an atomic sentence is always an *affirmative* sentence; that is, atomic sentences do not contain "nots." When you are translating from English into SL, therefore, always be on the lookout for explicit "nots."

---

[6]Logicians have also used '¬' (i.e. the hoe) to symbolize "not." Note that the minus symbol from mathematics is *not* used to symbolize negations.

If you spot one, then make sure that it is left out of your symbolization key. It will then reappear in the translation of the sentence as a '~.'

Negations are different from the other sentence operators we have encountered so far. In conjunctions and disjunctions, it is clearly the case that the '•' and the '∨' are *connecting* the component sentences: they bind them together, so to speak, to form a compound whole. This is not what is happening with negations—there is just *one* atomic sentence being operated upon. For this reason, the negation is what logicians refer to as a *monadic* sentence operator. All the other sentence operators—the two we have already been introduced to, and the two that we will be encountering later in the chapter—are called *dyadic* operators.

So far, then, we have introduced three of the five logical operators in SL. Before moving on, we can now explicitly articulate a method of translating sentences of English into sentences of SL:

Translating from English into SL

Step 1: Write out a symbolization key for the sentence. (That is, identify the atomic sentences involved, and assign a different upper-case letter to each atomic sentence. If there is just one atomic sentence, then the upper-case letter you assign to that sentence will be the translation of the English sentence. You do not need to proceed to **Steps 2** and **3**).

Step 2: Identify the operator words in the English sentence.

Step 3: Use the appropriate operator symbols to translate the rest of the sentence.

With practice, you will be able to move through these steps quickly. Starting out, though, it is important to be explicit about the steps we are taking. Let's work through some examples. Consider the following sentence:

I am going out to eat, but I will not be having dessert.

Step 1 asks us to write out a symbolization key. So, let's identify the atomic sentences involved, and assign an upper-case letter to each one:

G: I am going out to eat.
D: I will be having dessert.

Note that 'D' does not have the "not" that appears in the original sentence. **Step 2** asks us to identify the English operator words involved. We can be explicit about this and write down a semi-translated sentence:

G, but not-D

Step 3 involves using the appropriate symbols for the operator words identified in **Step 2**. In this case, we need to translate the words "but" and "not." As mentioned earlier, the word "but" indicates that what we have is a conjunction: the sentence is logically committed to both 'G' and also 'not-D.' Consequently, this is going to be a "dot" sentence. And, as we have just seen, the English word "not" gets translated with a tilde. Here, then, is the resultant sentence of SL:

G • ~D

Here, we have a compound sentence—a conjunction—in which a part of the sentence, i.e. the right-hand conjunct, is itself a compound sentence. This sort of thing happens a lot in SL. The '•' here is called the ***main operator*** in that it pulls all the pieces of the compound sentence together. When there is more than one logical operator in a sentence, we should be able to identify which one is the main operator. This can get complicated, however, and we will keep things fairly simple for now. Later in the chapter, we will spend more time on identifying a sentence's main operator.

Here is another example:

My team will win the tournament or I am mistaken.

Following **Step 1**, we articulate a symbolization key:

T: My team will win the tournament.
M: I am mistaken.

Notice that, even though saying that one is mistaken has a negative connotation, grammatically speaking, there is no "not" involved in the atomic sentence "I am mistaken." **Step 2** provides us with the following semi-translated sentence:

T or M

In **Step 3**, we use a '$\vee$' to translate the English "or," and we end up with the following compound sentence of SL:

T $\vee$ M

In some cases, **Step 1** will be already completed for you. The provided symbolization key will sometimes pertain to just one sentence; at other times, it will cover a bunch of sentences. Here is a brief example of the latter. (You will encounter more examples in Exercise Set 2.2). In this example, we will use upper-case letters with subscripts.

Symbolization Key
A_1: Adam is a lawyer.
A_2: Adam is a doctor.
B_1: Barbara is a lawyer.
B_2: Barbara is a doctor.

Let's now translate the following sentences into SL:

(a) Both Adam and Barbara are lawyers.
(b) Adam is not a lawyer, but he is a doctor.
(c) Either Adam is a doctor or Barbara is a lawyer.

Using the symbolization key, and working through **Steps 2** and **3**, we end up with the following translations:

(a) $A_1 \bullet B_1$
(b) $\sim A_1 \bullet A_2$
(c) $A_2 \vee B_1$

Exercise Set 2.2

Q1. Translate the following English sentences into SL. In each case, a symbolization key is provided. Write your answers in the space provided. The first one is done for you.

1. Either a Democrat or a Republican will get elected.

Symbolization Key:	**D:** A Democrat will get elected.
	R: A Republican will get elected.
Translation:	$D \vee R$

2. Ottawa is the capital city of Canada.

Symbolization Key:	**O:** Ottawa is the capital city of Canada.
Translation:	

3. Arnold is short or Graham is not short.

Symbolization Key:	**A:** Arnold is short.
	G: Graham is short.
Translation:	

4. Bob is not the smartest person in the room.

Symbolization Key:	**B:** Bob is the smartest person in the room.
Translation:	

5. Syracuse is cold in the winter, but it is warm in the summer.

Symbolization Key:	**W:** Syracuse is cold in the winter.
	S: Syracuse is warm in the summer.
Translation:	

6. Arnaud is not tall, but he is good at basketball.

Symbolization Key:	**A:** Arnaud is tall.
	B: Arnaud is good at basketball.
Translation:	

7. It is snowing today and, unfortunately, it will be snowing tomorrow as well.

Symbolization Key:	**S:** It is snowing today.
	T: It will be snowing tomorrow.
Translation:	

8. Lily is not the best public speaker, but she is not the worst either.

Symbolization Key:	**B:** Lily is the best public speaker.
	W: Lily is the worst public speaker.
Translation:	

9. Either Louis teaches kindergarten, or Miriam teaches in high school.

Symbolization Key:	**L:** Louis teaches kindergarten.
	T: Miriam teaches in high school.
Translation:	

10. Mount Everest, not Kilimanjaro, is the tallest mountain in the world.

Symbolization Key:	**E:** Mount Everest is the tallest mountain in the world.
	K: Kilimanjaro is the tallest mountain in the world.
Translation:	

Q2. Using the symbolization key provided, translate each English sentence into SL. Write your answers in the space provided. The first one is done for you.

L: Lily is a dog.
T: Tibbles is a cat.
M: Margaret is a goldfish.

1. Lily is a dog and Tibbles is a cat.

   > **Translation:**   L • T

2. Margaret is not a goldfish.

   > **Translation:**

3. Either Tibbles is a cat or Lily is a dog.

   > **Translation:**

4. Lily is not a dog, but Margaret is a goldfish.

   > **Translation:**

5. Either Tibbles is not a cat or Lily is not a dog.

   > **Translation:**

6. Margaret is either a goldfish or not a goldfish.

   > **Translation:**

7. Margaret is a goldfish, even though Tibbles is a cat.

   > **Translation:**

8. Lily is not a dog; unfortunately, Tibbles is not a cat either.

   > **Translation:**

9. Margaret is a goldfish; otherwise, Lily is a dog.

> **Translation:**

10. It is not the case that Tibbles is a cat, but it is the case that Margaret is a goldfish.

> **Translation:**

Q3. Translate the following English sentences into SL. Make sure you write out the symbolization key in each case. Write your answers in the space provided. The first one is done for you.

1. Today is Wednesday and it is raining.

> **Symbolization Key:**   **W:** Today is Wednesday.
> **R:** It is raining.
>
> **Translation:**   W • R

2. New York is not the capital of the United States.

> **Symbolization Key:**
>
> **Translation:**

3. I do not have a broken hand, but I do have a broken ankle.

> **Symbolization Key:**
>
> **Translation:**

4. Both Adam and Beatrice have read the Harry Potter books.

> **Symbolization Key:**
>
> **Translation:**

5. I am not hungry and I am not thirsty.

> **Symbolization Key:**
>
> **Translation:**

6. The Red Sox are awesome, but the Yankees suck.

> **Symbolization Key:**
>
> **Translation:**

7. Either I get some work done or I won't be able to go the mall.

> **Symbolization Key:**
>
> **Translation:**

8. It's either raining or not raining.

> **Symbolization Key:**
>
> **Translation:**

9. I love pizza; unfortunately, there is no pizza left.

> **Symbolization Key:**
>
> **Translation:**

10. It is not the case that Elvis Presley sold more records than anyone else.

> **Symbolization Key:**
>
> **Translation:**

11. Syracuse is not the biggest city in the world, but it is my favorite city in the world.

> **Symbolization Key:**
>
> **Translation:**

12. Murder is a horrible crime, but I don't believe in capital punishment.

> **Symbolization Key:**
>
> **Translation:**

13. Either the Bills won't win on Sunday or the Giants won't win on Sunday.

> **Symbolization Key:**
>
> **Translation:**

14. It's not you, it's me.

> **Symbolization Key:**
>
> **Translation:**

15. The Bible is the best-selling book of all time.

> **Symbolization Key:**
>
> **Translation:**

2.3 Conditional Sentences

Let's move on to the fourth sentence operator we will be using. Consider the following sentence of English:

If the Buffalo Bills win this game, then they will go to the playoffs.

Here is a symbolization key for the sentence:

B: The Buffalo Bills win this game.
P: The Buffalo Bills will go to the playoffs.

Note the absence of pronouns in the symbolization key. The word "they" in the second clause of the sentence refers to the Buffalo Bills. Here is the semi-translated sentence:

If B, then P

Obviously, there is no commitment here to the truth of both of these claims. That is, the sentence is not claiming that *both* the Bills will win the game *and* that they will go to the playoffs. Consequently, this sentence is not a conjunction. It's also not a disjunction: in a disjunction, there is a commitment to at least one of the disjuncts being true, and this is not what is going on here. As far as the person uttering this sentence is concerned, there is every possibility that the Buffalo Bills will not win the game and that they also will not go to the playoffs. Instead, the claim in this sentence is that there is some sort of *conditional* relationship between the two atomic sentences: *if* one is true, *then* so is the other. We introduce a new symbol to capture this kind of logical connection: the horseshoe, i.e. '⊃.' We end up with the following compound sentence of SL:

B ⊃ P[7]

Typically, this is read as "If B, then P." The "if" and the "then" that are present in the English sentence are packed into the '⊃' in the middle, so to speak. Such "horseshoe sentences" are called **conditional sentences**, or simply **conditionals**. Everything to the left of the horseshoe, i.e. the "if" part of the sentence (in this case 'B'), is called the **antecedent**; everything to the right of the horseshoe, i.e. the "then" part of the sentence (in this case 'P'), is called the **consequent**.

Conditional sentences can be confusing, so we need to be very careful. A first point to make is that conditional sentences are *not* arguments. You might be tempted to read the above sentence as "B, therefore P," for example, but this would be to mischaracterize the sentence. Here is a formal reconstruction of this argument[8]:

B
_____
∴ P

This argument includes the claim that the premise, i.e. 'B,' is true. It is also saying that the sentence 'P' is true. Finally, it insists that the latter sentence follows from the former sentence. In the above conditional sentence, however, there is no claim that 'B' is in fact true. There is also no claim that 'P' is true. Rather, the idea is that *if* 'B' is true, *then* so is 'P.' It is left open whether these atomic sentences are actually true. The argument "B, therefore P" does *not* leave this open. The point should be clear: conditional sentences are not arguments.

---

[7]Logicians have also used the single arrow, i.e. '→,' to symbolize "if-then" sentences.
[8]We are getting ahead of ourselves a little here. I give this example of the form of an argument to illustrate a specific point about conditional sentences. Later in the chapter, we will *officially* focus on presenting the logical form of arguments.

The next important point pertains to the order of things. How should we translate the following sentence, for example?

The Buffalo Bills will go to the playoffs if they win this game.

The atomic sentences here are the same as in the earlier sentence, so we will use the same symbolization key. In this case, however, the atomic sentences are in a different order. Notice, though, that the conditional relationship between the two atomic sentences is exactly the same: the Bills going to the playoffs is conditional on their winning the game. In other words, the "if" part of the sentence, i.e. the antecedent, is understood to be the same in both cases, which means the translation is exactly the same as before:

B ⊃ P

In general, no matter what the order of things in the English sentence is, once we identify the "if"-clause of the sentence, then that becomes the antecedent in the resultant translation in SL.

Another thing to note is that an English sentence can be appropriately translated as a conditional sentence in SL even if the words "if" and "then" are nowhere present in the English sentence. Here are some examples, using the same atomic sentences as provided earlier:

The Buffalo Bills will go to the playoffs provided they win this game.
The Buffalo Bills will go to the playoffs given that they win this game.
The Buffalo Bills winning this game implies that they will go to the playoffs.

In each of these cases, the conditional relationship between the two atomic sentences involved is the same as in the original sentence, so each sentence gets translated into SL in the same way:

B ⊃ P

With conditionals, then, we have to be very careful when deciding what to put before the horseshoe and what to put after the horseshoe. With conjunctions and disjunctions, no similar issue arises. For example, a sentence that is logically committed to the truth of both 'P' and 'Q' can be translated in two different ways, both of which preserve this logical commitment: 'P • Q' and 'Q • P.' In general, there is no need to tinker with the order of the conjuncts in this way—we should just put things in the order they appear in the English sentence—but we can clearly see that these translations mean the same thing. (In the next chapter, we will say that these two sentences are logically equivalent). The same goes for disjunctions: 'either P or Q' and 'either Q or P' basically mean the same thing. That is, 'P ∨ Q' and 'Q ∨ P' are logically equivalent. However, things are very different with conditionals! Let's use a different example to further illustrate this:

If Maria will order sushi, then Robert will be visiting her house this evening.

Here is a symbolization key for this sentence:

M: Maria will order sushi.
R: Robert will be visiting Maria's house this evening.

In the sentence, Maria's ordering of sushi implies Robert's visit to her house. The "if"-clause is clearly identifiable, and the sentence is translated into SL as follows:

M ⊃ R

Now, here is another sentence, using the same atomic sentences:

If Robert will be visiting Maria's house this evening, then Maria will order sushi.

The "if"-clause is different in this case, so we end up with

R ⊃ M

In this case, the conditional relationship is going the other way. Robert's visiting implies Maria's ordering of sushi. The sentences clearly differ in meaning.

This consideration leads us to a hugely important distinction—that between "if" and "only if." Let us take a closer look.

IF versus ONLY IF

Consider the following three sentences of English:

(a) I can vote in a US federal election if I am a US citizen.
(b) I can vote in a US federal election only if I am a US citizen.
(c) I can vote in a US federal election if and only if I am a US citizen.

We can use the following symbolization key for all of these sentences:

V: I can vote in a US federal election.
C: I am a US citizen.

This gives us the following semi-translated sentences:

(a) V if C.
(b) V only if C.
(c) V if and only if C.

At first glance, you might think that these three sentences are saying more or less the same thing: my being able to vote in a US federal election and my being a US citizen are conditionally linked. That is, there is "if" stuff going on in each case. However, further analysis reveals that the sentences are saying different things, and that each should be translated into SL in a different way.

To address this, let's first separate sentences (a) and (b) from sentence (c). Both (a) and (b) will be translated using a horseshoe. Sentences of type (c) will be considered later in the chapter. Consider, then, sentence (a):

(a) I can vote in a US federal election if I am a US citizen.

Using the symbolization key as articulated earlier, the "if"-clause here is clearly 'C,' and we end up with the following sentence of SL:

C ⊃ V

We have been focusing on capturing the logical form of sentences and haven't really concerned ourselves with whether the sentences at hand are true or false. And, of course, there is a good reason for this: our ultimate concern is validity, and we have discovered that the validity of an argument has little to do with the actual truth-values of the sentences that compose that argument. For the purposes of illustration, however, let's bring truth and falsity back into the picture for a bit. So, is (**a**) a true sentence? That is, does the fact that someone is a US citizen imply that that person can vote in a federal election? Or, alternatively: can a person be a US citizen and still *not* be permitted to vote in a US federal election? Well, yes! There are two clear-cut examples: you can be a US citizen under the age of 18, or you can be a US citizen who is a convicted felon—in both of these cases, US citizenship does *not* give you the right to vote. So, sentence (**a**) is false.

Now consider sentence (**b**):

(**b**) I can vote in a US federal election only if I am a US citizen.

Initially, this might look to be saying the same thing as the previous sentence—how much difference can that word "only" make? Well, as it turns out, it makes a huge difference! Before translating the sentence into SL, we should convince ourselves that it needs to be translated differently from the earlier sentence. Again, for the purposes of illustration, we will focus on the sentence's truth-value. Is it true that I can vote in a US federal election only if I am a US citizen? Well, yes! If I am not a US citizen, then I am not permitted to vote. Sentence (**b**), then, is true, whereas sentence (**a**) is false. This means that (**a**) and (**b**) must not be the same logical sentence: we assumed the Principle of Non-contradiction in Chapter 1, which means that no logical sentence is both true and false. Consequently, sentence (**b**) should be translated differently from sentence (**a**). So, how *do* we translate sentence (**b**)? Well, one approach would be to first paraphrase the sentence. To say that I can vote only if I am a US citizen is to say the following:

If I am not a US citizen, then I cannot vote in a US federal election.

This suggests the following sentence of SL:

~C ⊃ ~V

And this does capture the meaning of sentence (**b**). We can, however, provide a translation that does not have negations. Ask yourself: According to sentence (**b**), what is guaranteed to be the case if you can vote in a US federal election? Answer: you are guaranteed to be a US citizen. In other words, if I can vote in a US federal election, then I am a US citizen. And this gives us the following translation:

V ⊃ C

Both of these ways of translating an "only-if" sentence are correct. Arguably, however, we can formulate more palatable translation guidelines if we do not involve negations, so we will highlight the second of these ways of translating an "only-if" sentence. Here, then, is what we need to know when it comes to translating "if" sentences and "only if" sentences:

An "**if**"-**clause** of a sentence is always the **antecedent** of a conditional sentence.
An "**only if**"-**clause** of a sentence is always the **consequent** of a conditional.

Here is another example that serves to further illustrate the distinction. Take the following two sentences:

I am European if I was born in Ireland.
I am European only if I was born in Ireland.

These sentences might look to be saying more or less the same thing, but once again the "only" makes all the difference. Here is a symbolization key:

E: I am European.
I: I was born in Ireland.

To convince ourselves that these sentences assert different things, and therefore need to be translated differently, once again consider the truth-value of each sentence. The first sentence is clearly true: if I was born in Ireland, then yes, I am European. As always, the "if"-clause is the antecedent, and we end up with the following sentence of SL:

I ⊃ E

However, the second sentence is false: I can be European even if I am not born in Ireland. And if the sentences differ in truth-value, then the translations should be different. How do we translate this second sentence? Well, the "only if"-clause is clearly identifiable, and, as per the above guidelines, this becomes the consequent of the resultant conditional sentence:

E ⊃ I

This says that if I am European, then I must be Irish—which is clearly false, as required.

It may take some time for you to fully separate "ifs" from "only ifs." And that's OK—that's what practice sets are for!—but make sure you *do* end up appreciating the distinction. You might start off thinking that there really isn't much of a difference, which is understandable, given that we sometimes run "ifs" and "only ifs" together in everyday conversation. However, in logic, we are trying to capture the logical form of the sentence *as it is written or uttered*, even if this does not always align perfectly with what people *use* the sentence for. Other academic disciplines go beyond everyday circumstances in similar ways. In chemistry, for example, analysis has revealed that water is composed of hydrogen and oxygen. For everyday purposes, this fact is irrelevant; in other contexts, however, this kind of chemical analysis allows us to more completely understand the nature of water and how it behaves under various conditions. Likewise, we typically communicate successfully in English without having a detailed appreciation of the logical structure of the sentences we use; however, logical analysis enables us to more completely understand the nature of sentences and how they "behave" in arguments.

Exercise Set 2.3

Q1. Translate the following sentences of English into SL. Remember to provide a symbolization key in each case. Write your answers in the space provided. The first one is done for you.

1. If I pay my phone bill, then the phone company will not cut me off.

Symbolization Key:	**P:** I pay my phone bill.
	C: The company will cut me off.
Translation:	P ⊃ ~C

2. David will win the race if he can run fast enough.

    Symbolization Key:

    Translation:

3. A platypus is a mammal only if it has hair.

    Symbolization Key:

    Translation:

4. I will vote for the Democratic candidate if you do not vote for the Republican candidate.

    Symbolization Key:

    Translation:

5. I will go to the game only if Charles does not go to the game.

    Symbolization Key:

    Translation:

6. Only if Melanie studies hard will she pass the course.

    Symbolization Key:

    Translation:

7. Germany winning implies France losing.

> **Symbolization Key:**
>
> **Translation:**

8. Egypt will get involved in the conflict only if Saudi Arabia calls for a meeting of all states in the Middle East.

> **Symbolization Key:**
>
> **Translation:**

9. Marcus will create amazing art if he gets the chance to go to art school.

> **Symbolization Key:**
>
> **Translation:**

10. If the weather is not nice tomorrow, then we will not go for a picnic.

> **Symbolization Key:**
>
> **Translation:**

11. We will go for a picnic tomorrow only if the weather is nice.

> **Symbolization Key:**
>
> **Translation:**

12. If it's true that Ronan is a dog person, then he must not be a cat person.

> **Symbolization Key:**
>
> **Translation:**

13. Ralph could not have committed the crime, given that he does not own a car.

> **Symbolization Key:**
>
> **Translation:**

14. Five times six equals three times ten only if the laws of mathematics make sense.

> **Symbolization Key:**
>
> **Translation:**

15. If Nathan isn't going to the party, then neither will I.

> **Symbolization Key:**
>
> **Translation:**

Q2. Using the symbolization key, translate each English sentence into SL. Write your answers in the space provided. The first one is done for you.

I: I am a musical genius.
J: Justin Bieber is a musical genius.
K: DJ Khaled is a musical genius.

1. If Justin Bieber is a musical genius, then so am I.

> **Translation:** $J \supset I$

2. Justin Bieber is a musical genius only if I am a musical genius.

> **Translation:**

3. DJ Khaled is a musical genius if Justin Bieber is a musical genius.

> **Translation:**

4. If I am not a musical genius, then neither is DJ Khaled.

> **Translation:**

5. Justin Bieber is not a musical genius only if DJ Khaled isn't one either.

> **Translation:**

6. DJ Khaled is not a musical genius only if I am not a musical genius.

> **Translation:**

7. It is false to say that I am a musical genius, given that Justin Bieber is a musical genius.

> **Translation:**

8. If Justin Bieber is a musical genius, then it must be the case that DJ Khaled is a musical genius.

> **Translation:**

9. DJ Khaled's being a musical genius implies that I am a musical genius.

> **Translation:**

10. I am not a musical genius if Justin Bieber is one.

> **Translation:**

2.4 The Main Operator

As already indicated, the logical operators do not operate upon atomic sentences only. In fact, things can get somewhat complicated. Consider the following sentence, for example:

Bob will go to the mall, and either Natalya or Jacob will go to the concert.

There are three atomic sentences in play here:

B: Bob will go to the mall.
N: Natalya will go to the concert.
J: Jacob will go to the concert.

And here is a semi-translated version of the sentence:

B, and either N or J

This generates the following:

B • N ∨ J

This is not yet a complete translation into SL because the sentence is ambiguous. That is, there is more than one interpretation available. Ask yourself: Is this sentence a conjunction, or is it a disjunction? Given that there is more than one operator involved, we need to identify the ***main operator***. To do this, we are going to have to use grouping symbols, which in SL are parentheses: '(' and ').' But *where* shall we place the parentheses? There are two options available for the above sentence:

B • (N ∨ J)
(B • N) ∨ J

Remember that the main goal of translation is to capture the logical form of English sentences. The question, then, is: Which of these correctly captures the form of the original sentence? One suggestion here is to take note of the punctuation found in the original sentence. Readers and writers of English use punctuation symbols to group words and phrases. Commas and semicolons, for example, serve to inform a reader that a short pause is required; they allow him or her to separate what is *before* the punctuation mark from what comes *after* it. In the above semi-translated version of the sentence, there is just one item of punctuation—a comma following the 'B.' This suggests that the operator word closest to this comma, i.e. "and," is what pulls the sentence together. This means that the '•' is the main operator:

B • (N ∨ J)

The original sentence, then, is best represented as a conjunction: it is committed to Bob going to the mall, and it is also committed to either Natalya or Jacob going to the concert. Let's double-check our answer by translating the other candidate translation back into English and seeing how it fares in capturing the logical form of the original sentence. The sentence

(B • N) ∨ J

has the '∨' as the main operator, and can be phrased in English as follows: "Either Bob will go to the mall and Natalya will go to the concert, or Jacob will go to the concert." Disjunctions are not committed to the truth of *two* sentences; instead, we are guaranteed only that at least *one* of the disjuncts is true. This translation, therefore, doesn't insist on the truth of the left-hand disjunct, i.e. that Bob is going to the mall and that Natalya is going to the concert. Nor does it commit us to the truth of the right-hand conjunct, i.e. that Jacob is going to the concert. However, the original sentence *is* clearly committed to Bob going to the mall. Consequently, this candidate translation does not adequately capture the structure of the original sentence.

When translating a sentence of English into SL, it is hugely important that we correctly identify the sentence's main operator. So, let's add one more step to our translation method that was outlined earlier in the chapter:

Translating from English into SL

Step 1: Write out a symbolization key for the sentence.
Step 2: Identify the operator words in the English sentence.
Step 3: Use the appropriate operator symbols to translate the rest of the sentence.
Step 4: If **Step 3** results in an ambiguous sentence, then identify the main operator and group the rest of the sentence accordingly.

Step 4, as we have begun to discover, can be quite challenging. Here are some general guidelines:

Identifying the Main Operator in a Sentence

Step A: Closely examine any punctuation that is present in the English sentence. This often suggests how the different parts of the sentence ought to be grouped.
Step B: Once you have completed the grouping of the different parts of the sentence and identified a main operator, check to see how well the resultant translation captures the structure of the original sentence.

In general, do not be happy when you have a bunch of upper-case letters and operator symbols, each of which has a correlate in the original sentence. That is, do not be content with the completion of **Step 3**. Your translation is not complete until you arrive at a non-ambiguous sentence of SL that has appropriate grouping symbols and a clearly identifiable main operator.

Sometimes, the punctuation in an English sentence does not help that much. Consider the following:

If it rains tomorrow, then if I finish work early, then I can go to the park.

Here are the three atomic sentences in play here:

R: It rains tomorrow.
F: I finish work early.
P: I can go to the park.

And here is a semi-translation:

If R, then if F, then P

And it's horseshoes all the way here:

R ⊃ F ⊃ P

Clearly, the correct translation will be a conditional sentence, but *which* of the following conditional sentences?

$(R \supset F) \supset P$
$R \supset (F \supset P)$

Unfortunately, there are too many commas in the original English sentence to help us out here. But translating each candidate translation back into English, or even back into the semi-translated version, still helps:

$(R \supset F) \supset P$
[In semi-translation: 'If R then F, then P.' (Or, perhaps: 'R implies F, only if P.')]

$R \supset (F \supset P)$
[In semi-translation: 'If R, then if F, then P.']

The second candidate here is arguably a less awkward sentence, though this all by itself won't tell us that it is the correct translation. It does end up being the better of the two candidate translations, however. To see this, go back to the original sentence. The first word is "if," which tells us that there is going to be a horseshoe involved. Now, once you see an "if" there's got to be a "then," either explicit or implied, that relates to this "if." Everything between the "if" and this "then" will be the antecedent of the resultant conditional. In this case, this "if"-clause is the sentence "it rains tomorrow." This sentence, all by itself, is the antecedent. The "then"-clause of the sentence is itself a conditional, and is grouped accordingly within parentheses. All of this tells us that the second of the above translations is the correct one.

Here is another example:

It is not the case that if I go to the mall, then I will either buy some clothes or eat dinner there.

Here is a symbolization key for this sentence:

M: I go to the mall.
B: I buy some clothes.
D: I eat dinner at the mall.

Here is a semi-translation:

It is not the case that if M, then B or D

Adding symbols for our operator words we get the following:

$\sim M \supset B \vee D$

This, as you should notice, is ambiguous. One of the following is the correct translation:

- $\sim M \supset (B \vee D)$

- $\sim (M \supset B) \vee D$

- $\sim [M \supset (B \vee D)]$

(Notice that in the third of these candidate translations I have used brackets, i.e. '[' and ']', to make the grouping easier to follow). So, which one of these is the correct translation? The punctuation helps a bit here: given the comma after the 'M,' the "if"-clause in the conditional is going to involve just 'M.' This rules out the second candidate translation right away. Let's look at the first candidate translation, together with its semi-translated state:

- ~M ⊃ (B ∨ D)
  [In semi-translation: 'If not M, then either B or D.']

This won't do either, though, because in this case the antecedent is '~M.' It is clear from the English sentence that the only part of the sentence that goes with the "if" is 'M.' Consequently, the third candidate translation must be the correct one:

- ~[M ⊃ (B ∨ D)]
  [In semi-translation: 'not: if M, then either B or D.' Or: 'it is not the case that if M, then either B or D.']

To further understand what's going on here, we can appeal to what logicians call the *scope* of an operator. Notice that the disjunction 'B ∨ D' is the consequent of the conditional involved. The '∨' within the parentheses '(' and ')' operates on, or, as we will now say, "has scope over," the 'B' and the 'D'—*and nothing else*. That is, the parentheses serve to limit the effect of the '∨' to whatever is contained within them; the '∨' does not operate on anything outside of these parentheses. This means that the '∨' cannot be the main operator of the sentence: there are parts of the sentence that it has no effect on. In other words, it doesn't have sufficient, or wide enough, scope:

How about the '⊃'? The antecedent here is everything to the left of the '⊃' as far as the '['. The consequent is everything to the right of this '⊃' as far as the ']'. That is, the '⊃' has scope over everything within the brackets. So, the '⊃' has wider scope than the '∨' in that it operates on more parts of the sentence:

However, the '⊃' still does not operate on *everything* in the sentence—it does not touch the '~' to the left of the brackets. This means that the operator with the *widest* scope is this '~.' The way the parentheses and brackets are arranged indicates that the '~' operates on the entirety of the sentence. *Nothing* is left out:

What we have is a negation—*not* a conditional, and *not* a disjunction.

"Unless" Sentences

Here is another sentence for us to consider:

You will fail unless you study.

There seems to be a conditional built in here. But be careful: the sentence is not saying that if you study then you won't fail. Rather, it is saying the following:

If you don't study then you will fail.

Using the obvious atomic sentence letters, this gives us the following translation:

~S ⊃ F

Here is what we did to end up with this sentence of SL: we took the "unless" clause of the sentence, negated it, and then placed this as the antecedent of a conditional sentence, with the other clause being the consequent. And, in general, this will work to translate "unless" sentences. Here is another example:

You won't lose weight unless you reduce your calorie intake.

Once more, note what this sentence is *not* saying. It is not saying that you will lose weight if you reduce your calorie intake. So, using 'R' and 'L' as the atomic sentence letters, 'R ⊃ L' is not a correct translation. What it *is* saying is that if you don't reduce your calorie intake, then you will not lose weight. This gives us the following correct translation:

~R ⊃ ~L

Again, comparing this with the original sentence, we can see that we negated the "unless" clause, and then placed the resultant negation as an antecedent in a conditional sentence. We can formulate this as a general rule when translating "unless" sentences:

Translating "Unless" Sentences

Negate the "unless" clause and make the resulting negation the antecedent of a conditional; the other clause becomes the consequent of the conditional.
Example: 'P unless Q' is translated as '~P ⊃ ~Q.'

Translating can become complicated when we are using negations and conditionals at the same time, however; sentences that superficially look correct often end up being wrong! Fortunately, it turns out that there is a way to translate "unless" sentences that minimizes the risk of going astray. Let's look at the first example above again:

You will fail unless you study.

A fairly natural way to paraphrase this is as follows:

Either you study or you will fail.

This is a straightforward disjunction, symbolized as follows:

S ∨ F

As briefly noted earlier, we can swap the order of the disjuncts without unduly affecting the sentence. So, we can also translate the sentence as

F ∨ S

But looking at the original sentence and this most recent sentence of SL, all we really did was replace the word "unless" with '∨' and then translated around that. This suggests the following, simpler method of translating "unless" sentences:

Translating "Unless" sentences—Second Method

Translate the word "unless" with a '∨.'
Example: 'P unless Q' is translated as 'P ∨ Q'

Let's use this simpler method on the second of the above examples:

You won't lose weight unless you reduce your calorie intake.

Just replacing the word "unless" with '∨' gives us

~L ∨ R

Does this really get at what the sentence is saying? Well, moving from this sentence of SL back into English, we end up with

Either you won't lose weight or you reduce your calorie intake.

This might not seem exactly right, but let's flip the order of the disjuncts:

Either you reduce your calorie intake or you won't lose weight.

And this really does seem to capture the original sentence. So, replacing the "unless" with a '∨' successfully captures the form of the original sentence. And without any pesky conditionals or negations! How can two apparently very different sentences of SL, i.e. '~R ⊃ ~L' and '~L ∨ R,' amount to the same thing? For the moment, we will have to be satisfied with the fact that working through a couple of examples gives us both of these translations. In Chapter 4, we will develop the resources to show more precisely that these two sentences are, logically speaking, equivalent.

"Both Not" and "Not Both" Sentences

The following two statements, though superficially similar, turn out to be quite different:

- Both the Bills and the Eagles did not win on Sunday.
- Not both the Bills and the Eagles won on Sunday [or, equivalently: it is not the case that both the Bills and the Eagles won on Sunday].

Here is a symbolization key that will cover both sentences:

B: The Bills won on Sunday.
E: The Eagles won on Sunday.

If we semi-translate the first sentence, we get the following:

Both not-B and not-E

The first word here suggests that what we have is a conjunction. Each of the conjuncts will be a negation, so we end up with this sentence of SL:

~B • ~E

The '•' here is the main operator. What about the second of the above sentences? If we examine it carefully, we can see that it does *not* say that both teams lost on Sunday. Here is the semi-translated version:

It is not the case that both B and E

Notice that the phrase "it is not the case" comes before the "both." This tells us that the negation will have a wider scope than the conjunction, as follows:

~(B • E)

It is easy to just think that these two sentences of SL, i.e. '~B • ~E' and '~(B • E),' say the same thing—but they do not! To appreciate this, let's ask under what conditions the sentences are true or false. First, consider the second sentence: If it is true, does it leave open the possibility that one of the teams won? Yes, it does: the sentence says that not both of them won—but this can still be true if one of the teams did, in fact, win. However, the first sentence explicitly rules out the possibility of each team winning: it says that they *both* did not win. The sentences, therefore, are different—the parentheses are very important! Here are some guidelines for dealing with sentences like this:

"Both not" versus "not both"

Translate a "Both Not" sentence as a conjunction of two negations.
Example: 'Both not-P and not-Q' is translated as '~P • ~Q.'

Translate a "Not both" sentence as a negated conjunction.
Example: 'Not both P and Q' is translated as '~(P • Q).'

"Neither" Statements

Consider the following example:

Neither Sydney nor Melbourne is the capital city of Australia.

Here is a symbolization key for this sentence:

S: Sydney is the capital city of Australia.
M: Melbourne is the capital city of Australia.

If we take the English word "neither" to be a contraction of "not either," then the sentence can be restated as follows:

Not either Sydney or Melbourne is the capital city of Australia.

The first word here is "not," which suggests that what we have is a negation. The rest of the sentence, i.e. that which is being negated, is a disjunction. So, we end up with this sentence of SL:

~(S ∨ M)

In general, a "neither" sentence is translated as a negated disjunction just like this.

Note what this "neither" sentence does, though. It explicitly rules out two things: that Sydney is the capital city of Australia and also that Melbourne is the capital city of Australia. In effect, then, it says that Sydney is not the capital city of Australia and also that Melbourne is not the capital city of Australia, which can be captured as follows:

~S • ~M

So, a "neither" sentence says the same thing as a "both not" sentence:

Translating a "Neither" Sentence

Translate a "neither" sentence as either a negated disjunction or as a conjunction of two negations. *Example*: 'Neither P nor Q' is translated as either one of the following: '~(P ∨ Q)' or '~P • ~Q.'

Similar considerations would show us that a "not both" sentence says the same thing as a disjunction of two negations; that is, the sentences '~(P • Q) and '~P ∨ ~Q' are logically equivalent. Try to convince yourself that this is indeed the case!

Exercise Set 2.4

Q1. Translate the following sentences of English into SL. Provide a symbolization key in each case. Write your answers in the space provided. The first one is done for you.

1. I want to go the concert; however, I don't have enough money and I can't drive.

Symbolization Key:	**C:** I want to go to the concert.
	M: I have enough money.
	D: I can drive.
Translation:	C • (~M • ~D)

2. Either today is Tuesday, or I fell asleep Monday evening and slept for 36 hours.

    Symbolization Key:

    Translation:

3. If the United States is an ally of Germany and Germany is an ally of the United Kingdom, then the United States is an ally of the United Kingdom.

    Symbolization Key:

    Translation:

4. If Barbara wins, she goes through to the final, but if Carol wins, Carol goes through to the final.

    Symbolization Key:

    Translation:

5. I like coffee, I like tea, but I do not like chai.

    Symbolization Key:

    Translation:

6. Sophia will get a scholarship only if she applies for it and pays the application fee.

> **Symbolization Key:**
>
> **Translation:**

7. I know what the capital cities of Iraq and Iran are, but I don't know what the capital city of Syria is.

> **Symbolization Key:**
>
> **Translation:**

8. If I learn how to drive a truck, then, if I get a license, I can drive on the road.

> **Symbolization Key:**
>
> **Translation:**

9. Neither the Republican candidate nor the Democratic candidate will win on Tuesday.

> **Symbolization Key:**
>
> **Translation:**

10. Both Xavier and Yolanda will not go to the party unless it takes place on Friday.

> **Symbolization Key:**
>
> **Translation:**

11. If either a hurricane or an earthquake strikes Central New York, then I will emigrate to Canada.

> **Symbolization Key:**
>
> **Translation:**

12. The Cubs will win only if neither the Red Sox nor the Yankees win.

> **Symbolization Key:**
>
> **Translation:**

13. I sometimes eat salads; however, I don't like tomatoes, I don't like lettuce, and I don't like onions.

> **Symbolization Key:**
>
> **Translation:**

14. Either Japan or South Korea will be attacked, but they won't both be attacked.

> **Symbolization Key:**
>
> **Translation:**

15. The oceans will continue to warm unless we do something about climate change.

> **Symbolization Key:**
>
> **Translation:**

16. If James arrives at the airport first, then Elias will give him a ride home; but if Kevin arrives first, then Elias will give him a ride home.

> **Symbolization Key:**
>
> **Translation:**

17. It will rain, unless it doesn't.

> **Symbolization Key:**
>
> **Translation:**

18. Neither Iran nor Saudi Arabia will raise the price of oil.

> **Symbolization Key:**
>
> **Translation:**

19. Saoirse won't get the part unless she learns her lines and shows up to the audition.

> **Symbolization Key:**
>
> **Translation:**

20. I'm no geography expert, but if Kansas City is in Missouri, then Missouri City must be in Kansas.

> **Symbolization Key:**
>
> **Translation:**

21. I will get my gutters cleaned, unless it has already started snowing or I can't find my ladder.

> **Symbolization Key:**
>
> **Translation:**

22. Maple trees are deciduous and oak trees are deciduous, or I don't know anything about trees.

> **Symbolization Key:**
>
> **Translation:**

23. President Trump will not admit he was wrong; however, if he doesn't get Congress to pass a healthcare bill, then somebody in the Trump administration will have to admit to making a mistake.

> **Symbolization Key:**
>
> **Translation:**

24. Either Secretariat is the fastest horse ever or, if he isn't, then Red Rum is the fastest.

> **Symbolization Key:**
>
> **Translation:**

25. If either Tom Hanks or Tom Cruise is in this movie, then neither Ryan Gosling nor Ryan Reynolds is in it.

> **Symbolization Key:**
>
> **Translation:**

Q2. Consider the following symbolization key. For each of the sentences of SL that follow, write out a corresponding sentence of English. Do your best to come up with a grammatical, smooth sentence of English. The first one is done for you.

J: John plays basketball.
K: Kevin plays basketball.
L: Liam plays soccer.
M: Maria plays soccer.

1. J ⊃ ~K

> **English Sentence:**   If John plays basketball, then Kevin does not play basketball.

2. ~J ∨ K

> **English Sentence:**

3. ~(J • K)

> **English Sentence:**

4. L ⊃ (M ∨ J)

> **English Sentence:**

5. ~M • (J • K)

> **English Sentence:**

6. (J ∨ K) ⊃ ~(L ∨ M)

> **English Sentence:**

7. ~K ∨ ~(L ⊃ M)

> **English Sentence:**

8. K • [(~L • M) ⊃ J]

> **English Sentence:**

9. (M ⊃ L) • (~M ⊃ ~L)

> **English Sentence:**

10. [(M ⊃ L) ∨ (~M ⊃ ~L)] • ~(L ⊃ M)

> **English Sentence:**

2.5 If and Only If[9]

When discussing the difference between "if" sentences and "only if" sentences, we mentioned the following example:

I can vote in a US federal election if and only if I am a US citizen.

What is the difference between this sentence, and the associated "if" sentence? What is the difference between it and the associated "only if" sentence? Well, let's see. Using the same symbolization key as above gives us the following semi-translated sentence:

V if and only if C

Notice what we've got here: there is an "if," an "only if," and also an "and." Luckily, we know how to deal with each of these! Let's paraphrase to make things clearer:

V if C and V only if C

This is the most complicated sentence we've seen so far, but we can deal with it! The "and" here seems to be doing most of the work in that it pulls the different parts of the sentence together to form a whole. Consequently, what we have is a conjunction, with both the left-hand conjunct and the right-hand conjunct being conditional sentences. We end up with the following sentence of SL:

(V ⊃ C) • (C ⊃ V)

This, then, is one way to correctly translate an "if and only if" sentence. Such sentences are committed to there being a conditional relationship between two sentences that goes *both* ways, and not just *one* way as in a conditional sentence. Logicians tend to abbreviate this kind of sentence by introducing a new logical operator, using the symbol '≡,' i.e. a triple bar. The result is the following sentence of SL:

V ≡ C[10]

This kind of sentence is called a ***biconditional sentence***, or just a ***biconditional***. Everything to the left of the triple bar is simply called ***the left-hand side of the biconditional***. Everything to the right of the triple bar is called ***the right-hand side of the biconditional***. As just indicated, it is possible to do without the '≡' operator as we are developing our language SL. However, it is important to be able to indicate that two sentences are related in this way.

Necessary and Sufficient Conditions

Consider the following sentence:

Having the flu is a sufficient condition for feeling miserable.

Clearly, there is some "conditional stuff" going on here. What is conditional on what? Using the obvious atomic sentence letters, here is the correct translation:

F ⊃ M

---

[9]Philosophers sometimes abbreviate "if and only if" as "iff."
[10]Logicians have also used the double arrow, i.e. '↔,' to symbolize "if and only if" sentences.

This says that if I have the flu, then I am miserable. That is, having the flu is sufficient for feeling miserable. And this is true, right? What about the other way around? Consider:

M ⊃ F

This says that if I am miserable, then I have the flu. But this is false! If I am miserable, there is no guarantee at all that I have the flu. There are lots of ways of being miserable that don't involve me having the flu. In other words, being miserable is *not* a sufficient condition for having the flu. This serves to further illustrate how important the order of things is when it comes to conditionals!

We can formulate a general rule for sufficient conditions as follows:

The antecedent of a conditional sentence is a ***sufficient condition*** for the consequent of that conditional. *Example*: In the sentence 'P ⊃ Q', 'P' is a sufficient condition for 'Q.'

Now take a look at this sentence:

The presence of oxygen is a necessary condition for human life.

This is true: for there to be human life there must be oxygen in the vicinity. How should we capture this? 'O ⊃ H' won't do it (using the obvious atomic sentence letters): this says that if there is oxygen, then there is human life. The original sentence is true, but the sentence represented by this symbolization is false: there can be oxygen in a room, for example, without there being any living humans in that room. So, what do we do? Well, to say that something is a necessary condition for something else is basically to say that without the first you don't get the latter:

~O ⊃ ~H

That is, if there's no oxygen, then there's no human life. And this captures the meaning of our sentence. However, as we saw a short time ago when discussing "only if" sentences, this can also be written as follows:

H ⊃ O

And this is the most straightforward way to translate sentences involving necessary conditions. Again, we can turn this into a general rule:

The consequent of a conditional sentence is a ***necessary condition*** for the antecedent of that conditional *Example*: In the sentence 'P ⊃ Q', 'Q' is a necessary condition for 'P.'

Notice that the sentence 'H ⊃ O' is the same translation we would get for the sentence "H only if O." That is, describing 'O' as a necessary condition for 'H,' is basically to say the following: 'H only if O.'
What about the following sentence?

Being an avid reader is a necessary and sufficient condition for being a good conversationalist.

Well, let's rephrase:

Being an avid reader is a necessary condition for being a good conversationalist and being an avid reader is a sufficient condition for being a good conversationalist.

This is a conjunction we can handle:

$(G \supset R) \bullet (R \supset G)$

But we've just come across something like this—it's a biconditional:

$R \equiv G$

Consequently, to say that 'R' is both a necessary and sufficient condition for 'G' is simply to say the following: 'R if and only if G':

Necessary and Sufficient Conditions are translated as biconditionals.
Example: 'P is a necessary and sufficient condition for Q' is translated as 'P $\equiv$ Q'

Exercise Set 2.5

Q1. Translate the following English sentences into SL. At this point, you may be able to get away with not explicitly writing out the symbolization key. I have, however, provided you with obvious atomic sentence letters for each question. Write your answers in the space provided. The first one is done for you.

1. Becky driving a Ferrari is a sufficient condition for her being super cool. (F, C)

> **Translation:** $F \supset C$

2. Tom liking Juanita is a sufficient condition for Alexa to be jealous, but it is not a necessary condition. (T, A)

> **Translation:**

3. It is not the case that if you are a moral person, then you must be a religious person. (M, R)

> **Translation:**

4. Dinosaurs were not stupid reptiles nor were they cold-blooded. (L, C)

> **Translation:**

5. Bob won't win the election unless he outspends his opponent on advertising and goes door to door more than her. (B, O, D)

> **Translation:**

6. I will move to California if and only if I can sell my house and save some money. (C, H, M)

> **Translation:**

7. If health insurance companies cut costs, then either more people will sign up for health insurance or the companies will go out of business. (H, S, B)

> **Translation:**

8. Iran's diplomatic engagement with the United States is a necessary and sufficient condition for the United States' diplomatic engagement with Iran. (I, U)

> **Translation:**

9. Alice's graduating from college is a necessary condition for her getting a good job. (A, G)

> **Translation:**

10. Tom will go to the movies if and only if Jerry does not go to the movies. (T, J)

> **Translation:**

11. Yolanda is not doing well in math, but she will graduate if she does well in English. (Y, G, E)

> **Translation:**

12. Politicians are neither honest nor socially responsible, but they do work long hours. (H, S, W)

> **Translation:**

13. North Korea developing a nuclear weapon is a necessary condition for Japan increasing the size of its army only if Japan changes its constitution. (N, A, C)

> **Translation:**

14. The flu virus can be deadly, but a person can die from it only if his immune system is compromised or he is old. (F, D, I)

> **Translation:**

15. Life on earth will survive unless there is a nuclear war or something from outer space collides with the planet. (L, N, S)

> **Translation:**

16. If Amazon keeps charging for shipping, then more people will shop at brick-and-mortar stores; but if that happens, then Amazon will go out of business and there will be nowhere to buy books online. (C, S, B, O)

Translation:

17. Alfonso reads a lot of books, though most of the books he reads are very short; meanwhile, Barbara doesn't read many books, but one of them had 1,500 pages. (A, S, B, P)

Translation:

18. If Megan plays neither the banjo nor the bouzouki, then she probably doesn't play the oud either. (B, Z, O)

Translation:

19. Both of the following are false: if it isn't raining, then it isn't cold, and if it's cold, then it is snowing. (R, C, S)

Translation:

20. I downloaded the latest software update, but then my phone stopped working, my computer stopped working, and I ended up with bats in my attic. (D, P, C, B)

Translation:

21. Neither Pomeranians nor Chihuahuas are good hunters, but if you train Corgis, then they become good hunters unless you start training them when they are too old. (P, C, T, H, O)

Translation:

22. The fact that birds are descended from dinosaurs implies two things: dinosaurs did not really die out and there are flying dinosaurs in my back yard right now. (B, D, F)

Translation:

23. I will eat cabbage and Brussels sprouts if and only if they both help me live longer. (C, B, L)

> **Translation:**

24. Martin should stop his antisocial behavior; otherwise, he will have to be punished, and neither I nor Martin like that idea. (M, P, I, L)

> **Translation:**

25. It is not the case that either LeBron James is the best basketball player and the Cavaliers will win the championship or that Stephen Curry is the best basketball player and the Warriors will win the championship. (L, C, S, W)

> **Translation:**

2.5 The Grammar of SL

Every language, whether natural or formal, has a grammar. That is, in every language, some things count as meaningful and some things are meaningless. When we are proficient in a language, we have at least some working knowledge of the difference between a meaningful sentence and a meaningless sentence. A community of language users can do very well without there ever being an *explicit* articulation of what these grammar rules are, however. Any attempt to articulate the rules of grammar comes "after the fact," so to speak. And it can get complicated: in English, for example, there are some standard ways for saying that something happened in the past—but then there are hundreds of exceptions, i.e. irregular verbs.

What about the language of SL? As we've seen, SL has a bunch of symbols, i.e. its grammar: upper-case letters, the five sentence operators, and parentheses. Sometimes, putting a bunch of these symbols together will result in something meaningful, and sometimes it will not. After spending some time with SL, it becomes fairly easy to tell the difference. Here are some examples:

P ∨ Q
~J
G • ∨ QS
~K~

The first two strings of symbols here are meaningful, whereas the second two are not. However, when it comes to grasping the grammar of SL, we do not ultimately have to depend on what is or is not obvious. There is a very precise way of articulating when we have something meaningful and when we do not. To get to this point, we first need to provide some definitions:

> An **EXPRESSION** is any string of symbols in SL.
> A **WELL-FORMED FORMULA (wff)** is a meaningful expression in SL.

All of the above strings of symbols are expressions. The first two expressions are meaningful, and so qualify as wffs. The grammar of SL should be able to capture why this is the case. The last two expressions are not meaningful, and so do not qualify as wffs: they are *ill*-formed formulas. Again, the grammar of SL should be able to tell us exactly why this is the case. Of course, we can't just list off all the possible wffs and insist that any expression on the list is well formed, while any expression not on the list is ill-formed—there are an infinite number of possible wffs! Instead, we will write out a small number of rules that will allow us to *generate* all possible wffs, and that will never generate an ill-formed formula.

But before articulating these grammar rules, we also need a way of referring to sentences of SL *in general*. Consider, for example, the following sentences of SL:

A • B
F • ~ G
(S ∨ T) • U
[X ≡ (Y • Z)] • [J ⊃ (K ⊃ L)]

In each of these sentences, the main connective is the '•.' That is, they are all conjunctions. We can represent this by using what are called *sentence variables*. In mathematics, we use variable letters, like 'x,' as a kind of placeholder: we don't know x's value, and it could end up being anything. In a similar way, we can use the letters '$\mathcal{P}$' and '$\mathcal{Q}$' as placeholders for *any* sentences of SL. When we do this, each of the above sentences of SL can be understood to take the following form:

$\mathcal{P} • \mathcal{Q}$

In fact, if '$\mathcal{P}$' and '$\mathcal{Q}$' are sentence variables, then '$\mathcal{P} \bullet \mathcal{Q}$' represents *any* conjunction in SL. Likewise, we can use '$\mathcal{P} \vee \mathcal{Q}$' to represent any disjunction in SL, '$\sim\mathcal{P}$' to represent any negation in SL, and so on. Note the different font we use when labeling the sentence variables: this is to indicate that '$\mathcal{P}$' and '$\mathcal{Q}$' are not themselves sentences of SL. This means that '$\mathcal{P} \bullet \mathcal{Q}$,' '$\mathcal{P} \vee \mathcal{Q}$,' '$\sim\mathcal{P}$,' and so on, are not sentences of SL either. 'P • Q,' 'P ∨ Q,' '~P,' however, *are* sentences of SL. This is a very important point, so take the time to absorb it well!

With the idea of sentence variables on board, we can now proceed to the grammar of SL. The first point to make is that all individual upper-case letters are automatically wffs, given that they represent atomic sentences. Our rules will also have to allow for the generation of conjunctions, disjunctions, negations, conditionals, and biconditionals. We will also have to exclude the possibility that there are other kinds of meaningful expressions in SL. We end up with the following:

1. Every atomic sentence, as represented by an individual upper-case letter, is a wff.
2. If $\mathcal{P}$ is a wff, then $\sim\mathcal{P}$ is a wff of SL.
3. If $\mathcal{P}$ and $\mathcal{Q}$ are wffs, then $(\mathcal{P} \bullet \mathcal{Q})$ is a wff.
4. If $\mathcal{P}$ and $\mathcal{Q}$ are wffs, then $(\mathcal{P} \vee \mathcal{Q})$ is a wff.
5. If $\mathcal{P}$ and $\mathcal{Q}$ are wffs, then $(\mathcal{P} \supset \mathcal{Q})$ is a wff.
6. If $\mathcal{P}$ and $\mathcal{Q}$ are wffs, then $(\mathcal{P} \equiv \mathcal{Q})$ is a wff.
7. All and only wffs of SL can be generated by applications of these rules.

Having this precise articulation of what it takes in SL for an expression to be a wff means that we don't have to depend on our intuition. Even if we can usually tell the difference between a wff and a non-wff just by looking at it, it is an advantage to be able to articulate this so concisely. In addition, such a precise formulation enables entities that have no logical intuitions—like a computer, for example—to follow instructions that are coded in such this way. Consider: our interest in evaluating arguments motivated us to develop a formal logical language like SL. Such a language is, at bottom, an attempt to capture the form of human reasoning. If the grammar of SL can be precisely articulated, and if you can code a machine to follow these grammar rules, then the following possibility arises: a machine that can simulate or mirror human reasoning. We would also be able to communicate and interact with such a machine. This is one way of understanding what a computer does, or tries to do. There is a lot more to building a computer, of course, but this does capture a central feature of computer science—and it is part of the reason that a logic course is typically required in a computer science program.

What is the difference between a sentence and a wff? In SL, there really is no difference: the above formulation of SL's grammar will always generate an expression that is either true or false, something that is at the core of the definition of a sentence. Consequently, we will still refer to the wffs of SL as *sentences*. (The wffs of a logical system are not always sentences in that system, however. The language of Predicate Logic, which we will begin considering in Chapter 7, is one such system).

Notice that in the above list of rules, most of the wffs we can legitimately generate are surrounded by parentheses. For example, rule 3 tells us that if '$\mathcal{P}$' and '$\mathcal{Q}$' are sentences of SL, then so is '$(\mathcal{P} \bullet \mathcal{Q})$.' This is to remove the possibility of ambiguous wffs. Consider the following two sentences of SL, for example:

A • B
C ⊃ D

Rule 3 says that I can generate the following conjunction:

A • B • C ⊃ D

However, without parentheses, this expression is not obviously a conjunction—it may be a conditional sentence. Building the use of parentheses into the formulation of the grammar rules removes the possibility of such ambiguity. The above compound sentences would already have surrounding parentheses:

(A • B)
(C ⊃ D)

Chapter 2 Logical Form

Then these sentences allow us to generate the following, via rule 3:

$(A \bullet B) \bullet (C \supset D)$

And this is clearly a conjunction.

Of course, up to now we have largely omitted parentheses that surround the entirety of a sentence. And doing so means that, strictly speaking, we have not been dealing with wffs of SL. But this is OK, as long as we keep in mind that we are taking this liberty, and as long as we make sure to use parentheses when it is necessary for removing ambiguity.

Note also that the list of grammar rules do not mention brackets (i.e. '[' and ']'), even though we have used them when writing out some sentences of SL. Again, however, this need not unduly worry us: we use brackets to make a sentence more readable, and we can continue to do this – let's just remember that, if the grammar police come calling, all brackets we use would turn into parentheses. We can also use braces (i.e. '{' and '}'), to make especially long sentences more readable.

Exercise Set 2.5

Q1. Which of the following expressions in SL are, *strictly speaking*, well-formed formulas? Which of them do we normally consider to be wffs, given the just-mentioned liberties we take with the grammar of SL?

1. P ⊃ ~~S
2. ~~~~~~~F
3. L • ∨ Q
4. H ⊃ [T₁ ⊃ T₁]
5. R ≡ S ≡ D
6. (A ∨ A)
7. x • y
8. M ⊃ [(M • (N ≡ R))]
9. ~[P ∨ (P ∨ ~P)]
10. If J then P
11. a = b
12. A = B
13. ~G ∨ {Y ⊃ [Z • (T ∨ ~~C)]}
14. H ⊃ (L ≡ (K ⊃ (J ⊃ (M • F)))
15. 𝒫 ∨ ~𝒬
16. O ⊃ O ⊃ O ⊃ O

2.6 Translating Arguments

It is possible to get bogged down in all the sentence translation we have been doing. We should always keep the ultimate goal in mind, however. Remember what, fundamentally, the discipline of logic is all about: we are focusing on the following distinction:

> good *reasoning*   versus   bad *reasoning.*

Since an argument is a unit of reasoning, this amounts to focusing on the following:

> good *arguments*   versus   bad *arguments.*

We are dealing with deductive arguments and deductive validity, so our focus becomes this distinction:

> *valid* arguments   versus   *invalid* arguments.

How can we tell the difference between valid and invalid arguments? Well, as we noted at the start of this chapter, we can understand the validity of an argument as pertaining to its logical form. Consequently, we should develop the skill of capturing the following:

> the *logical form* of *arguments*.

And, seeing as an argument is a collection of sentences, the fundamental skill we need is capturing this:

> the *logical form* of *sentences*.

This is why we have spent so much time translating sentences of English into sentences of SL. Now, based on all of this, let us develop a convention for presenting the logical form of arguments. We begin with a straightforward example. Here is an argument in English:

Either a bat or a cat is making a lot of noise in my attic. It's not a cat doing so. Therefore, it's a bat making a lot of noise in my attic.

As we have seen when translating sentences, the first thing to do in the translation process is identify the atomic sentences involved, so that we can articulate a symbolization key. The same goes for translating arguments, though in this case we have to go through more than just one sentence. Surveying all of the sentences in this argument, we end up with the following symbolization key:

B: A bat is making lots of noise in my attic.
C: A cat is making lots of noise in my attic.

Both of these atomic sentences are present in the first sentence of the argument. The atomic sentence 'C' is also present in the second sentence of the argument, inside a negation, and there is no need to rewrite it in the symbolization key. The atomic sentence 'B' is present in the last sentence of the argument; again, there is no need to rewrite it in the symbolization key.

A useful next step is to articulate a semi-translated version of the argument, using the atomic sentences as laid out in the symbolization key:

Either B or C. Not-C. Therefore, B.

At this point, I hope you agree that each of these sentences is easy to translate. However, remember that an argument is not *just* a list of sentences—we also need to be able to isolate the *premises* and the *conclusion*. There is nothing too complicated about this task in this instance, though: the conclusion is whatever is attached to the "therefore," i.e. the last sentence of the argument. Note that the word "therefore" does *not* get translated by a logical operator—it is merely a word that picks out a sentence as the conclusion. Using our convention of writing out arguments from Chapter 1, and using the symbol '∴' to indicate that a sentence is a conclusion, we end up with the following:

B ∨ C
~C
_____
∴ B

This is the logical form of the above argument in SL. Of course, we have not yet developed a means of using this logical form to check for validity; that will come later. For now, let's just focus on making sure that we correctly capture the logical form of the arguments we encounter.

Here, then, is a distillation of the method we have just used to capture the logical form in SL of an argument:

Capturing the Logical Form of an Argument

Step 1: Read through the entirety of the argument and pick out the atomic sentences. Write out a symbolization key that assigns an upper-case letter to each atomic sentence.

Step 2: Rewrite the argument using the symbolization key.

Step 3: Identify the conclusion of the argument; the other sentences will be the argument's premises.

Step 4: Write out the logical form of the argument.

With some practice, **Steps 2** and **3** here may end up being performed at the same time, and ultimately inside your head. This is perfectly fine, as long as you end up with a neatly articulated symbolization key and the logical form of the argument. Let's look at another example:

> If Bob was involved in the crime, then so was Alice. If Alice was involved in the crime, then so were Carol and David. However, David was not involved. So, we can conclude that Bob was not involved.

Let's work through the steps we just articulated.

Step 1 tells us to read through the entirety of the argument and pick out the atomic sentences. Then we need to list these atomic sentences in a symbolization key. Here is what we end up with:

> **A:** Alice was involved in the crime.
> **B:** Bob was involved in the crime.
> **C:** Carol was involved in the crime.
> **D:** David was involved in the crime.

Again, some of these atomic sentences appear more than once in the argument, but we only need to record them once in the symbolization key. **Step 2** asks us to rewrite the argument using this symbolization key:

> If B, then A. If A, then C and D. Not-D. Therefore, not-B.

Step 3 is to identify the conclusion. This is straightforward here: the conclusion is the last sentence, i.e. 'not-B.'

Finally, with **Step 4** we end up with the logical form, in SL, of this argument:

> $B \supset A$
> $A \supset (C \bullet D)$
> $\sim D$
> _____
> $\therefore \sim B$

And that's it! As already mentioned, most of the hard work has been done figuring out how to translate individual sentences. All we have to do here is make sure that we display the form of the argument correctly, which fundamentally means correctly identifying the argument's conclusion and its premises.

Let's do just one more example:

> I have the power to pardon criminals only if I am the president. So, I am not the president, because I do not have the power to pardon criminals!

Here is the symbolization key we get from performing **Step 1**:

> **C:** I have the power to pardon criminals.
> **P:** I am the president.

Step 2 provides us with the following:

> C only if P. So not-P, because not-C.

Step 3 asks us to identify the conclusion. You might be tempted to include all of the last sentence of the argument in the conclusion, but this would be a mistake! Yes, the word "so" indicates that what follows is a conclusion. However, the word "because" here serves as a premise indicator, so the last clause of this sentence is another premise: it is presented as one of the reasons, along with the first sentence, for thinking that 'not-P' is true. We end up, then, with the following argument form:

C ⊃ P
~C
───────
∴ ~P

Again, we can ignore the issue of whether this is a valid argument.

Exercise Set 2.6

Q1. Translate the following arguments into SL. Make sure to provide a symbolization key in each case. Write your answers in the space provided. Ignore the issue of whether the argument is valid or sound. The first one is done for you.

1. Ostriches are birds only if they can fly. Ostriches can fly. Therefore, they are birds.

   Symbolization Key: **B:** Ostriches are birds.
   F: Ostriches can fly.

   Translation: B ⊃ F
   F
   ―――――――
   ∴ B

2. Alice admitted to committing the crime, but so did Bob. They didn't both commit the crime. So, either Alice is lying or Bob is lying.

   Symbolization Key:

   Translation:

3. I think, therefore, I am.

   Symbolization Key:

   Translation:

4. If there is a total eclipse of the sun, then it will go completely dark. But if it goes completely dark, then the birds will be confused. Consequently, if there is a total eclipse of the sun, then the birds will be confused.

   Symbolization Key:

   Translation:

5. Cairo is the capital of Egypt. Therefore, either Cairo is the capital of Egypt or the moon is made of green cheese.

> **Symbolization Key:**
>
> **Translation:**

6. If the crime happened in the kitchen, then there is evidence somewhere in the kitchen. Therefore, it is not the case that both the crime happened in the kitchen and there is no evidence somewhere in the kitchen.

> **Symbolization Key:**
>
> **Translation:**

7. Electricity is the movement of electrons. If this is the case, then there must be a huge number of electrons in the universe. And if this is the case, then there must be a huge number of protons in the universe. Consequently, there must be a huge number of protons in the universe.

> **Symbolization Key:**
>
> **Translation:**

8. Either the Wildcats or the Scarlet Knights will not get to the championship game. If the Wildcats don't get to the championship game, then Mary will be disappointed. If the Scarlet Knights don't get to the championship game, then Danny will be disappointed. Therefore, either Mary or Danny will be disappointed.

> **Symbolization Key:**
>
> **Translation:**

9. Either the local football team or the local basketball team won. However, they didn't both win. We can conclude that the local basketball team won.

> **Symbolization Key:**
>
> **Translation:**

10. The Nile is the longest river in Africa. In fact, the Nile is the longest river in the world. If both of these things are true, then the Amazon is neither the longest river in Africa nor the longest river in the world. Therefore, the Amazon is not the longest river in the world.

> **Symbolization Key:**
>
> **Translation:**

11. History is Johnny's favorite subject in school only if he knows everything about the US Civil War. And Geography is Sarah's favorite subject only if she knows all of the US state capitals. However, Johnny does not know everything about the Civil War and Sarah does not know all of the US state capitals. Consequently, History must not be Johnny's favorite subject and Geography must not be Sarah's favorite subject.

> **Symbolization Key:**
>
> **Translation:**

12. Titus will not win the pole-vaulting competition unless he breaks his own personal record or his main rival drops out. His main rival will not drop out, however. Therefore, if Titus does not break his own personal record, he will not win the pole-vaulting competition.

> **Symbolization Key:**
>
> **Translation:**

13. The election was clearly stolen. If it wasn't, then a lot of dead people from District 9 voted—which obviously did not happen.

    Symbolization Key:

    Translation:

    ---

14. Heejung, Barbara, and Lily are well-behaved children. But if they are well-behaved children, then the vase must have jumped off the shelf all by itself. I guess I'll have to conclude that the vase must have jumped off the shelf all by itself.

    Symbolization Key:

    Translation:

    ---

15. If Mark is my friend, then he bought me a present. If Martha is my friend, then she bought me a present. However, neither Mark nor Martha bought me a present. I must conclude, then, then neither of them is my friend.

    Symbolization Key:

    Translation:

Chapter 3

Truth Tables: Sentences

In Chapter 2, we emphasized that the validity of an argument can be understood primarily in terms of that argument's logical form. With this in mind, we developed a way of capturing the logical form of an argument: we translate it into the language of Sentential Logic (SL). In this chapter, we will introduce truth tables, a tool that will ultimately allow us to check an argument for validity in terms of the logical form of the argument.

Here is the general idea behind truth tables. We have five logical operator symbols on board that help us formulate sentences of SL: '•,' '∨,' '~,' '⊃,' and '≡.' Sentences in SL that use these symbols are meant to capture the logical form of English sentences. The understanding is that each symbol corresponds to a distinct type of sentence operator that appears naturally in the English language: the '•' is used to symbolize "and" sentences, the '∨' is used to symbolize "either-or" sentences, and so on. However, we can do more to show that sentences of SL really do adequately capture the form of English sentences. We do this by offering precise conditions under which each type of sentence in SL—conjunctions, disjunctions, etc.—is true and when it is false. We will mostly not be focusing on whether the sentences of English are *actually* true or false; instead, we will be trying to be more precise about what a conjunction *means*, what a disjunction *means*, and so on, in terms of when these kinds of sentences are true and when they are false.

Here is another way to appreciate the project we are about to embark upon. In Chapter 2, we laid out a *vocabulary* for the language of SL (i.e., what symbols we can use) and some *rules of grammar* for SL (i.e., what strings of symbols will constitute meaningful expressions, or well-formed formulas). Together, these provided us with the formal language's *syntax*. However, natural languages don't just have a syntax, they also have a *semantics*. That is, grammatically correct words, phrases, and sentences *mean* something. In formal logic, the semantics of a language is typically defined in terms of truth-value; i.e. we define the meaning of sentences in terms of their possible truth-values. For compound sentences, this requires us to say something about when conjunctions, disjunctions, and so on are true and when they are false. And this is precisely what truth tables will enable us to do.

So, let's get started. We will take each operator symbol one at a time.

3.1 Truth Table for Conjunctions, Negations, and Disjunctions

Conjunctions

Consider the following sentence:

Washington DC is the capital of the United States and Paris is the capital of France.

Here is a symbolization key for this sentence:

W: Washington DC is the capital of the United States.
P: Paris is the capital of France.

And translating this sentence into SL, we get the following:

W • P

Now, let's ask a further question: Is this compound sentence *true*? Well, the claim is that *both* Washington DC is the capital of the United States *and* Paris is the capital of France; and given that it is the case that Washington DC is the capital of the United States and that Paris is the capital of France, this is indeed a true sentence. That is, 'W • P' is true because 'W' (the left-had conjunct) is true and 'P' (the right-hand conjunct) is true. We can capture this as follows:

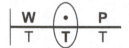

Here, 'W' is true: it is assigned a T; 'P' is true: it is assigned a T; and because both conjuncts of 'W • P' are true, the *entire* conjunction is true, i.e. the '•' is assigned a F. What we have here is a *partial* truth table. We have information on the truth-value of each atomic sentence of the sentence, which turns out to be sufficient for us to figure out the truth-value of the entire compound sentence.

Now consider another sentence:

Washington DC is the capital of the United States and Pittsburgh is the capital of Canada.

This is another conjunction. Using 'W' and 'P' as the atomic sentence letters, we get the following sentence of SL:

W • P

Is *this* sentence true? Well, this time the claim is that *both* Washington DC is the capital of the United States *and* Pittsburgh is the capital of Canada; however, only *one* of these is true. Consequently, the sentence is false. Again, we can figure this out based on our knowledge of the truth-values of the component atomic sentences. Let's capture this as follows:

$$
\begin{array}{c|c|c}
W & \cdot & P \\
\hline
T & F & F
\end{array}
$$

This is another partial truth table. 'W' is true, so it is assigned a T; 'P' is false, so it is assigned an F. And because it is not the case that both conjuncts of 'W • P' are true, the entire conjunction is false, i.e. the '•' is assigned an F.

There are two more possible scenarios to consider. Perhaps the first conjunct is false, while the second conjunct is true, as in the following sentence:

Warsaw is the capital of the United States and Paris is the capital of France.

This sentence is clearly false: it is *not* the case that both Warsaw is the capital of the United States and Paris is the capital of France. Again using 'W' and 'P' as the atomic sentence letters, we can represent this as follows:

$$
\begin{array}{c|c|c}
W & \cdot & P \\
\hline
F & F & T
\end{array}
$$

Finally, there will be cases where both conjuncts are false. For example:

Warsaw is the capital of the United States and Pittsburgh is the capital of Canada.

Once more, it is clearly not the case that both of the conjuncts are true here. So, again, we have a false conjunction (using the same atomic sentence letters):

W	•	P
F	F	F

In each of the above four cases, notice that we figured out the truth-value of the compound sentence, i.e. the conjunction, based on our knowledge of the truth-values of the component atomic sentences involved. Note, also, that these four cases exhaust the possibilities. That is, there are no more ways of combining truth-values for 'W' and 'P.' These two facts allow us to construct a *complete* or *full* truth table for the conjunction:

W	•	P
T	T	T
T	F	F
F	F	T
F	F	F

The column under the main operator is highlighted, and we will continue to do this as we work with truth tables. This truth table pertains to just one specific sentence of SL, of course. Using sentence variables, however, which we introduced in Chapter 2, we can generalize and offer a truth table for *all* sentences of SL that have the '•' as the main operator:

$\mathcal{P}$	•	$\mathcal{Q}$
T	T	T
T	F	F
F	F	T
F	F	F

This, then, is how we will understand the meaning of the '•.' It might also help to if we articulated this in English:

> A conjunction is true whenever both conjuncts are true; it is false otherwise.

So, we can figure out the truth-value of *any* wff in SL that has a '•' as the main operator as long as we know the truth-value of each of the conjuncts involved. Here is another way of putting this: the truth-value of a conjunction is *wholly a function of* the truth-values of the conjuncts involved. The '•,' then, is what is called a *truth-functional operator*. Here is a definition:

> A sentence operator is **TRUTH FUNCTIONAL** if and only if the truth-value of a compound sentence in which that operator is the main operator is wholly a function of the truth-values of the component atomic sentences.

It is the truth-functionality of the '•' that allows us to easily construct a full truth table for a sentence that has the '•' as its main logical operator. And, as it turns out, each of the five logical operators we introduced in Chapter 2 can be treated in this way. That is, each logical operator we use in SL is truth-functional. In this way, we can also refer to the language of SL as a truth-functional language.

Negations

Consider the following sentence:

Mount Everest is not the highest mountain in the world.

A little knowledge of geography will tell us that this sentence is false. The atomic sentence here is as follows:

E: Mount Everest is the highest mountain in the world.

So, we end up with the following sentence of SL:

~E

Now, 'E' represents a sentence that is true. Consequently, to say that it is not the case that 'E' is true is to say something false. We can capture this as follows:

Here, 'E,' as a true sentence, is assigned a T. Because the compound sentence, i.e. the negation sentence, asserts that something true is not the case, the '~' gets assigned an F.

There is just one other possible kind of scenario with negations: scenarios in which something false is negated, resulting in a true sentence. For example:

Erie, Pennsylvania is not the biggest city in the world.

This sentence is, of course, true. The atomic sentence in this case is:

E: Erie, Pennsylvania is the biggest city in the world.

So, again we end up with the following sentence in SL:

~E

This time, 'E' represents a false sentence. Consequently, to assert that a false sentence is not the case is to say something true:

	~	E
	T	F

Combining both possible scenarios, and using sentence variables, we can create the complete truth table for the negation '~E':

	~	E
	F	T
	T	F

And once more we can generalize, using sentence variables:

$$
\begin{array}{c|c}
\sim & \mathcal{P} \\
\hline
F & T \\
T & F \\
\end{array}
$$

We can articulate this truth table in English as follows:

A negation is false whenever the sentence being negated is true; a negation is true whenever the sentence being negated is false.

Again, we are interpreting the '~' as truth-functional: a negation's truth-value can be calculated as long as we have information on the truth-value of the component atomic sentences.

Disjunctions

Consider the following sentence:

Either Lady Gaga is a musician or LeBron James is a musician.

This, I hope you'll agree, is a true sentence. Using the obvious atomic sentence letters, we can translate this sentence into SL as follows:

G ∨ J

We saw earlier that a conjunction is true if and only if both conjuncts are true. However, disjunctions have "lower standards" than conjunctions, so to speak: it is enough if just *one* of them is true, as in this case. So, the following represents why the above sentence is true:

$$
\begin{array}{c|c|c}
G & \vee & J \\
\hline
T & T & F \\
\end{array}
$$

There are, of course, three other possible kinds of scenarios for disjunctions. Here is one more:

Either Lady Gaga is an athlete or LeBron James is an athlete.

This is also a true sentence. Here is the translation into SL (using the same atomic sentence letters as the previous sentence):

G ∨ J

Again, this is true because of the "low standards" of "either-or" sentences: at least one of them is true, so the whole thing is true. We can represent this as follows:

$$
\begin{array}{c|c|c}
G & \vee & J \\
\hline
F & T & T \\
\end{array}
$$

And here is a scenario in which both disjuncts are false:

Either Lady Gaga is an astronaut or LeBron James is an astronaut.

And again, using the same atomic sentence letters, we end up with the following sentence in SL:

G ∨ J

This time, the fact that both disjuncts are false entails that the *entire* disjunct is false:

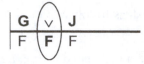

G	∨	J
F	**F**	F

The one remaining scenario is the one in which both disjuncts are true. Here is an example of a sentence like that:

Either Lady Gaga or Michael Jackson is a musician.

And one final time (using the same atomic sentence letters) we end up with the following sentence of SL:

G ∨ J

Is this sentence true or false? Our intuitions could go both ways on this one. Each disjunct is true in this case, and this might lead us to say that the whole disjunction is true. Every *part* of the sentence is true, so arguably it would be weird to think of the *entire* sentence as false. However, we often use "either-or" sentences to assert that one or the other of two things is the case, *but not both*. If this is what's going in here, then the fact that both of the disjuncts are true entails that the entire disjunction is false. Both interpretations of a disjunction in English are legitimate, though logicians have typically chosen to interpret the '∨' along the lines of the first interpretation here. Here is how we can represent this:

G	∨	J
T	**T**	T

This is called the ***inclusive*** interpretation of a disjunction, or ***inclusive-OR***, in that taking the disjunction to be true includes the possibility of both disjuncts being true. In this book we will follow convention and take all disjunctions to be inclusive disjunctions, unless it is explicitly stated otherwise. We end up, then, with the following complete truth table for the above sentence:

G	∨	J
T	**T**	T
T	**T**	F
F	**T**	T
F	**F**	F

Generalizing once more and using sentence variables, we get the following interpretation that is applied to all sentences in which the '∨' is the main operator:

𝒫	∨	𝒬
T	**T**	T
T	**T**	F
F	**T**	T
F	**F**	F

We can describe this truth table in English as follows:

A disjunction is false whenever both disjuncts are false; it is true otherwise.

If a disjunction excludes the possibility that both disjuncts are true, then we have what's called an ***exclusive*** interpretation of the disjunction, or ***exclusive-OR***. If we interpreted disjunctions in this way, the top row of the truth table would have an 'F' under the '∨.' Again, sometimes this is the appropriate way to interpret what is going on in an "either-or" sentence of English, but in SL we will *never* interpret the '∨' in this way. How, then, should we handle sentences of English that are clearly intended to be exclusive disjunctions? Consider, for example, the following sentence:

Either a Republican or a Democrat will win the election.

Using the obvious atomic sentence letters, we end up with the following sentence of SL:

D ∨ R

Now, in an everyday context, this sentence is typically offered as an exclusive disjunction: we tend not to consider the possibility that *both* a Republican *and* a Democrat will win an election. However, as a general guideline, if this is not made explicit in the English sentence, we simply translate the sentence using a '∨,' and interpret this '∨' as inclusive, as outlined above. To get at the exclusive interpretation of the disjunction, we insist on an *explicit* indication of this in the sentence. For example:

Either a Republican or a Democrat will win the election, but not both.

This sentence is clearly *not* entertaining the possibility that both the Republican and the Democrat might win the election. We cannot, however, translate this in the same way as we translated the earlier sentence: the "but not both" part of the sentence is not included in the meaning of '∨.' Instead, we explicitly include this phrase in the translation. Here is the semi-translation:

Either R or D, but not both R and D.

This, then, becomes a conjunction, as follows:

(R ∨ D) • ~(R • D)

So, we can still symbolize what is going on in an explicitly exclusive disjunction—it's just a little more complicated than an inclusive disjunction. We are not yet in a position to construct a complete truth table for this compound sentence, but we will get there shortly.

Before moving on to developing truth-functional interpretations for the remaining sentence operators, i.e. the '⊃' and the '≡,' let's take a look at what our first three truth tables, i.e. for the '•,' the '~,' and the '∨,' can do for us. The first thing to notice is that we should be able to figure out the truth-value of *any* conjunction, *any* disjunction, and *any* negation. Consider, for example, the following sentence of SL:

~S • G

Is this sentence true or false? Well, as it stands, there really is no way of knowing! I do not know what 'S' symbolizes and I do not know what 'G' symbolizes. More importantly, I have no idea if 'S' represents something that is true or if 'G' represents something that is true. I just don't have enough information to determine if this sentence is true or false. Compare a situation in math where you don't have enough information to give an answer. For example, let's say you are asked if the following equation is true or false:

$$2x = 3y$$

Without information on what the values of '*x*' and '*y*' are, there is just no way you can make a judgment on this.

So, let's add some information, and assume that 'S' represents a sentence that is true, and that 'G' represents a sentence that is false. With this knowledge of the truth-values of the atomic sentences involved, and given that both the '•' and the '~' are truth-functional, we should be able to work out the truth-value of the entire conjunction. Here's how to do this. First let's assign these truth-values to each of the atomic sentences:

~ S	•	G
T		F

At this point, there are two gaps in the truth table: under the '~' and under the '•.' Figuring out the truth-value of the entire sentence means filling in these gaps correctly. Before doing this, however, we must identify the sentence's main operator. Remember that the main operator of a sentence is the operator that has the widest scope; it is the operator that "pulls the entire sentence together." Clearly, this is the '•' in the above sentence. It is a good idea to explicitly label a sentence's main operator:

The truth-value of the compound sentence will be whatever truth-value we end up assigning to the main operator of the sentence, something we always fill in last. We start off by assigning truth-values to those operators of the sentence that have the narrowest scope. In this case, there is just one of these, the '~.' What should we put in there? Well, if 'S' is labeled as true, then the truth-value of '~S' is obvious: it is false. So, we put an F under the '~':

```
        *
 ~ S  •  G
 F T     F
```

This, in effect, identifies the left-hand conjunct as false. I will now use this new F to help me figure out the truth-value of the entire conjunction. We know from earlier that a conjunction is true whenever both conjuncts are true, but that it is false otherwise. In this situation, we have two false conjuncts; we have just labeled the left-hand-conjunct as false; the right-hand conjunct, i.e. 'G,' was already labeled as false. This means that the entire conjunction is false. Consequently, we place an F under the '•,' and highlight it, as follows:

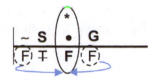

I have crossed out the T under the 'S' to indicate that we do not use it once we have generated the F under the '~.' In general, once we have used a truth-value assignment to generate another truth-value assignment like we've done here, then, from that point on, we will never make use of that original truth-value assignment. (The arrows and the circles here are for illustration purposes only and are not part of the truth table).

Based on this example, let us articulate a method for calculating the truth-value of a compound sentence:

Calculating the Truth-value of a Compound Sentence

Step 1: Assign the given truth-values to the atomic sentences.
Step 2: Identify and label the main operator of the compound sentence.
Step 3: Starting with the operator with the narrowest scope, assign truth-values to all of the operators of the sentence.
Step 4: The operator with the widest scope should be the last one to get a truth-value assignment. Highlight this truth-value assignment—this is the truth-value of the entire compound sentence.

To reiterate: if you do not have access to the truth-values for the atomic sentences, you will not be able to complete **Step 1** here, and so will not be able to calculate the truth-value of the compound sentence.

Let's do another example. Assume that 'A' is true and that 'B' is false, and consider the following sentence:

~A ∨ ~B

Step 1 asks us to assign truth-values to the atomic sentences:

$$\begin{array}{cccc} \sim & \textbf{A} & \vee & \sim & \textbf{B} \\ \hline & T & & & F \end{array}$$

Step 2 asks us to identify and label the main operator. In this case, each '~' has scope over just an atomic sentence, whereas the '∨' has scope over the entire sentence. That is, what we have is a disjunction:

$$\begin{array}{cccc} & & * & & \\ \sim & \textbf{A} & \vee & \sim & \textbf{B} \\ \hline & T & & & F \end{array}$$

Now we need to start filling in the gaps, starting with those under each '~.' If 'A' is true, then '~A' is false; and if 'B' is false, then '~B' is true:

$$\begin{array}{cccc} & & * & & \\ \sim & \textbf{A} & \vee & \sim & \textbf{B} \\ \hline F & T & & T & F \end{array}$$

What we have now is a disjunction with the left-hand disjunct, i.e. '~A,' false, and the right-hand disjunct, i.e. '~B,' true. Checking in with our interpretation of how a disjunction works in this kind of scenario, we end up with the following:

$$\begin{array}{cccc} & & * & & \\ \sim & \textbf{A} & \vee & \sim & \textbf{B} \\ \hline F & T & T & T & F \end{array}$$

The disjunction, then, is true, based on the original truth-value assignments. One final example, with the same truth-value assignments for 'A' and 'B' as above:

~ (A ∨ B)

Performing **Steps 1** and **2**, and being careful to understand the role of the parentheses in the sentence, we arrive at the following:

```
        *
     |— ~  (A  ∨  B)
     |_____
            T     F
```

We calculate the truth-value of the '∨' first:

```
        *
     |— ~  (A  ∨  B)
     |_____
           T̶  T  F̶
```

Then this truth-value allows us to calculate the truth-value of the entire sentence: we negate the truth-value of what is inside the parentheses, as indicated by the arrow in the following:

```
        *
     |— ~  (A  ∨  B)
     |_____
       F    F  T  T
```

Exercise Set 3.1

Q1. Assume these truth-values for the SL atomic sentences 'A,' 'B,' and 'C':

    A: true
    B: false
    C: true

Now, using truth tables, determine the truth-values of the following SL compound sentences. Construct the truth tables in the space provided. I have done the first one for you. *Make sure to show how you arrived at your answer.*

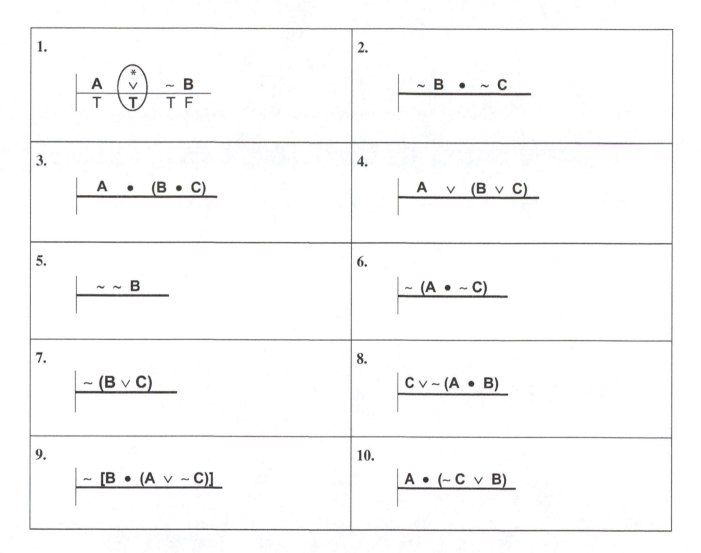

Chapter 3   Truth Tables: Sentences   **115**

3.2 Truth Tables for Conditional Sentences

So far, we have used truth tables to give truth-functional definitions for the first three operator symbols. We turn next to conditional sentences: when is a conditional sentence true, and when is it false? Consider the following sentence, for example:

If John mows the lawn, then John can go to the party.

Here is a symbolization key:

L: John mows the lawn.
G: John can go to the party.

And here is the resultant sentence of SL:

L ⊃ G

How should we decide if this sentence is true or false? To work through this, let's imagine that it is John's dad who is uttering the above sentence to John: "if you mow the lawn, then you can go to the party." There are four possible scenarios:

Scenario 1: John mows the lawn, and he can go to the party (i.e., true antecedent, true consequent).
Scenario 2: John mows the lawn and he cannot go to the party (i.e., true antecedent, false consequent).
Scenario 3: John does not mow the lawn and he can go to the party (i.e., false antecedent, true consequent).
Scenario 4: John does not mow the lawn, and he cannot go to the party (i.e., false antecedent, false consequent).

Let's explore each of these in turn. **Scenario 1** has John mowing the lawn and going to the party. In this case, when John's dad uttered the conditional, was he telling the truth? That is, was the sentence he uttered true? It appears so: John satisfied the **IF** part of the sentence, and his dad followed through with the **THEN** part. So, we get the following top row of the truth table for the '⊃':

L	⊃	G
T	T	T

Scenario 2 has John mowing the lawn, but not being able to go to the party. If this is how things turned out, then when John's dad uttered the conditional, was he telling the truth? John mows the lawn, but then his dad does not let him go to the party; that is, John satisfied the **IF** part of the sentence, but then his dad did not follow through with the **THEN** part. This means that John's dad was lying to John, and the conditional is false. Here, then, is the second row of the truth table for the conditional:

L	⊃	G
T	F	F

So, the first two rows of the truth table for '⊃' are relatively straightforward. What about **Scenario 3**, in which John does not mow the lawn and can go to the party? Did John's dad say something true or false in this case when he uttered the conditional? Well, uttering the conditional sentence commits John's dad to what happens *if* John mows the lawn. However, the sentence does not say anything about what happens if John does *not* mow the lawn. That is, John's dad did not insist that John can go to the party *only if* he mows the lawn—remember the distinction between "if" sentences and "only if" sentences from Chapter 2! Consequently, if it turns out that John gets to go the party even if he does not mow the lawn, this does not entail that John's dad lied when he uttered the conditional sentence. In this case, then, the sentence is not false. And, in SL, if something is not false, then there's only one other option: it must be true. (Recall that we are assuming the Principle of Bivalence, which insists that every sentence is either true or false). This, then, gives us the third row of the truth table for '⊃':

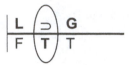

Similar considerations come into play for the **Scenario 4**, in which John does not mow the lawn and is not able to go to the party. Once more, John's dad does not commit himself to anything if John did *not* wash the car, and so the sentence is not false. This means that it must be true:

We end up, then, with the following truth table for the above sentence:

L	⊃	G
T	**T**	T
T	**F**	F
F	**T**	T
F	**T**	F

Generalizing from this example, like we have done with the earlier operators, we end up with the following complete truth table for conditional sentences:

P	⊃	*Q*
T	**T**	T
T	**F**	F
F	**T**	T
F	**T**	F

We can capture this truth table in English as follows:

> A conditional sentence is false whenever the antecedent is true and the consequent is false; it is true otherwise.

The above truth table defines what is called the ***Material Conditional***. It is the standard truth-functional interpretation for conditional sentences. We should note, however, that, notwithstanding the generation of each row of the truth table based on the above example, there is no universal agreement among logicians that this is the best way to capture the logical form of conditional sentences. The controversy surrounding this issue is beyond the scope of this book, however. Your task is to familiarize yourself with the above truth table. So, let's get some practice in. Assume that 'M' is true, 'N' is false, and 'O' is true. What is the truth-value of the following sentence?

M ⊃ (N ⊃ ~O)

Let's follow the steps outlined above. Assigning the truth-values to each atomic sentence, and then identifying and labeling the main operator, we get the following:

$$
\begin{array}{ccc}
 & * & \\
\mathbf{M} \supset & (\mathbf{N} \supset \sim \mathbf{O}) \\
\hline
\mathbf{T} & \mathbf{F} & \mathbf{T}
\end{array}
$$

The negation operates only on the 'O' here. And notice that the second of the two horseshoes here has scope only over what is inside the parentheses; consequently, it is the first of the horseshoes that is the main operator. Next, given that 'O' has been assigned a 'T,' we can assign an 'F' to the '~' that is to the left of 'O.' The conditional sentence inside the parentheses, therefore, must be assigned a 'T': a false antecedent and a false consequent generates a true conditional:

$$
\begin{array}{ccc}
 & * & \\
\mathbf{M} \supset & (\mathbf{N} \supset \sim \mathbf{O}) \\
\hline
\mathbf{T} & \mathbf{F} \; \mathbf{T} \; \mathbf{F} \; \mathbf{T}
\end{array}
$$

The entire sentence, then, has a true antecedent and a false consequent, which means that it is false:

As indicated, the truth table for conditional sentences is somewhat counterintuitive, so make sure to complete Exercise Set 3.2.

Exercise Set 3.2

Q1. Assume these truth-values for the SL atomic sentences 'M,' 'N,' and 'O':

M: true
N: false
O: true

Now, using truth tables, determine the truth-values of the following SL compound sentences. Construct the truth tables in the space provided. I have done the first one for you. *Make sure to show how you arrived at your answer.*

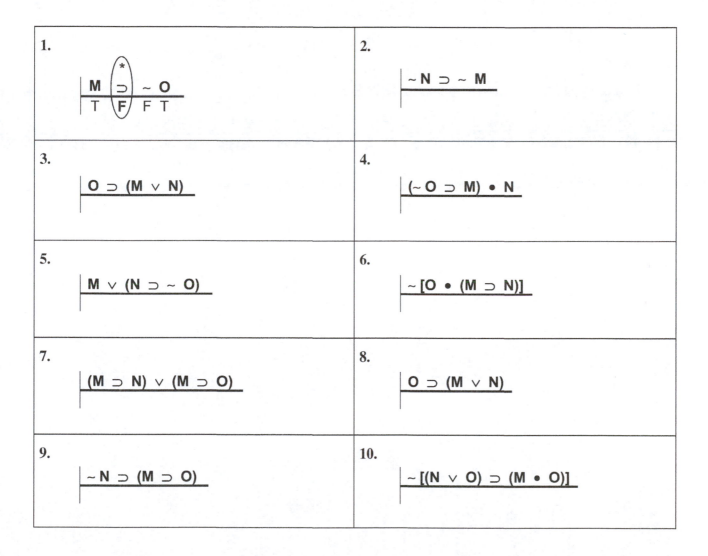

3.3 Complete Truth Tables for Compound Sentences

We still have to introduce the truth table for one more sentence operator, i.e. the biconditional, but that truth table will make more sense if we look at *complete* truth tables first. So far, we have seen that we can calculate the truth-value of a compound sentence as long as we have the truth-value of each atomic sentence involved. This, after all, is what it means for the sentence operators to be truth-functional. What can we do when we have no information on the truth-value of the atomic sentences? Well, we cannot calculate the *actual* truth-value of the compound sentence; however, we can still lay out all the *possible* ways things could turn out for the compound sentence. We do this by constructing a ***complete*** truth table for the compound sentence. Let's work through an example. Consider the following sentence of SL:

A • ~B

We have no information on the truth-value of 'A' or the truth-value of 'B,' but we can explore the possible truth-value combinations for these atomic sentences. There are four possible ways things could turn out:

Scenario 1: A is true, and B is true.
Scenario 2: A is true, and B is false.
Scenario 3: A is false, and B is true.
Scenario 4: A is false, and B is false.

We can use a truth table to lay out each of these possibilities as follows:

	A	B	A • ~ B
Scenario 1 →	T	T	
Scenario 2 →	T	F	
Scenario 3 →	F	T	
Scenario 4 →	F	F	

Each row[1] of a complete truth table corresponds to a possible combination of truth-values for the atomic sentences. We do not know which of these rows corresponds to the way things *actually* are, but that's OK—we are going to explore all the possibilities.

The next step is to identify the main logical operator of the sentence. What we have here is clearly a conjunction; the column under the '•' will consist of the four possible truth-values for this sentence. This, however, will be the final piece of the puzzle; at this stage, we can merely fill in the column under each atomic sentence letter in the compound sentence. On the first row, 'A' is assigned a T, and 'B' is assigned a T; on the second row, 'A' is assigned a T, and 'B' is assigned an F; and so on for rows three and four:

A	B	A	• *	~	B
T	T	T			T
T	F	T			F
F	T	T			T
F	F	T			F

[1] The convention is to label horizontal lines as ***rows***. Vertical lines in truth tables will be referred to as ***columns***.

At this point, then, we have some gaps: the column under the '~' needs to be filled in, as does the column under the '•.' As before, we deal with the main operator last. So, let's do the '~' column. Wherever 'B' is assigned a T, the '~' is assigned an F; and wherever 'B' is assigned an F, the '~' is assigned a T:

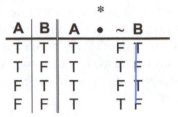

We cross out the 'B' column to indicate that we will no longer be using it to generate other columns. At this point, we are in a position to insert truth-values into the column underneath the main operator: the column under the 'A' is the left-hand conjunct, the column under the '~' is the right-hand conjunct:

A	**B**	**A**	**•**	**~**	**B**	
T	T	T	F	F	T	
T	F	T	T	T	F	
F	T	T	F	F	T	
F	F	T	T	T	F	

We highlight the entire column under the main connective; the truth-values listed in this column are the possible truth-values for the compound sentence. To reiterate, we have no way of knowing if the sentence is *actually* true or false. However, we now know the circumstances under which the sentence is true (rows 2 and 4) and the circumstances under which it will turn out to be false (rows 1 and 3). And this is useful information to have.

Here, then, is the procedure for constructing complete truth tables:

Constructing Complete Truth Tables

Step 1: Write out the possible combinations of truth-values for the atomic sentences involved. Each row corresponds to one such possible combination.

Step 2: Based on the result of **Step 1**, complete the columns under the atomic sentences as they appear in the compound sentence.

Step 3: Identify and label the main operator of the compound sentence.

Step 4: Starting with the operator with the narrowest scope, complete each column of the truth table.

Step 5: The column under the main operator will be the last one to be completed. Highlight this column.

Not all complete truth tables will have four rows. The number of rows depends on the number of atomic sentences in the compound sentence you are presented with. In the sentence '~~S,' for example, there is just one atomic sentence, i.e. 'S,' which is possibly true and possibly false. There are no other possibilities, so a complete truth table for this sentence will have just two rows:

S	**~**	**~**	**S**
T			T
F			F

The main operator here is the left-most '~.' Consequently, we fill in the column under the other '~' first, and then generate the main operator column based on that:

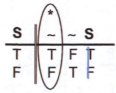

Our next example will enable us to construct a complete truth table for biconditionals. Recall that the sentence 'A ≡ B,' for example, is an abbreviation of the sentence '(A ⊃ B) • (B ⊃ A).' Consequently, if we can construct a complete truth table for the latter sentence, we will have constructed a complete truth table for the former. So, let us do that, following the above procedure.

Step 1 asks us to write out the possible combinations of truth-values for the atomic sentences involved:

A	B	(A ⊃ B) • (B ⊃ A)
T	T	
T	F	
F	T	
F	F	

We can now complete the columns under each atomic sentence in the compound sentence. Let's also do **Step 3** and label the main operator:

A	B	(A	⊃	B)	•	(B	⊃	A)
T	T	T		T		T		T
T	F	T		F		F		T
F	T	F		T		T		F
F	F	F		F		F		F

Now, we need to complete the columns under each horseshoe:

A	B	(A	⊃	B)	•	(B	⊃	A)
T	T	T	T	T		T	T	T
T	F	T	F	F		F	T	T
F	T	F	T	T		T	F	F
F	F	F	T	F		F	T	F

Again, we can draw a line through those columns that will not be used from this point on; they have already been used to generate new columns. The new columns will then generate the column under the main operator:

A	B	(A	⊃	B)	•	(B	⊃	A)
T	T	T	T	T	**T**	T	T	T
T	F	T	F	F	**F**	F	T	T
F	T	F	T	T	**F**	T	F	F
F	F	F	T	F	**T**	F	T	F

The column under the main operator informs us of the conditions under which this conjunction is true and under which it is false. And, as indicated, this provides us with the complete truth table for biconditional sentences (using sentence variables):

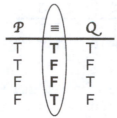

As we have done with the truth tables for the other logical operators, we can formulate this in English as well:

A biconditional is true whenever its left-hand side and its right-hand side have identical truth-values; it is false otherwise.

We now have complete truth tables for each sentence operator of SL. These, together with their English formulations, are also listed in Appendix A.

A complete truth table for a compound sentence lays out all the possible ways things can turn out, and gives details about when that sentence would be true and when it would be false. The size of a truth table depends on the number of atomic sentence letters that are involved in the compound sentence. As we have seen, when there is just one atomic sentence letter, then all we need is a two-row truth table. Most of our examples so far have been compound sentences containing two atomic sentence letters, resulting in four-row truth tables. What about a compound sentence that has three different atomic sentences, for example 'M ∨ (N ⊃ W)'? It turns out that there are *eight* different permutations in this case:

M	N	W	M ∨ (N ⊃ W)
T	T	T	
T	T	F	
T	F	T	
T	F	F	
F	T	T	
F	T	F	
F	F	T	
F	F	F	

There is, in fact, a straightforward formula for calculating the number of rows that your truth table will have: raise 2 to the power of the number of different atomic sentence letters that are in your compound sentence. In this case, we have $2^3 = 8$ rows. Earlier, we had $2^2 = 4$ rows, and $2^1 = 2$ rows. A sentence with four different atomic sentence letters will have $2^4 = 16$ rows. And so on. We can also make use of a simple algorithm to quickly ensure that all of the truth-value combinations are covered. For this most recent sentence, for example, the column under 'W' has T's and F's on every second row. The column under 'N' has T's and F's in pairs—the first two rows are T's, the second two rows are F's, and so on. Finally, the column under 'M' does things in fours—the first four rows are T's and the next four rows are F's. Taking this approach to assigning truth-values to the atomic sentences quickly guarantees that all possible scenarios are covered, without having to go row by row to assure ourselves that this is the case.

Back to the sentence at hand: let's label the main operator and fill in the columns under each atomic sentence letter:

M	N	W	M	∨	(N	⊃	W)
T	T	T	T		T		T
T	T	F	T		T		F
T	F	T	T		F		T
T	F	F	T		F		F
F	T	T	F		T		T
F	T	F	F		T		F
F	F	T	F		F		T
F	F	F	F		F		F

The complete truth table ends up as follows:

M	N	W	M	∨*	(N	⊃	W)
T	T	T	T	T	T	T	T
T	T	F	T	T	T	F	F
T	F	T	T	T	F	T	T
T	F	F	T	T	F	T	F
F	T	T	F	T	T	T	T
F	T	F	F	F	T	F	F
F	F	T	F	T	F	T	T
F	F	F	F	T	F	T	F

Tautologies, Contradictions, and Contingent Sentences

The ability to construct complete truth tables and give details about when a compound sentence would be true and when it would be false is very useful. Ultimately, it will allow us to do what we've set out to do, namely check to see if an argument is valid. Before we get to that point, however, we will explore some of the other things truth tables can do for us. First on this list is the fact that truth tables allow us to classify sentences into three different types. Consider the following sentence of English, for example:

Either it is raining or not raining.

Is this sentence true or false? What do we have to do to figure it out? Looking outside will tell us one of two things: that it is, in fact, raining, or that it is, in fact, not raining. However, we don't need to look outside to figure out if the above sentence is true. The sentence is true *no matter what* the weather is doing right now: it just *has* to be either raining or not raining at this moment. What we have, then, is a necessarily true sentence. In other words, the sentence is a ***necessary truth:***

A sentence is a **NECESSARY TRUTH** if and only if it is impossible for it to be false.

Using the obvious atomic sentence letter, and constructing a truth table for the resultant sentence of SL, we get the following:

R	R	∨*	~	R
T	T	T	F	T
F	F	T	T	F

Notice that the column under the main operator is all T's. And remember that each row of a truth table corresponds to a possible scenario, and that the rows taken together exhaust all of these possibilities. Consequently, this truth table tells us that it is not possible for this sentence to be false. What we have, then, is an accurate reflection of our take on the original sentence: it is a necessary truth. In logic, such sentences are typically called *tautologies*. Here's a definition:

> A sentence in SL is a **TAUTOLOGY** if and only if the column under the main operator is composed exclusively of T's.

A tautology is true no matter what the facts on the ground are. And we can identify a tautology without *knowing* these facts. That is, in some instances, knowing the logical form of a sentence is sufficient for knowing that that sentence is true. If you reflect on this fact for a moment, you will realize how remarkable it is!

In some other cases, knowing the logical form of a sentence is sufficient for knowing that that sentence is *false*. Consider the following sentence of English, for example:

Syracuse is the capital of the United States and Syracuse is not the capital of the United States.

This sentence should strike us as a bit odd: it is both affirming and denying that Syracuse is the capital of the United States. Surely *both* cannot be true! So, it looks like the conjunction is false. What we have here is a necessarily false sentence, what logicians call a *contradiction:*

> A sentence is a **CONTRADICTION** if and only if it is impossible for it to be true.

Let's explore this in SL. Using the obvious atomic sentence letter, and constructing a truth table for the resultant sentence of SL, we get the following:

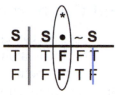

As we can see, there is no possibility in which this sentence turns out to be true. Once more, what we have is an accurate reflection of our take on the original sentence: it is a contradiction. Here's a definition in terms of truth tables:

> A sentence in SL is a **CONTRADICTION** if and only if the column under the main operator is composed exclusively of F's

Note that this aligns with one of our basic assumptions in this book—the Principle of Non-Contradiction— according to which there are no true contradictions.

In the case of both tautologies and contradictions, then, it is possible to determine the sentence's truth-value *solely in virtue of the logical form* of that sentence alone. We do not need to know what the atomic sentence letters represent, and we do not need to know if what they represent is actually true or false.

There is, of course, one possibility remaining: sentences that are neither necessarily true nor necessarily false. Consider the following:

Either Bob will win or Sally will win.

This sentence is true if either Bob wins, or Sally wins, or both win. However, we have no guarantee that one of these will be the case. Perhaps neither Bob nor Sally will win, in which case the sentence is false. So, the truth-value of this sentence depends upon what *actually* turns out to be the case. In English, we sometimes say that something's being true or false is *contingent upon* something else being true or false. Consequently, such sentences are called ***Contingent Sentences***:

> A sentence is **CONTINGENT** if and only if it is neither necessarily true nor necessarily false.

Here is a complete truth table for the above sentence:

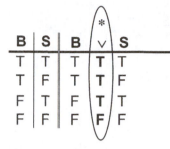

Here, the column under the main operator is a mixture of T's and F's. And, in this case, the logical form of the sentence does *not* guarantee the truth-value of the sentence. Instead, the truth-value of the sentence is *contingent upon* what is actually the case. That is, we can't know what the sentence's truth-value is unless we have knowledge of the facts on the ground. Here is a definition, in truth-table terms:

> A sentence of SL is a **CONTINGENT SENTENCE** if and only if the column under the main operator has at least one T and at least one F.

At this point, then, not only can we construct complete truth tables for individual sentences of SL, we can read some information off these truth tables: namely, we can ascertain if the sentence is a tautology, a contradiction, or a contingent sentence. The above examples are fairly straightforward, but many sentences are less obviously tautologies, contradictions, or contingent sentences. Let us articulate a truth-table test based on the foregoing:

> ### What Kind of Sentence Do I Have?
>
> **Step 1:** Construct a complete truth table for the sentence.
> **Step 2:** Check the column under the main operator. There are three possibilities:
>   **a.** This column is composed exclusively of T's. In this case, the sentence is a **TAUTOLOGY.**
>   **b.** This column is composed exclusively of F's. In this case, the sentence is a **CONTRADICTION.**
>   **c.** The column has at least one T and at least one F. In this case, the sentence is a **CONTINGENT SENTENCE.**

Shortcuts

When first learning any skill, it is not a good idea to start off by taking shortcuts. However, at this point, you may be familiar enough with truth tables to take advantage of some shortcuts. Let's see if we can generate some for when we are checking to see if a sentence is a tautology, a contradiction, or a contingent sentence:

To show that a sentence is . . .	You may use the following shortcut . . .
. . . a Tautology?	No shortcut possible. All rows of the truth table must be completed.
. . . a Contradiction?	No shortcut possible. All rows of the truth table must be completed.
. . . a Contingent Sentence?	Complete just two rows, one of which has a T under the main operator, the other having an F under the main operator.

All shortcuts come with a warning, of course: be very, very careful!

Exercise Set 3.3

Q1. Create a complete truth table for each of the following sentences. Check to see if the sentence is a **TAUTOLOGY**, a **CONTRADICTION**, or a **CONTINGENT SENTENCE**. Construct your truth tables in the space provided. The first one is done for you.

1.

W	~ W • W
T	F T **F** T
F	T F **F** F

This is a **CONTRADICTION**

2.

X	~ X ∨ X
T	
F	

3.

J	J ⊃ ~J
T	
F	

4.

M	M ≡ M
T	
F	

5.

Y	~ (Y ∨ ~ Y)
T	
F	

6.

Z	~ (Z • ~ Z)
T	
F	

7.

A	B	A ⊃ ~B
T	T	
T	F	
F	T	
F	F	

8.

C	D	C ⊃ (B ⊃ C)
T	T	
T	F	
F	T	
F	F	

9.

R	S	~R ∨ (R • S)
T	T	
T	F	
F	T	
F	F	

10.

G	H	~ [G ∨ (H ∨ ~H)]
T	T	
T	F	
F	T	
F	F	

11.

A	S	E	(S ⊃ A) ∨ (S ⊃ E)
T	T	T	
T	T	F	
T	F	T	
T	F	F	
F	T	T	
F	T	F	
F	F	T	
F	F	F	

12.

D	V	Z	(D ⊃ V) ⊃ (Z ⊃ D)
T	T	T	
T	T	F	
T	F	T	
T	F	F	
F	T	T	
F	T	F	
F	F	T	
F	F	F	

Q2. Create a complete truth table for each of the following sentences on a separate sheet of paper. Check to see if the sentence is a **TAUTOLOGY**, a **CONTRADICTION**, or a **CONTINGENT SENTENCE**.

1. L ⊃ (L ∨ ~L)
2. ~R ⊃ ~R
3. ~~~M
4. J ⊃ (K • ~K)
5. ~[(P ⊃ (Q ⊃ P)]
6. S ≡ (~S ∨ U)
7. (J ∨ L) ∨ ~(J ∨ L)
8. (X ⊃ Y) ∨ (Y ⊃ X)
9. (Q • ~Q) ⊃ S
10. G ⊃ (H ∨ ~H)
11. (N • O) ⊃ (O ∨ P)
12. [~A ∨ (C ∨ E)] ≡ [A ⊃ (C ∨ E)]

Chapter 4

Truth Tables: Comparing Sentences and Arguments

Once we can construct truth tables for individual sentences of Sentential Logic (SL), we can also *compare* and *contrast* the truth tables for sets of sentences. Ultimately, this means we will be able to use truth tables to check an argument for validity – and this is what we will end up doing in this chapter. First things first, however. Let's start with simple comparisons between two sentences.

4.1 Logical Equivalence

Consider the following sentence of English:

Neither Martin nor Zak is taking French this year.

Using the obvious letters for the atomic sentences, we can translate this into SL as follows:

~ (M ∨ Z)

In Chapter 2, we indicated that a "neither-nor" sentence can also be translated as follows:

~M • ~Z

We are now in a position to show that the two candidate translations really do amount to the same thing. The basic idea is to construct a complete truth table for each sentence and compare the columns under each main operator. Let's place the truth tables side by side:

M	Z	~(M ∨ Z)	~ M • ~ Z
T	T	F T T T	F T F F T
T	F	F T T F	F T F T F
F	T	F F T T	T F F F T
F	F	T F F F	T F T T F

131

As you can see, the columns under the main operator are identical. When the first sentence is true, so is the second one, and vice versa. And when the first sentence is false, so is the second one, and vice versa. In other words, they never deviate in truth-value. From a logical point of view, then, these sentences are logically equivalent:

> Two sentences are **LOGICALLY EQUIVALENT** if and only if the columns under the main operators are identical.

We can also check for logical equivalence by using our understanding of the biconditional truth table. Let us again use an example from Chapter 2 to illustrate the point: the two ways of translating "unless" sentences. Recall that a sentence like "P, unless Q" can be translated in either of two ways:

P ∨ Q

~Q ⊃ P

To check for logical equivalence this time, we will form a biconditional out of the two sentences and construct a complete truth table for it:

P	Q	(P ∨ Q)	≡*	(~ Q ⊃ P)
T	T	T T T	**T**	F T T T
T	F	T T F	**T**	T F T T
F	T	F T T	**T**	F T T F
F	F	F F F	**T**	T F F F

As you can see, the biconditional is a tautology. Remember, though, that a biconditional is true whenever its left-hand side and its right-hand side have identical truth-values. The fact that the above biconditional sentence is a tautology, then, tells us that the left-hand side and the right-hand side must always have the same truth-value. And this, of course, means that the sentence that constitutes the left-hand side of the biconditional and the sentence that constitutes the right-hand side of the biconditional are logically equivalent.

One final example before moving on. Recall that the truth table for the material conditional is somewhat counterintuitive: its last two rows just "default" to being true. However, we can do a little more to justify this choice of truth table by noting that it basically guarantees the following: a conditional sentence is never true if the IF part of the conditional is met and the THEN part of it is not met. Or, to put this another way: 'A ⊃ B' should be logically equivalent to '~(A • ~B).' Let's see if this is the case:

A	B	A ⊃ B	~(A • ~ B)
T	T	T **T** T	**T** T F F T
T	F	T **F** F	**F** T F T F
F	T	F **T** T	**T** F F F T
F	F	F **T** F	**T** F F T F

The two sentences are, indeed, logically equivalent. Again, it is not appropriate in an introductory logic text to thoroughly explore the issue of whether the material conditional's truth table adequately captures what is going on in a conditional sentence. Hopefully, though, this most recent consideration will help you understand conditionals just a bit more.

It is time to formulate our test for logical equivalence:

The Truth-table Test for Logical Equivalence

Step 1:   Construct a complete truth table for each sentence.

Step 2:   Compare the column under the main operator of each sentence. There are two possibilities to watch out for:

   a.   The columns are identical. In this case, the sentences are LOGICALLY EQUIVALENT.

   b.   The columns are not identical. In this case, the sentences are NOT LOGICALLY EQUIVALENT.

Shortcuts

Be on the look-out for the following shortcuts:

To show that a pair of sentences are . . .	You may use the following shortcut . . .
. . . *Logically equivalent*	No shortcut possible. All rows of the truth table must be completed.
. . . *Not Logically Equivalent*	Complete just one row in which the sentences differ in truth-value.

Again: taking shortcuts can be dangerous—so be very careful!

Exercise Set 4.1

Q1. Use truth tables to check the following pairs of sentences for **LOGICAL EQUIVALENCE**. Construct your truth tables in the space provided. The first one is done for you.

1.

R	S	R ⊃ S	~ S ⊃ ~ R
T	T	T **T** T	F T **T** F T
T	F	T **F** F	T F **F** F T
F	T	F **T** T	F T **T** T F
F	F	F **T** F	T F **T** T F

These sentences are
LOGICALLY EQUIVALENT

2.

R	S	R ⊃ S	~ R ⊃ ~ S
T	T		
T	F		
F	T		
F	F		

3.

G	J	J ∨ ~ G	~ J ∨ G
T	T		
T	F		
F	T		
F	F		

4.

M	N	M ∨ ~ M	~ (M • ~ M)
T	T		
T	F		

5.

W	X	X ≡ W	(X • W) ∨ (~ X • ~ W)
T	T		
T	F		
F	T		
F	F		

6.

A	B	~ A ∨ ~ B	~ B ⊃ A
T	T		
T	F		
F	T		
F	F		

7.

C	D	E	C ⊃ (D ⊃ E)	(C • D) ⊃ E
T	T	T		
T	T	F		
T	F	T		
T	F	F		
F	T	T		
F	T	F		
F	F	T		
F	F	F		

8.

N	P	Q	(N ∨ P) ⊃ (N ∨ Q)	(N ∨ Q) ⊃ (N ∨ P)
T	T	T		
T	T	F		
T	F	T		
T	F	F		
F	T	T		
F	T	F		
F	F	T		
F	F	F		

9.

X	Y	Z	X ⊃ (Y ⊃ Z)	Y ⊃ (~ X ∨ Z)
T	T	T		
T	T	F		
T	F	T		
T	F	F		
F	T	T		
F	T	F		
F	F	T		
F	F	F		

10.	A	B	C	A ≡ (B ≡ C)	(A ≡ B) ≡ C
	T	T	T		
	T	T	F		
	T	F	T		
	T	F	F		
	F	T	T		
	F	T	F		
	F	F	T		
	F	F	F		

Q2. Use truth tables to check the following pairs of sentences for **LOGICAL EQUIVALENCE**. Construct your truth tables on a separate sheet of paper.

1. P ∨ Q, Q ∨ P

2. ~(D • E), ~D • ~E

3. ~(S ∨ U), ~S ∨ ~U

4. A ⊃ ~B, B ⊃ ~A

5. C ≡ Z, ~Z ≡ ~C

6. J ⊃ ~(K ∨ L), K ⊃ (L ⊃ J)

7. P • (Q • R), (P • Q) • R

8. J • (K ∨ L), (J • K) ∨ L

9. M ⊃ ~(N ∨ O), (N • O) ⊃ ~M

10. X ⊃ (Y ≡ ~Z), ~[X • ~(Y ≡ ~Z)]

4.2 Logical Consistency

We will look at one more way in which sentences of SL can relate to one another. Here is a definition to get us started here:

> Two or more sentences are **LOGICALLY CONSISTENT** if and only if it is possible for all of them to be true at the same time.

Consider the following pair of English sentences, for example:

Abdul has 17 dollars in his wallet.
Abdul has more than 10 dollars in his wallet.

Intuitively, focusing on the content of the sentences, both of these sentences can be true at the same time. We might not know who Abdul is, and he might have no money in his wallet—but it is still the case that both sentences *could be* true at the same time. Consequently, these sentences are logically consistent.

Figuring out if two sentences are logically consistent isn't always so straightforward, however. Consider the following pair:

If John gets paid on Friday, then he will buy a ticket for the show.
If John does not get paid on Friday, then he will buy a ticket for the show.

How are these two sentences related? They certainly don't seem to be logically equivalent. Are they consistent? Let's check. Here is a symbolization key:

P: John gets paid on Friday.
S: John will buy a ticket for the show.

And let's place the complete truth table for each resultant translated sentence side by side:

P	S	P ⊃ S	~ P ⊃ S
T	T	T **T** T	F T **T** T
T	F	T **F** F	F T **T** F
F	T	F **T** T	T F **T** T
F	F	F **T** F	T F **F** F

The two marked rows of the table are rows in which both sentences are true. Remember that each row of a truth table corresponds to a possible scenario; so, this tells us that it is possible for both sentences to be true under the same circumstances. This provides us with a definition of logical consistency in truth-table terms:

> Two (or more) sentences are **LOGICALLY CONSISTENT** if and only if there is at least one row in which there is a T under each main operator.

Once we complete the truth table for each sentence, it is important that we mark any row in which all of the sentences are true. If we do not find a row like this, then the sentences are ***logically inconsistent***.

When checking for logical consistency, we can place more than two sentences side by side to see if it is possible that they are all true at the same time. Here is an example of this:

J	K	L	J	⊃	K	L	⊃	~	J	~	K	•	J
T	T	T	T	T	T	T	F	F	T	F	T	F	T
T	T	F	T	T	T	F	T	F	T	F	T	F	T
T	F	T	T	F	F	T	F	F	T	T	F	T	T
T	F	F	T	F	F	F	T	F	T	T	F	T	T
F	T	T	F	T	T	T	T	T	F	F	T	F	F
F	T	F	F	T	T	F	T	T	F	F	T	F	F
F	F	T	F	T	F	T	T	T	F	T	F	F	F
F	F	F	F	T	F	F	T	T	F	T	F	F	F

Checking each row one by one, we do not find any row in which there is a T under each main operator. So, these sentences are logically inconsistent. Another way of putting this is to say that the *set* consisting of these sentences is logically consistent. This shows that any sentences of English whose forms are captured by the above sentences of SL cannot all be true at the same time. This can be very useful information! If we find ourselves believing each claim that these sentences make, then this makes our *beliefs* logically inconsistent. Logically speaking, then, we ought to give up on *at least one* of these beliefs. If we persist in believing all three claims in the full knowledge that the sentences are logically inconsistent, then we are being illogical.

Shortcuts

Once more, let's consider if there are any shortcuts available:

To show that a set of sentences is . . .	You may use the following shortcut . . .
. . . *Logically consistent*	Complete just one row in which each sentence has a T under the main operator.
. . . *Not logically consistent*	No shortcut possible. All rows of the truth table must be completed.

Exercise Set 4.2

Q1. Check each of the following sets of sentences for **LOGICAL CONSISTENCY**. Construct your truth tables in the space provided. If you determine that a set of sentences is logically consistent, then mark the row of the truth table that indicates this. The first one is done for you.

1.

A	B	A ∨ B	~A ∨ ~B
T	T	T **T** T	F T **F** F T
✖ T	F	T **T** F	F T **T** T F
✖ F	T	F **T** T	T F **T** F T
F	F	F **F** F	T F **T** T F

These sentences are
LOGICALLY CONSISTENT

2.

P	Q	P • Q	P ∨ Q
T	T		
T	F		
F	T		
F	F		

3.

G	H	G ⊃ H	G • ~H
T	T		
T	F		
F	T		
F	F		

4.

M	N	M ⊃ N	~M ⊃ ~N
T	T		
T	F		
F	T		
F	F		

5.

J	K	~J⊃~K	~J•~K
T	T		
T	F		
F	T		
F	F		

6.

X	Y	X⊃Y	Y⊃X	~X∨~Y
T	T			
T	F			
F	T			
F	F			

7.

D	E	F	D⊃(F⊃E)	(D•E)⊃~F
T	T	T		
T	T	F		
T	F	T		
T	F	F		
F	T	T		
F	T	F		
F	F	T		
F	F	F		

8.

S	R	U	S ∨ U	S ⊃ R	~ U ⊃ ~ R
T	T	T			
T	T	F			
T	F	T			
T	F	F			
F	T	T			
F	T	F			
F	F	T			
F	F	F			

9.

A	B	C	A ⊃ B	A ⊃ C	~ B ⊃ ~ (A ∨ C)
T	T	T			
T	T	F			
T	F	T			
T	F	F			
F	T	T			
F	T	F			
F	F	T			
F	F	F			

10.	U	V	W	U ≡ (V ∨ W)	U • ~V	W ⊃ ~U
	T	T	T			
	T	T	F			
	T	F	T			
	T	F	F			
	F	T	T			
	F	T	F			
	F	F	T			
	F	F	F			

Q2. Use truth tables to check the following sets of sentences for **LOGICAL CONSISTENCY**. Construct your truth tables on a separate sheet of paper. If you determine that a set of sentences is logically consistent, then mark the row, or rows, of the truth table that indicates this.

1. X • ~Y, ~X • Y
2. N ∨ ~N, ~N
3. Q • ~Q, Q
4. Y ⊃ Y, ~Y ⊃ ~Y, Y
5. J ⊃ (K ∨ ~K), J ⊃ (K • ~K)
6. F ∨ G, G ∨ C, C ⊃ ~F
7. W • D, C ⊃ ~D, C
8. P ∨ ~S, S ∨ ~R, R ∨ ~P
9. (Z ∨ D) ≡ G, Z ⊃ ~(D ∨ L), L ⊃ G, D ⊃ L
10. A ⊃ B, B ⊃ C, C ⊃ D, ~(A • ~D)

4.3 Validity: Complete Truth Tables

Our primary motivation for isolating the logical form of sentences and arguments was to develop a way of checking for validity that focuses on the logical form of an argument. Finally, we are at the point where we can do this. Note that the fact that we can construct truth tables for sets of sentences means that we can construct truth tables for arguments: arguments are, after all, sets of sentences. But once we have an argument's truth table drawn up, we will have to pay special attention to how those sentences that are identified as the *premises* of the argument relate to the sentence that is identified as the *conclusion* of the argument. In particular, we will have to focus on whether the form of the argument is such that the truth of the premises guarantees the truth of the conclusion.

The key thing to remember is that constructing a complete truth table for sentences in SL allows us to lay out all the possible scenarios for those sentences. Each row corresponds to a possible way things can turn out. If we set the sentences (both the premises and the conclusion) of an argument alongside each other, and construct a complete truth table for each sentence, then we should be able to tell if it is possible for all the premises to be true and the conclusion false. Let us work through an example. Here is an argument, already translated into SL:

D ∨ E

D

_____

∴ E

Arguments in SL are also often laid out horizontally, as follows:

D ∨ E, D ∴ E

Here, the premises are separated by commas. The conclusion is the sentence that comes after our symbol for "therefore," i.e. '∴'. When using truth tables to check for validity, we will also lay the argument out horizontally, as follows:

				*
D	E	D ∨ E	D	∴ E
T	T			
T	F			
F	T			
F	F			

Note that the sentence identified as the conclusion of the argument is over on the right of the truth table. This will always be the case. I have also included the '∴' before this sentence to further indicate that it is the conclusion, though note that '∴' is *not* a sentence operator, so it does *not* get its own column in the truth table. Now let's construct a truth table for each sentence of the argument:

D	E	D ∨ E	D	∴ E
T	T	T T T	T	T
T	F	T T F	T	F
F	T	F T T	F	T
F	F	F F F	F	F

The basic task, then, is the same. Now, however, we need to examine the truth table closely. Can it tell us if the truth of the premises guarantees the truth of the conclusion? That is, is it possible for the premises to be true and the conclusion false? Well, seeing as each row corresponds to a possibility, this amounts to asking the following question: Are there any rows on the truth table in which all the premises are true and the conclusion is false? In this case, there *is* one such row. Let's mark this row:

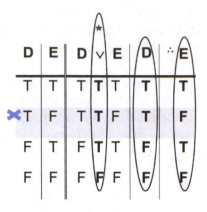

This row tells me that this argument is invalid. (Note: it would be incorrect to say that the row itself is invalid.) Let us summarize the reasoning here:

1. Each row of the argument's truth table corresponds to a possible scenario.
2. All the rows of the argument's truth table taken together exhaust all the possible scenarios.
3. One of the rows has all true premises and a false conclusion. That is, there is a T under the main operator of each of the premises, and an F under the main operator of the conclusion.
4. Therefore, it is possible for all the premises to be true and the conclusion false.
5. Therefore, given our definition of validity, this is an invalid argument.

This, then, suggests the following truth-table test for validity:

Truth-Table Test for Validity

Step 1: Write out the premises and conclusion of the argument alongside each other.
Step 2: Construct a complete truth table for each sentence of the argument.
Step 3: On each row, check the truth-value of each sentence under its main operator:
  - If there is *at least one* row in which each premise is assigned a T under the main operator and the conclusion is assigned an F under its main operator, then the argument is **INVALID.**
  - If there is *no* row in which each premise is assigned a T under the main operator and the conclusion is assigned an F under its main operator, then the argument is **VALID.**

In short, once you complete an argument's truth table, you are looking for all true premises and a false conclusion, i.e. one row with "all T's and an F." This is the *only* possibility you are interested in. If you find such a row, then the argument is invalid. If you do not find such a row, then the argument is valid. The fact that one row has all true premises and a true conclusion does *not* all by itself indicate than an argument is valid. (Recall that in Chapter 1 we encountered invalid arguments in which all the premises and the conclusion were true). Likewise, the fact that one row has all false premises and a false conclusion does *not* all by itself indicate that an argument is invalid. (Revisit Chapter 1 for an example of a valid argument in which the premises and the conclusion are false). Again, the only scenario that we are interested in is the "All T's and an F" scenario.

Here's another example, which requires an eight-row truth table:

A ⊃ ~B, B ∨ ~C, B ∴ A ∨ C

First, let's lay out the premises and conclusion as instructed in **Step 1** of the above method:

			*	*		*
A	B	C	A ⊃ ~B	B ∨ ~C	B	∴ ~A ∨ C
T	T	T				
T	T	F				
T	F	T				
T	F	F				
F	T	T				
F	T	F				
F	F	T				
F	F	F				

And here is the full truth table:

			*	*	*	
A	B	C	A ⊃ ~B	B ∨ ~C	B	∴ ~A ∨ C
T	T	T	T F F T	T T F T	T	F T T T
T	T	F	T F F T	T T T F	T	F T F (F)
T	F	T	T T T F	F F F T	F	F T T T
T	F	F	T T T F	F T T F	F	F T F (F)
F	T	T	F T F T	T T F T	T	T F T T
F	T	F	F T F T	T T T F	T	T F T F
F	F	T	F T T F	F F F T	F	T F T T
F	F	F	F T T F	F T T F	F	T F T F

This time, there is *no* row in which all of the premises are assigned a T and the conclusion is assigned an F. Consequently, this argument is valid. Notice that as you look for a row in which all the premises are true and the conclusion is false, you can immediately just focus your attention on the two rows indicated—these are the only rows in which the conclusion is false, so these are the only rows that have a chance of having all true premises and a false conclusion. To reiterate, you should have a one-track mind when checking for validity: Is there a row with all T's and an F? Nothing else matters!

Shortcuts

Again, be very careful:

To show that an argument is . . .	You may use the following shortcut . . .
. . . Valid	No shortcut possible. All rows of the truth table must be completed.
. . . Invalid	Complete just one row in which all of the premises have a T under the main operator and the conclusion has an F under its main operator.

Exercise Set 4.3

Q1. Construct complete truth tables for each of the following arguments in the space provided. Then check each one for **VALIDITY**. If you judge that an argument is invalid, mark the row, or rows, that indicates this. Construct your truth tables in the space provided. The first one is done for you.

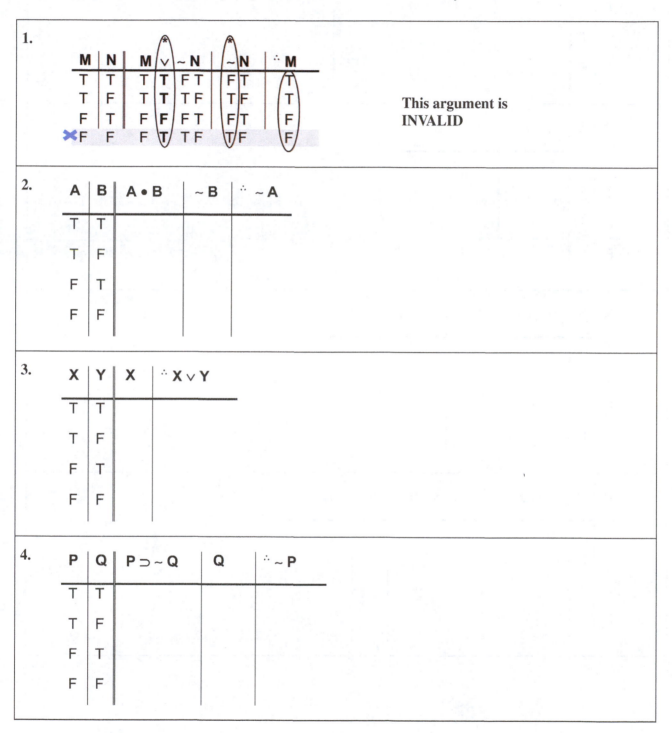

1.

M	N	M ∨ ~ N	~ N	∴ M
T	T	T **T** F T	F T	T
T	F	T **T** T F	T F	T
F	T	F **F** F T	F T	F
✖ F	F	F **T** T F	T F	F

This argument is
INVALID

2.

A	B	A • B	~ B	∴ ~ A
T	T			
T	F			
F	T			
F	F			

3.

X	Y	X	∴ X ∨ Y
T	T		
T	F		
F	T		
F	F		

4.

P	Q	P ⊃ ~ Q	Q	∴ ~ P
T	T			
T	F			
F	T			
F	F			

5.

G	Z	G ∨ Z	Z ⊃ ~G	G ⊃ ~Z	∴ Z
T	T				
T	F				
F	T				
F	F				

6.

D	E	D ≡ E	D	∴ E
T	T			
T	F			
F	T			
F	F			

7.

R	S	R ⊃ (R ⊃ S)	R ∨ S	∴ S
T	T			
T	F			
F	T			
F	F			

8.

U	V	U ⊃ V	~U ⊃ ~V	V	∴ U
T	T				
T	F				
F	T				
F	F				

9.

A	B	C	A ⊃ B	B ⊃ C	C	∴ A
T	T	T				
T	T	F				
T	F	T				
T	F	F				
F	T	T				
F	T	F				
F	F	T				
F	F	F				

10.

G	H	I	G ≡ H	G ≡ I	~ G ∨ ~ I	∴ H
T	T	T				
T	T	F				
T	F	T				
T	F	F				
F	T	T				
F	T	F				
F	F	T				
F	F	F				

Q2. Construct a complete truth table for each of the following arguments on a separate sheet of paper. Then check each one for **VALIDITY**. If you judge that an argument is invalid, mark the row, or rows, that indicates this.

1. P, ~Q ∨ P ∴ ~Q

2. ~A ⊃ ~B, ~B ∴ ~A

3. H ∴ H ∨ ~Y

4. S ⊃ W, W ⊃ S ∴ S

5. ~R ∨ ~Q, ~~R ∴ ~Q

6. J • ~K, K ⊃ ~J ∴ ~K

7. ~(W • X), W ∴ ~X

8. D ⊃ E, E ⊃ D ∴ D ∨ E

9. Z ∨ ~Z ∴ E

10. P ≡ ~S, S ∴ ~P

11. ~(G ⊃ D), ~(D ⊃ G) ∴ ~(D ∨ G)

12. U • ~U ∴ V

13. X ≡ Y, Y ≡ Z ∴ ~Z ≡ ~X

14. U ∨ A, U ⊃ C, A ⊃ ~D ∴ C ∨ ~D

15. K ⊃ (L ⊃ M), ~M, ~L ∴ ~K

16. (P • Q) ⊃ R, (P • R) ⊃ Q ∴ (Q • R) ⊃ P

17. ~(S ∨ D), ~(D ∨ W), D ∴ ~S ∨ ~W

18. A ≡ ~(B ∨ C), C ⊃ ~A, B ⊃ ~A ∴ ~A

19. G ⊃ H, H ⊃ I, I ⊃ J ∴ ~G ⊃ ~J

20. ~U ∨ X, ~X ⊃ Q, ~Q ∨ ~W ∴ ~(Q ∨ X)

4.4 Validity: Brief Truth Tables

To show that an argument is invalid, we show that there is one row of that argument's truth table in which all of the premises are true and the conclusion is false. And, as already indicated, identifying just *one* such row is sufficient; the presence of more rows like this does not make an argument any *more* invalid! Showing that there is *no* such row tells us that the argument is valid. A thorough appreciation of all of this allows us to develop what is called the ***Brief Truth-Table Method*** for checking an argument for validity. Consider the following argument, for example:

~M ⊃ ~N, M ∴ N

Here is the complete truth table for this argument:

M	N	~	M	⊃	~	N	M	∴	N
T	T	F	T	T	T	F	T		T
T	F	F	T	T	F	T	T		F
F	T	T	F	F	F	T	F		T
F	F	T	F	T	T	F	F		F

The argument, as you can see is invalid: the second row has all true premises and a false conclusion. The brief truth-table method tries to pick out this row of the complete truth table without having to construct all of its rows. In a sense, the method is an attempt to work backward from this kind of row. Let's consider the argument again, and *pretend* that if I were to complete a complete truth table, then I would end up with a row that has all true premises and a false conclusion:

M	N	~	M	⊃	~	N	M	∴	N
				T			T		F

Basically, what we've done here is assume that the argument is invalid: we assigned a T to the main operator of each premise, and an F to the main operator of the conclusion. (Of course, there's only one compound sentence in the argument, but the general point remains: when assigning T's and F's in this manner, make sure to place them under the main operator). How can we convince ourselves that such a row *would* appear in a complete truth table if we were to complete the complete truth table? Answer: we try to complete that row and see what happens. As it stands, there are six gaps that need to be filled in:

So, let's fill these gaps. First, we are assuming that 'M' is true, so wherever 'M' is, let's assign it a T:

Now we're down to four gaps. What else can be filled in at this point? Well, the antecedent of the conditional is '~M,' so given that 'M' is true, we can assign an F to the '~':

That's all we do based on my assumption that 'M' is true. There are still three gaps remaining. When we assumed the argument was invalid, however, we also assumed that 'N' is false. So, wherever 'N' is, let's assign it an F:

There is just one gap remaining, that under the '~' in the consequent of the conditional. If 'N' gets an F, then this '~' gets a T:

At this point, then, all the gaps have been filled in. We have completed the row on which we assumed the premises are true and the conclusion is false. And notice that this row is identical to the row which, in the complete truth table, informed us that the argument is invalid.

The key part of this brief truth-table method of checking for validity is that we can complete the row *without contradiction*. In the above example, any row with all true premises and a false conclusion must have 'M' being true and 'N' being false. This allowed us to fill in all the gaps surrounding the '⊃' in the first premise. Once we do this, we can check to see if the conditional, which we started out assuming to be true, *remains* true. That is, do the truth-values of the antecedent and the consequent that our assumption forced us to assign to them generate a true conditional? In this case, yes, they do: the truth-value of the antecedent is F, and the truth-value of the consequent is T. In this case, then, we can complete the row without contradicting ourselves—or "stepping on our toes," so to speak. With other arguments, we will not be able to complete the row without contradiction, enabling us to conclude that the argument at hand is valid. Let's work through an example of this. First, the argument:

S ∨ ~W, W ∴ S

And let's assume that if we were to do a complete truth table test, then we would find it to be invalid. That is, assign a T to all the premises, and an F to the conclusion:

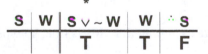

Now, let's try to complete this row. Based on our assumption, we know that 'W' gets a T, and also that 'S' gets an F. We can start with either of these; let's do 'S':

That is all we can do with 'S.' Now, let's turn to 'W':

There is one remaining gap: the '~' in the right-hand disjunct of the first premise. The fact that 'W' is assigned a T forces our hand here: the '~' must be assigned an F:

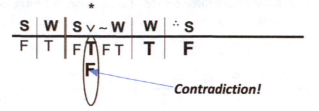

We have completed the row, but notice what has happened with the first premise. We assumed that it was true by assigning a T to the '∨.' However, based on this assumption, each side of the '∨' in the first premises has become an F, which means that the '∨' should be assigned an F! In other words, our attempt to complete the row has resulted in a contradiction: the first premise was assumed to be true, but now it's false:

S	W	S ∨ ~ W	W	∴ S
F	T	F (T) F T	T	F
		F		

Contradiction!

What we have shown, then, is that if we were to construct a complete truth table for this argument, then there would not be a row with all true premises and a false conclusion. That is, we can conclude that our assumption that the argument is invalid was incorrect. Therefore, the argument is valid.

Let's articulate all of this as a method for checking for validity:

The Brief Truth-Table Method of Checking for Validity

Step 1: Assume the argument is invalid. That is, place a T under the main operator of each premise, and an F under the main operator of the conclusion.

Step 2: Complete the row based on the assumption in **Step 1**. There are two possibilities to watch out for:

    a. If you can complete the row without contradiction, then your assumption in **Step 1** was true, i.e. the argument is **INVALID**.

    b. If you cannot complete the row without contradiction, then your assumption in **Step 1** was false, i.e. the argument is **VALID**. Make sure to indicate where the contradiction arises.

Using the brief truth-table method for the above arguments doesn't save us that much time or space: we generated one row of a truth table instead of completing a four-row truth table. However, this method has the potential to save us a lot of time and space. Consider the following argument, for example:

P ⊃ Q, Q ⊃ R, ~S ⊃ ~R, S ∴ P

There are four different atomic sentences here, which means that a complete truth table for the argument would have 16 rows. If we can check for validity by working with just one row, then that would be awesome! So, let's try it. **Step 1** tells us to assume that the argument is invalid:

				*	*	*		
P	Q	R	S	P⊃Q	Q⊃R	~S⊃~R	S	∴P
				T	T	T	T	F

Step 2 asks us to complete the row. Let's first fill in for 'S' and 'P':

				*	*	*		
P	Q	R	S	P⊃Q	Q⊃R	~S⊃~R	S	∴P
F			T	F **T**	T	F T **T**	T	F

At this point, we are guaranteed that both the first and third conditional premises will remain true, no matter what: a false antecedent makes for a true conditional, no matter what the truth-value of the consequent is. However, we have to make sure that the second conditional remains true. Given that we haven't yet been forced to choose a truth-value for 'Q' and 'R,' we have three options here—there are three combinations of antecedent and consequent truth-values that generate a true conditional. Choosing just one of these gives us the following:

				*	*	*		
P	Q	R	S	P⊃Q	Q⊃R	~S⊃~R	S	∴P
F	T	T	T	F **T** T	T **T** T	F T **T** F T	T	F

So, we have completed the row without contradiction, which means that our original assumption that the argument is invalid is correct. Note that we could have completed the row in two other ways, but we just need to show that *one* of these rows is possible. If we were to construct a complete truth table for the argument, then there would be three rows with all true premises and a false conclusion.

Exercise Set 4.4

Q1. Use the brief truth-table method to check each of the following arguments for **VALIDITY**. If you judge that an argument is valid, make sure to indicate where in your truth table a contradiction arises. Construct your truth tables in the space provided. The first one is done for you.

1.

G	H	G ∨ ~H	~H	∴ G
F	T	F **T** T F	**T** F	**F**

    (with * above G∨~H and * above ~H)   This argument is INVALID.

2.

P	S	P ⊃ ~S	S ⊃ P	∴ P

3.

J	K	J ≡ K	J	∴ ~K

4.

A	B	~B • ~A	∴ ~A ∨ S

5.

L	M	N	L ∨ ~M	M ∨ ~N	∴ ~L ⊃ ~N

6.

X	Y	Z	(X • Y) ⊃ Z	X	~Y	∴ ~Z

7.

D	E	F	(D ∨ F) ⊃ E	~E	~D	∴ F

8. | P | Q | S | $(P \lor Q) \supset (P \lor S)$ | P | ∴ S

9. | O | A | U | $(O \equiv A) \supset {\sim}U$ | $O \lor U$ | ${\sim}A$ | ∴ ${\sim}O$

10. | H | I | B | $(H \supset I) \supset B$ | $(B \supset H) \supset I$ | ${\sim}H$ | ∴ $B \lor I$

11. | S | G | X | Y | $S \supset G$ | $S \supset Y$ | ${\sim}X \supset {\sim}G$ | ∴ ${\sim}S$

12. | C | D | J | K | ${\sim}C \lor D$ | ${\sim}D \equiv K$ | ${\sim}(J \bullet C)$ | ∴ ${\sim}(D \bullet K)$

13. | P | Q | R | S | $(P \lor Q) \supset S$ | ${\sim}(R \supset S) \supset P$ | ${\sim}(R \equiv S) \supset {\sim}G$ | ∴ $S \lor {\sim}P$

14. | M | Z | B | U | $M \lor Z$ | ${\sim}B \lor {\sim}U$ | $M \supset B$ | $U \supset Z$ | ∴ ${\sim}(B \lor U)$

15. | L | M | S | Y | $L \equiv {\sim}M$ | $S \supset {\sim}Y$ | $L \lor Y$ | ${\sim}M \lor {\sim}S$ | ∴ ${\sim}[L \bullet ({\sim}S \lor {\sim}Y)]$

Q2. Use the brief truth table method to check each of the following arguments for **VALIDITY**. If you judge that an argument is valid, make sure to indicate where in your truth table a contradiction arises. Construct your truth tables on a separate sheet of paper.

1. S ⊃ (Q ⊃ U), S, Q ∴ U
2. J • (K ∨ L), L ∴ K
3. ~(G ⊃ D) ∴ ~(G ≡ D)
4. M ⊃ (N ⊃ O), O, N ∴ M
5. [(P ∨ Q) ∨ R] ⊃ S], ~P, ~Q, ~R ∴ ~S
6. X ∨ ~Y, Y ∨ ~Z, Z ∨ ~A ∴ ~A ⊃ ~X
7. A ⊃ (B ⊃ ~C) ∴ ~(B ∨ C) ⊃ ~A
8. ~(E ∨ V), ~(E • W), V ∴ ~W
9. R ≡ (P • ~D), D ≡ (P • ~R) ∴ P ⊃ (D ∨ R)
10. (G ∨ H) ⊃ (J • K), ~G, ~H ∴ ~J ∨ ~K
11. A ⊃ B, ~C ∨ D, (B ∨ D) ⊃ L, ~L ∴ ~(A ∨ B)
12. W ⊃ X, X ⊃ Y, ~Z ⊃ W, ~Y ∴ Z
13. (M ∨ N) ⊃ ~(S • R), (O ∨ P) ⊃ (S • R) ∴ ~S ∨ ~R
14. ~(D ≡ K), ~(L ≡ D), ~(L ≡ K) ∴ D
15. B ⊃ (J ⊃ K), K ⊃ (U ⊃ V), U ⊃ (V • K), J ⊃ (B • K) ∴ ~B ∨ (J ∨ K)

4.5 Translating Arguments and Checking for Validity

So far, the arguments we have been looking at have already been translated for us. We do not normally encounter arguments like this, however; rather, most arguments we encounter will be in a natural language like English. It is important to appreciate how we can go from an argument that is presented to us in English all the way through to checking it for validity via truth tables. Let us work through an example. Consider the following argument:

If either the Jets or the Cowboys win, then the Bills will go to the playoffs. Neither the Jets nor the Cowboys will win. So, the Bills will not go to the playoffs.

In Chapter 2, we developed a convention for translating arguments. First, we present a symbolization key:

J: The Jets win.
C: The Cowboys win.
B: The Bills will go to the playoffs.

And then we translate into SL:

(J ∨ C) ⊃ B, ~(J ∨ C) ∴ ~B

(I have presented the argument horizontally in this case, given how the truth-table test for validity works). And at this point our truth-table method (either complete or brief) kicks in. Let's construct a complete truth table for the argument:

J	C	B	(J ∨ C) ⊃ B	~ (J ∨ C)	∴ ~ B
T	T	T	T T T **T** T	**F** T T T	**F** T
T	T	F	T T T **F** F	**F** T T T	**T** F
T	F	T	T T F **T** T	**F** T T F	**F** T
T	F	F	T T F **F** F	**F** T T F	**T** F
F	T	T	F T T **T** T	**F** F T T	**F** T
F	T	F	F T T **F** F	**F** F T T	**T** F
✗ F	F	T	F F F **T** T	**T** F F F	**F** T
F	F	F	F F F **T** F	**T** F F F	**T** F

The original argument, therefore, is invalid. If you are surprised by this result, then this just serves to illustrate how important it is to be able to check for validity by focusing on the form of an argument.

As you can see, moving from an argument that is written in English all the way through to checking that argument for validity using truth tables involves nothing new: it is just a matter of carefully putting together skills we already have on board. It is, however, very important that we get the first part of this right; if we make a mistake when translating the argument from English into SL, then we will be checking the wrong argument for validity! Make sure to be aware of this as you work through the exercises.

Exercise Set 4.5

Q1. Translate the following arguments into Sentential Logic (SL), and then use truth tables to check each argument for **VALIDITY**. You may use either the complete truth-table method or the brief truth-table method. Write your answers in the space provided. The first one is done for you.

| 1. | If Paul will go to the gym, then so will Quentin. But Quentin will not go to the gym. Therefore, Paul will not go the gym |

Symbolization Key: P: Paul will to the gym.
Q: Quentin will go to the gym.

Translation: P ⊃ Q, ~Q ∴ ~P

Truth table:

			*	*	*
P	**Q**	**P ⊃ Q**	**~ Q**	**∴ ~ P**
T	T	T T T	F T	F T
T	F	T F F	T F	F T
F	T	F T T	F T	T F
F	F	F T F	T F	T F

This argument is **VALID.**

| 2. | If it is snowing, then it must be cold outside. It is cold outside, so it's got to be snowing. |

Symbolization Key:

Translation:

Truth table:

This argument is _____.

3.   I will read a book or watch a movie this evening. If I read a book, I will probably fall asleep by 9 pm. If I watch a movie, then I will probably fall asleep by 9 pm. It looks like I will be probably fall asleep by 9 pm!

Symbolization Key:

Translation:

Truth table:

This argument is _____.

4.   If there are more high-school graduates next year or the economy collapses, then more people will enroll in college courses. There will be more high-school graduates next year; however, the economy will not collapse. So, it looks like there won't be more people enrolling in college courses.

Symbolization Key:

Translation:

Truth table:

This argument is _____.

5.	There are no rainforests in North Korea. Therefore, either there are no rainforests in North Korea or there are no rainforests in South Korea. **Symbolization Key:** **Translation:** **Truth table:** This argument is _____.

Q2. Translate the following arguments into SL, and then on a separate sheet of paper, use truth tables to check the argument for **VALIDITY**. You may use either the complete truth-table method or the brief truth-table method.

1.	If your friend Samantha works at Google, then she must be rich. However, she does not work at Google. Consequently, she must not be rich.

2.	If quantum computers come on the market, then I will buy one. But quantum computers will come on the market only if computer scientists know how to make them. However, computer scientists do not know how to make quantum computers. Consequently, I will not be buying one.

3.	Either my iPhone update has slowed down my phone or I don't know anything about phone software. Of course, I don't know anything about phone software, so my iPhone update must have slowed down my phone.

4.	I will vote for the Green Party candidate unless the Independence Party candidate convinces me to vote for her. If this happens, then I will either vote for the Independence Party candidate or not vote at all. However, I will vote. I guess I'm voting for the Independence Party candidate.

5.	If abortion is morally permissible, then so is infanticide. But if infanticide is morally permissible, then murder is morally permissible. And if murder is morally permissible, then everything is morally permissible. But surely it is not the case that everything is morally permissible. We ought to conclude, then, that abortion is not morally permissible.

6.	Abortion is not morally permissible only if an unborn fetus has the right to life. But this latter is true only if an unborn fetus is a person, which isn't the case. Therefore, abortion is morally permissible.

7.	If Einstein's theory of relativity is correct, then time travel is not possible. However, time travel is possible. So, Einstein's theory of relativity must be incorrect.

8.	The tax bill going through Congress right now is either good for wealthy people, good for the middle class, or good for poor people. It is not good for either the middle class or for poor people. We must conclude, then, that the tax bill going through Congress right now is good for wealthy people.

9.	If all my actions are causally determined, then I don't have free will. If I don't have free will, then I cannot choose to ignore this exercise set. However, I can choose to ignore this exercise set. Consequently, it is not the case that all of my actions are causally determined.

10.	Peace talks between the Orcs and the Elves are a necessary condition for there to be no war on Middle Earth. However, they are not a sufficient condition for this. Peace talks and Gandalf working his magic would work, though. Therefore, there will be no war on Middle Earth if and only if there are peace talks between the Orcs and the Elves and Gandalf works his magic.

Q3. Label each of the following statements as **TRUE** or **FALSE**. In each case, explain *why* you chose your answer. Note: 'P,' 'Q,' and 'R' are sentence variables, i.e. they represent any sentence of Sentential Logic, both simple and compound.

1. If sentences P and Q are logically equivalent, then they are also logically consistent.

2. If sentences P and Q are both tautologies, then P and Q are logically equivalent.

3. The negation of a tautology is a contradiction.

4. For the argument P, Q $\therefore$ R . . .

    a. If R is a tautology, then the argument must be valid.

    b. If R is a contradiction, then the argument must be invalid.

    c. If P is a tautology, then the argument must be valid.

    d. If P is a contradiction, then the argument must be invalid.

    e. If P and Q form an inconsistent set of sentences, then the argument must be invalid.

    f. If the conditional $(P \cdot Q) \supset R$ is a tautology, then the argument must be valid.

    g. If the conditional $(P \cdot Q) \supset R$ is contingent, then the argument must be valid.

Chapter 5
Sentential Logic Proofs: Basic Inference Rules

So far in this book, we have encountered two approaches to checking an argument for validity:

1. **The Counterexample Method**
   We used this method in Chapter 1. Here, we focus on the content of the argument, and try to imagine a scenario in which all the premises are true and the conclusion is false. If we can describe even one such scenario, then we conclude that the argument is invalid. If we cannot imagine a scenario like this, then we either try harder or eventually conclude that such a scenario is impossible and the argument is valid. If you have had some difficulty with the last couple of chapters, then one obvious advantage to this way of checking for validity is that there are no pesky symbols involved! However, the counterexample method of checking for validity is quite limited. When we focus on the content of an argument, we run the risk of getting bogged down in what the argument is talking about: we may not fully understand the claims being made in the argument, for example, or our biases may prevent us from evaluating the argument correctly. Relatedly, the method is overly dependent on our powers of imagination.

2. **The Truth-Table Method**
   When we came to understand validity in terms of the *form* of an argument, and not its content, then we developed this other way of checking an argument for validity. We looked at this method in Chapter 3. There are two steps involved:

   (a) Translate the argument into Sentential Logic (SL).
   (b) Perform a truth-table test for validity.

Step **(a)** here allows us to capture the logical form of the argument in question. Step **(b)**, then, focuses on this form.

As a way of checking for validity, the truth-table method has a lot going for it:

- It enables us to arrive at a definitive answer on the question of an argument's validity, without having to engage with the content of the argument.
- It is a totally mechanical method, i.e. once we learn how to construct truth tables, and how to check for validity using truth tables, then applying the method requires no special insight by the person using the method.
- It is a reliable method. The person using the method might make a mistake, but the method itself, if applied correctly, will *always* provide you with the correct answer.

You might think that this means our job is done: we have come up with a mechanical, reliable way of checking an argument for validity. The truth-table method has some disadvantages as well, however:

- It can be cumbersome. An argument's truth table can involve a lot of rows. An argument with ten different atomic sentence letters, for example, requires a 1028-row truth table! The shortcuts mentioned in Chapter 4, including the brief truth-table method, help, of course, but things can still take a while.
- It is easy to make mistakes. This is the flip side of the last advantage of the truth-table method mentioned above. Sure, the *method* is 100% reliable, but a simple lack of concentration on behalf of the person constructing the truth table can result in a mistake that throws everything off.

- It is very artificial. This is the flip side of the second of the above-mentioned advantages of the truth-table method, i.e. that it is totally mechanical. We can fairly easily learn how to use truth tables to check for validity, but it is not something that we naturally do when we encounter an argument, and it does nothing to reveal the argument's reasoning. In other words, the method tells us *that* an argument is valid, but it doesn't say anything about *why* it is valid.

These disadvantages of the truth-table method of checking an argument for validity push us, in this chapter, to develop a *third* way of approaching the question of an argument's validity:

3. ***The Proof Method***
   Like the truth-table method, this is also a two-step procedure:

   (a) Translate the argument into SL.
   (b) Construct a proof in a natural deduction system.

As before, step (a) provides us with the logical form of the argument in question. We have already developed the skill of translating arguments into SL, so step (b) will be the primary focus in this chapter and in Chapter 6.

5.1 Developing a Natural Deduction System

As just indicated, the Proof Method involves constructing proofs in a natural deduction system. Two obvious questions arise: What is a *proof*? And what is a *natural deduction system*? We are not immediately in a position to provide definite answers to these questions, but we can make some progress if we reflect on our everyday understanding of the terms involved:

- To **prove** something is to show that it is true. In a court of law, for example, we try to show, beyond reasonable doubt, that the defendant is guilty, or that he or she is not guilty. In mathematics, the standard of proof is higher: we try to show that some statement is true beyond *any* doubt. Unsurprisingly, given that we have highlighted logic's affinity with mathematics, we will be understanding the concept of a proof in this latter way in this chapter.
- **Deduction** is the process of concluding something on the basis of some other claims. That is, we **deduce** one claim from some other claims. In Chapter 1, we defined a **deductive argument** as an argument in which the premises are intended to prove that the conclusion is true—so, deduction and proof are clearly related concepts. We have also already encountered the related idea of an **inference**: to deduce something is to "make" or "draw" an inference. A valid inference is one in which the sentence inferred follows necessarily from other sentences. Logicians also use the term **derivation**: some sentences can be validly **derived** from other sentences. More informally, we will talk of "getting" one sentence from others, and of some sentences "giving us" another.
- In general, we can understand a **system** to be an organized whole composed of some parts; each part is related to other parts, and to the whole, in an organized way. The Proof Method we will be developing is systematic in this sense.
- The term **natural** has a number of meanings. In the current context, however, we will understand the claim that something is natural to be the opposite of the claim that it is artificial or contrived in some way. The truth-table method of checking for validity is *not* natural in this sense, but the system we will be developing in this chapter *is* natural in that it largely corresponds to valid forms of reasoning that we use in everyday settings. Of course, our natural reasoning is often invalid, so we will have to make sure that our system does not allow for all forms of natural reasoning!

There is one more concept we need to outline before we can offer a precise definition of a proof, and of the natural deduction system within which we will be constructing proofs. The system we will be developing will have rules in place called *valid inference rules*. A valid inference rule is a rule of reasoning that, when followed correctly, ensures that we draw a valid inference. In principle, *any* valid form of reasoning can be viewed as a valid inference rule. That is, if we discover that an argument form is valid via the truth-table test, then we know that any instance in which this argument form is used will be an instance of valid reasoning.

There are an infinite number of valid argument forms, which means that there are potentially an infinite number of valid inference rules—but who wants to operate within a system that has an infinite number of rules?! What we will end up doing, then, is selecting a relatively small number of valid forms of reasoning and using those to generate a small selection of valid inference rules. Most of these inference rules correspond to valid forms of reasoning that we use in everyday life, thus making our deduction system a *natural* deduction system.

It is now time for some definitions. We will then get going on providing examples of the natural deduction system at work.

A **VALID INFERENCE RULE** is a statement of a valid argument form. Each valid inference rule can be legitimately used in the construction of a proof in a natural deduction system.

NATURAL DEDUCTION is a method of constructing a proof in which the conclusion of an argument is derived from the premises of that argument by appealing to valid inference rules that correspond to our natural forms of reasoning.

A **PROOF** is a sequence of sentences in SL. Each sentence is either a premise of an argument or has been derived from earlier sentences in the proof using the valid inference rules. The last sentence of the sequence is the conclusion of the argument.

Here, then, is the general idea: given an argument, if we can trace a valid path from the premises to the conclusion, using only the valid inference rules, then we have shown that the argument is valid. We still need to decide what valid inference rules we will have on board, however. The approach we take is quite straightforward. We have identified five different types of sentence in SL: conjunctions, disjunctions, negations, conditionals, and biconditionals. Our deduction system ought to be able to derive sentences of each type. Consequently, we will have five so-called *Introduction Rules*, i.e. rules that will allow us to validly infer, or "introduce," sentences of each type. We will also include rules that allow us to validly "break apart" sentences of each of these five types to derive other sentences. We will call these rules *Elimination Rules*. Together, the Introduction rules and the Elimination rules will provide us with ten valid inference rules. Adding one more inference rule (which we will get to in due course) will result in eleven so-called *Basic* inference rules. (There will also be *Derived* inference rules and *Substitution* rules, but first things first!) See Appendix A for a list of all of the inference rules.[1]

As just mentioned, our natural deduction system is supposed to correspond to our natural way of reasoning—at least to some degree. However, you might not be immediately convinced that this is indeed the case! Consequently, we will take some time to introduce each inference rule. The more familiar you are with the rules, the easier it will be to construct proofs that appeal to them. I should also note that there can be a big difference between (*a*) understanding how proofs work by looking at an already-constructed proof, and (*b*) being able to construct a proof all by yourself. Make sure to keep this in mind as you work your way through this chapter.

Let us turn then to the inference rules. First up are the conjunction rules and the disjunction rules.

Conjunction and Disjunction Inference Rules

If I know that today is Thursday, and I also know that it is raining, then I can validly infer that the following conjunction is true: "Today is Thursday and it is raining." This obviously valid inference is the basis for our first inference rule, which we can state in terms of the sentence variables 'P' and 'Q': if sentence 'P' is true and sentence 'Q' is true, then I can validly infer that the conjunction '$P \cdot Q$' is true. (All of the inference

---

[1]The natural deduction system developed in this chapter is just one way of organizing a list of valid inference rules that can be used in constructing proofs. As we work our way through the system, I will share some alternative names for the valid inference rules we encounter.

rules will be stated using sentence variables). We call this the ***Conjunction Introduction*** (•**I**) rule. It can be articulated as follows:

Conjunction Introduction (•I)[2]

$$\mathcal{P}$$
$$\underline{\mathcal{Q}}$$
$$\therefore \mathcal{P} \bullet \mathcal{Q}$$

This inference rule tells me that if I have two sentences on separate lines of a proof, then I can validly infer, and therefore write down, the conjunction of these two sentences on another line of the proof. Let's use this inference rule to construct our first proof. Consider the following argument:

S, T ∴ S • T

From the premises (i.e., 'S,' and 'T,') we are to trace a valid path to the conclusion (i.e., 'S • T.') You can think of it in terms of an app like Google Maps: your starting point consists of the premises; your destination is the conclusion. The question, then, is: How can you get from the former to the latter, using only valid inferences along the way?

One immediate concern you might have here is that tracing a valid path from the premises to the conclusion doesn't even seem necessary for this argument. After all, isn't it *obvious* in this case that the conclusion follows from the premise? Well, yes, it is obvious. However, one important task of any proof is to record *every* inference that you make when showing that an argument is valid. Even when you can see straightaway that an argument is valid, you are still making an inference—and you need to record that inference. More specifically, you should record the inference in terms of the valid inference rules that we are using in our natural deduction system. Forcing ourselves to do this reduces the risk of reasoning mistakes creeping in, even though it may slow the process down a bit. Note also that what is obvious to one person will not be obvious to someone else, which again gives us good reason to make sure that we articulate *all* the inferences that are being made in a proof. This is such an important aspect of the natural deduction system that it is worthwhile writing it out as our basic requirement of proof construction:

The Basic Requirement of Proof Construction

When constructing a proof, record every inference that you make. Each inference must be an instance of one of the valid inference rules that we are using in our natural deduction system.

To drive home this point, it can be useful to pretend (as best you can!) that you are a computer. *Nothing* is obvious to a computer; it can just perform the tasks that you have coded for. Imagine, then, that you have been coded with the inference rules, and nothing else but the inference rules—and you are then being asked to prove that some argument is valid. The inference rules describe the only allowable steps, and outside of explicitly following these inference rules, nothing can go in a proof.

Back to the proof for the argument at hand. We always begin a proof by writing out our premises in numbered lines, as follows:

1. S
2. T

The sentences on lines 1 and 2 are understood to be *assumptions*: we do not need to appeal to an inference rule to show where we got them from. We indicate this by drawing a horizontal line under them. From now on in the proof, however, for every sentence we write down, we will have to explain how we validly derived that sentence using one of the inference rules. Note that we have also written out the conclusion of the argument in

---

[2]This valid form of reasoning is sometimes simply called the ***Conjunction*** inference rule.

the top right-hand corner of the proof. Strictly speaking, this is not a part of the proof; we include it because it is a good idea to always know what our destination is in a proof.

So, how do we validly get from the premises on lines 1 and 2 to the conclusion of the argument? Notice that the conclusion is a conjunction, and our first rule tells us how to "make," i.e. validly infer, conjunctions: we take sentences from two separate lines of the proof and put a dot between them. We also need to record that it is this •I rule that we are using to draw this inference. Here's how it goes in our first example:

Line 3 says that we derived the conjunction 'S • T' by taking the sentences that are on lines 1 and 2 and applying the •I rule to them. The right-most column of a proof is referred to as the *justification column*, in that it offers a justification on each line for the sentence that is written on that line.

The above, then, qualifies as a complete proof. It is a sequence of sentences, and each sentence is either a premise of an argument or has been derived from earlier sentences using the inference rules; the last sentence of the sequence is the conclusion of the argument. We have, therefore, shown that the argument is valid: we used only valid inference rules along the way, and if every step of the proof is valid, then the inference from the premises to the conclusion (i.e., the last line of the proof) is also valid.

It can be useful to understand the •I rule as a sort of conjunction-making machine, which may be represented as follows:

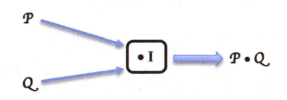

Whenever you need a specific conjunction, look around for the appropriate raw materials and then insert them into your conjunction-making machine. Once you turn the handle on this machine, it spits out the conjunction you need.

Let's work through another, slightly more complicated, example. Here is the argument that needs proving:

G, H, L ∴ (G • H) • L

Again, the first step is to write out all the premises as follows:

1. G   (G • H) • L
2. H
3. L

As before, our task is to trace a valid path from the assumptions laid out in lines 1–3 to the conclusion that is written out in the box. (Again, it seems obvious that the argument is valid, but remember that we cannot just go straight from the assumptions to the conclusion on these grounds alone. Each step we take along the way must align with one of the valid inference rules). The first thing to notice is that the conclusion is a conjunction—which is awesome, because we have an inference rule that allows us to validly construct conjunctions! However, we need to be careful: the •I rule says that we can construct a conjunction only if we have each of its conjuncts.

The main operator in the conclusion is the second '•,' which means that the left-hand conjunct is 'G • H' and the right-hand conjunct is 'L.' We already have 'L' on line 3; however, we do *not* have 'G • H' on any line of the proof at this point. We do, however, have the *resources* to derive 'G • H'—each conjunct of *this* conjunction is already on a line in the proof: 'G' is on line 1 and 'H' is on line 2. Line 4 of the proof can now be written out:

1.	G	(G • H) • L
2.	H	
3.	L	
4.	G • H	•I 1, 2

The sentence on line 4 is the left-hand conjunct of the conclusion. And, as already noted, the sentence on line 3 is the right-hand conjunct of the conclusion. Consequently, we can write out the conclusion on line 5:

1.	G	(G • H) • L
2.	H	
3.	L	
4.	G • H	•I 1, 2
5.	(G • H) • L	•I 4, 3

And we're done! Notice the justification column on line 5: the first line number we write out (in this case line 4) refers to the line that has the left-hand conjunct of the conjunction we just derived; the right-hand conjunct comes from the other line, i.e. line 3.

This proof should remind us that the inference rules are stated using sentence variables. When applying •I, given *any* sentence (either atomic or compound) of SL, for example '$\mathcal{P}$,' and *any other* sentence (either atomic or compound) of SL, for example '$\mathcal{Q}$,' we can validly infer the conjunction '$\mathcal{P} \bullet \mathcal{Q}$.' In line 5, the '$\mathcal{P}$' of the •I rule is 'G • H,' so to speak; the '$\mathcal{Q}$' is 'L,' and the '$\mathcal{P} \bullet \mathcal{Q}$' is '(G • H) • L.'

You should also appreciate the general strategy employed here. After writing down the premise lines, we made sure to take note of the *kind* of sentence that we needed to derive—in this case, we needed to derive a conjunction. Keeping this in mind, we then scanned the sentences we already have in the proof—the premises—to see if we could find the resources that would enable us to derive, via one of the inference rules, the conjunction that we needed. In general, before rushing headlong into a proof, we should always take a breath, focus on where we need to go, and then see if any sentences we already have can, via the inference rules, get us there. This general approach deserves to be articulated as a proof strategy:

Proof Strategy #1

When constructing a proof, always keep in mind where you are going. If the argument is valid, then the sentences you already have will provide you with the resources to get there. Scan these sentences to see if they map onto any of the inference rules.

More proof strategies will be highlighted as we proceed through this chapter. All of them are listed at the end of Chapter 6.

Let's move on to the rule that allows us to validly "break apart" conjunctions in proofs: ***Conjunction Elimination*** (•E). A simple illustration can also motivate this inference rule: if I know that this conjunction is true—"the New York Yankees won and the Boston Red Sox won"—then I can easily, and validly, infer that each conjunct of this conjunction all by itself is true: "the New York Yankees won" is true, and "the Boston Red Sox won" is true. More generally, if I know that the conjunction '$\mathcal{P} \bullet \mathcal{Q}$' is true, then I can validly infer that each conjunct by itself is true, i.e. '$\mathcal{P}$' is true and '$\mathcal{Q}$' is true. This can be articulated as follows:

Conjunction Elimination (•E)[3]

$$\frac{\mathcal{P} \bullet \mathcal{Q}}{\therefore \mathcal{P}} \qquad \frac{\mathcal{P} \bullet \mathcal{Q}}{\therefore \mathcal{Q}}$$

This rule tells me that if I have a conjunction on one line of a proof, then I can validly write down each of the conjuncts on separate lines. The •E rule, then, can be viewed as a machine that breaks conjunctions apart:

Putting a conjunction into this •E machine and turning the handle will provide you with the component parts of that conjunction. (Or, to use a chemistry analogy, the •E rule enables you to "break the bond" that is holding the conjuncts together, i.e. the '•,' and "release" the conjuncts). Note, by the way, that it is the '•' that is eliminated; it would be wrong to think of either conjunct as being eliminated.

Let's work through a proof that appeals to both conjunction rules. Here is a valid argument:

J • K, L ∴ K • L

And we begin in the usual way:

1. J • K   ┌─────┐
              │ K • L │
2. L   └─────┘

Remembering our first proof strategy, let's first pause and consider the conclusion. It is a conjunction, so we know that having 'K' on one line and 'L' on another will allow us to validly derive 'K • L.' And, looking over the premises, we can see that we already have 'L' on line 2; we do not have 'K' by itself on any line yet. However, our new rule, •E, provides us with the resources to get 'K' from line 1:

1. J • K   ┌─────┐
              │ K • L │
2. L   └─────┘
─────────────
3. K   •E 1

At this point, then, we can use the raw materials that are on lines 2 and 3 to generate the conclusion:

1. J • K   ┌─────┐
              │ K • L │
2. L   └─────┘
─────────────
3. K   •E 1
4. K • L   •I 3, 2

And that is the complete proof. Using the •E rule on line 1 would also have given us 'J,' of course, but because we were paying due attention to where we were going, we knew we didn't need to do this. It would not have been incorrect to have 'J' on a line somewhere in the proof; in general, as long as every line is validly

[3]This valid form of reasoning is sometimes referred to as the *Simplification* inference rule.

derived, via one of the inference rules, from earlier lines in the proof, then the proof will be legitimate. However, in this case, including this line would have been more than what was required.

Let us turn now to the disjunction inference rules. Recall from Chapter 3 that a disjunction is true whenever at least one of its disjuncts is true. Given this, we can validly derive a disjunction as long as we have a guarantee that at least one of its disjuncts is true. This describes the ***Disjunction Introduction*** (∨I) inference rule:

Disjunction Introduction (∨I)[4]

This inference rule is a disjunction-making machine: putting any sentence into the machine and turning the handle will give you any disjunction that has the inputted sentence as one of its disjuncts:

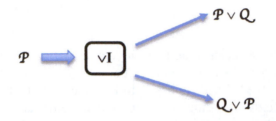

At first glance, this might appear to be an invalid inference: Where are we getting the 'Q' from?! Remember, though, that in a disjunction there is no commitment to both disjuncts being true, so we do not end up *asserting* that 'Q' is true. Rather, we are asserting that the disjunction '$P \lor Q$' is true, and this is guaranteed once it is assumed that 'P' is true. In other words, given any sentence of SL, the ∨I rule allows you to generate *any* disjunction that has this sentence as one of its disjuncts. For example, given the sentence 'A,' we could use the ∨I rule to validly infer each of the following:

- A ∨ B
- C ∨ A
- A ∨ (T ⊃ S)
- A ∨ [L • (M ≡ N)]
- [J ∨ (K ∨ L)] ∨ A
- . . .

'A' is a disjunct in each of these disjunctions, and the information that 'A' is true guarantees that each of these disjunctions is true. There are, of course, an infinite number of disjunctions that can be formed like this; when constructing a proof, however, usually it will be clear which specific disjunction we need to create. Let's work through an example. Here is the start of a proof:

1. A • B $\boxed{A \lor C}$

_____

As usual, we take a close look at where we need to end up. This time we need to derive a disjunction, and our new rule allows us to do that. How do we get started, though? Well, notice that 'A' is one of the disjuncts in the conclusion, and 'A' is also present in our one premise. The other disjunct of the conclusion, i.e. 'C,' is nowhere to be found in the premise. If we can get 'A' on its own, though, then our new rule, ∨I, will generate the disjunction we need. Here is the complete proof:

1. A • B $\boxed{A \lor C}$
_____
2. A   •E 1
3. A ∨ C   ∨I 2

_____

[4]This valid form of reasoning is sometimes referred to as the ***Addition*** inference rule.

When we began constructing this proof, we noticed that a component of the conclusion was nowhere to be found among the premises. As it turns out, the proof we end up with in this kind of scenario will typically make use of the ∨I rule at some stage. Recognizing this can prevent panic: instead of asking "where the heck are we going to get the 'C' from?" we understood that getting the other disjunct of the conclusion would be sufficient for generating the disjunction we needed. Let's formulate this as a proof strategy that pertains specifically to this rule:

> ## Proof Strategy #2
>
> If your goal in a proof includes a component that is nowhere to be found in the premises, then it is likely that at some point you will have to use the ∨I rule. Look for an opportunity to do this.

Let's move on to the ***Disjunction Elimination*** (∨E) rule.[5] Given that the disjunction '$\mathcal{P} \vee \mathcal{Q}$' is true, what can we say about '$\mathcal{P}$,' and what can we say about '$\mathcal{Q}$'? Well, not much! All we can really say is that at least one of them is true. We have no guarantee that '$\mathcal{P}$' by itself is true, and we have no guarantee that '$\mathcal{Q}$' by itself is true. A disjunction, then, is not like a conjunction: we cannot immediately break it down into its component parts. Instead, to validly break apart a disjunction, we need to know that something *else* is also the case. If, for example, we know that '$\mathcal{P} \vee \mathcal{Q}$' is true, and we also know that '$\sim\mathcal{P}$' is true (i.e., if we know that '$\mathcal{P}$' is false), then it has to be the case that '$\mathcal{Q}$' is true. In other words, if we are told that a disjunction is true, and *also* that one of its disjuncts is false, then we can validly infer that the other disjunct is true—if this latter were false, then this would render the disjunction false, contradicting our first assumption. Here is a formal statement of the inference rule:

Disjunction Elimination (∨E)

The ∨E rule is a machine for "breaking apart" disjunctions. Inserting just a disjunction into the ∨E machine will not generate any output, however; it will only work if you insert a disjunction *and* the negation of one of its disjuncts:

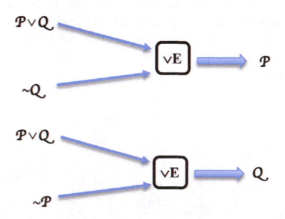

Note that the truth of a disjunction together with the negation of *either* of its disjuncts allows us to infer that the remaining disjunct is true. Let us use this new rule in a proof. Here is the beginning of the proof:

1. X ∨ Z   ☐ X
2. Y • ~Z

---

[5] This valid form of reasoning is also referred to as ***Disjunctive Syllogism***.

How can we get 'X' out of lines 1 and 2? Well, notice that 'X' is one of the disjuncts of line 1; however, we can't just conclude that 'X' is true based solely on line 1. As far as the disjunction 'X ∨ Y' is concerned, 'X' *might* be true, but it also might be false. To be *guaranteed* that 'X' is true, we need '~Z' to be true—this would allow us to use the ∨E rule. We don't have '~Z' on a line by itself at this point, but a quick look at line 2 shows that we have the *resources* to get '~Z' by itself: we just have to use the •E rule. Here is the completed proof:

1.	X ∨ Z	X
2.	Y • ~Z	
3.	~Z	•E 2
4.	X	∨E 1,3

Remember, we did not get the 'X' on line 4 from just line 1; we also needed the '~Z' on line 3. Notice also that the elements of the ∨E rule do not have to appear in the proof on consecutive lines: as long as any two lines of the proof align with the ∨E rule as formally stated earlier, then we can use the rule. As usual, when constructing a proof, we should always be scanning all the sentences we already have to see if anything lines up with one of the inference rules.

It is important that we appeal to the rules of inference only when lines in our proof *exactly* align with the rule. Here is the beginning of another proof for us to consider:

1.	N ∨ ~M	N
2.	M	

At first glance, it might look like lines 1 and 2 align nicely with the ∨E rule. However, they do not! Yes, there is a disjunction in line 1, but line 2 does *not* have the negation of one of these disjuncts: the negation of 'N' is '~N,' and the negation of '~M' is '~~M.' Without one of these negated disjuncts, we cannot legitimately use the ∨E rule. Of course, the sentence on line 2, i.e. 'M,' is in a sense the "opposite" of one of the disjuncts, namely '~M.' And it is obvious that 'M' and '~~M' are logically equivalent, making the inference from the premises to the conclusion valid. As we emphasized earlier, however, judging that an inference is obviously valid is still making an inference, and the basic requirement of our natural deduction system is that we record *all* inferences that we make. Taking the two premises to correspond to the ∨E rule conceals an inference—the inference that 'M' and '~~M' are logically equivalent—and is therefore illegitimate. As written, then, we cannot construct a proof for the above argument given just the four inference rules we have on board so far. (We will be able to construct a proof for the argument later in this chapter, however). We *can* construct a proof for the following argument, however:

N ∨ ~M, ~~M ∴ N

Here is the proof:

1.	~M ∨ N	N
2.	~~M	
3.	N	∨E 1, 2

In this case, the sentence on line 2 *is* the negation of one of the disjuncts of the disjunction on line 1, so we can legitimately appeal to the ∨E rule.

Exercise Set 5.1

Q1. Fill in the gaps in each of the following proofs. Remember, except for assumption lines, each line of a proof should have three elements: the line number, a sentence of SL that is derived from earlier sentences in the proof via one of the valid rules of inference, and a record of the rule that is being used to derive that sentence together with the line numbers of the proof to which the inference rule is being applied.

1.
1. X $\boxed{X \bullet (Y \bullet Z)}$
2. Y
3. Z
4.   •I 2, 3
5. X • (Y • Z)

2.
1. (M • N) • (S • T) $\boxed{S}$
2. S • T
3.   •E 2

3.
1. G • H $\boxed{H \vee Q}$
2.   •E 1
3.   ∨I 2

4.
1. A ∨ B $\boxed{A}$
2. B ∨ C
3. ~C
4. B
5. A

5.
1. D ⊃ E $\boxed{(D \supset E) \vee (E \supset D)}$
2. (D ⊃ E) ∨ (E ⊃ D)

6.
1. M • (N • O) $\boxed{(M \bullet N) \bullet O}$
2. M
3. O   •E 1
4. (M • N) • O
5.   •E 3
6.
7.   •I 2, 4

7.

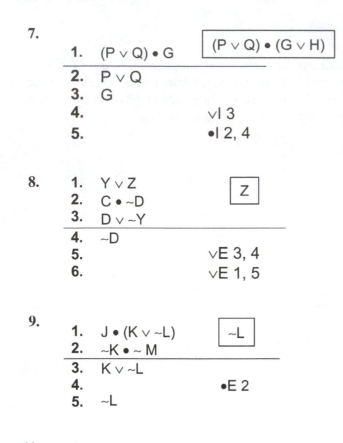

1. $(P \lor Q) \bullet G$ $(P \lor Q) \bullet (G \lor H)$
2. $P \lor Q$
3. G
4. $\lor I \ 3$
5. $\bullet I \ 2, 4$

8.

1. $Y \lor Z$ $\boxed{Z}$
2. $C \bullet \sim D$
3. $D \lor \sim Y$
4. $\sim D$
5. $\lor E \ 3, 4$
6. $\lor E \ 1, 5$

9.

1. $J \bullet (K \lor \sim L)$ $\boxed{\sim L}$
2. $\sim K \bullet \sim M$
3. $K \lor \sim L$
4. $\bullet E \ 2$
5. $\sim L$

10.

1. $\sim A \lor B$
2. $\sim B \lor C$
3. $\sim C \lor D$ $\boxed{\sim A}$
4. $(E \bullet \sim D) \bullet F$
5. $\bullet E \ 4$
6. $\sim D$
7. $\sim C$
8. $\sim A$
9. $\lor E \ 2, 7$

Q2. On a separate sheet of paper, construct a proof for each of the following valid arguments.

1. $J, K \bullet \sim Q, R \lor Q \quad \therefore J \bullet R$

2. $P \bullet (\sim S \bullet J), T \lor S \quad \therefore T$

3. $F, G \quad \therefore (F \bullet G) \lor H$

4. $L, M \quad \therefore (L \lor R) \bullet (M \lor T)$

5. $(R \bullet S) \lor T, U \bullet \sim (R \bullet S) \quad \therefore T \bullet U$

6. $P \supset T \quad \therefore (P \supset T) \lor [G \equiv (S \bullet \sim L)]$

7. $X \bullet \sim Y, Z \bullet (A \lor Y) \quad \therefore A$

8. $H \lor (J \lor I), \sim H \bullet \sim J \quad \therefore I \lor M$

9. $S \quad \therefore (S \lor G) \lor (S \lor H)$

10. $\sim B \bullet (\sim C \bullet \sim D), C \lor E, D \lor F \quad \therefore E \bullet F$

5.2 Conditional Elimination

If I know that a sentence of the form '$P \supset Q$' is true, then what can I conclude about 'P' and 'Q'? Well, nothing! The truth of a conditional sentence does not guarantee the truth of either the antecedent or the consequent. Here is an example in English: the sentence "if today is Friday then tomorrow is Saturday" is a true conditional sentence, but I cannot conclude from this alone that today is Friday, nor can I conclude that tomorrow is Saturday. As in the case of disjunctions, then, to validly break apart a conditional sentence, I am going to need some extra piece of information. Recall our treatment of conditional sentences in Chapter 3: when a conditional sentence is true, then the only way it remains true when the antecedent is true is when the consequent is also true. That is, if I know that a conditional is true, and I *also* know that the antecedent of that conditional is true, then I can conclude with certainty that the consequent is true. Here, then, is a statement of the **Conditional Elimination** ($\supset$E) rule:

Conditional Elimination ($\supset$E)[6]

$$P \supset Q$$
$$P$$
$$\therefore Q$$

The $\supset$**E** rule allows us to validly break apart conditionals:

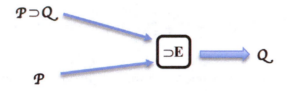

Putting just a conditional sentence into this $\supset$**E** machine and turning the handle will not give us any output; we need *both* a conditional sentence *and* its antecedent. Then, and only then, does cranking the handle generate output, namely the consequent of the conditional. Also, note that the rule does not work the other way around: a conditional sentence together with its consequent does *not* allow us to validly infer that the conditional's antecedent is true.

Here is the beginning of a proof in which we will use the $\supset$**E** inference rule:

1. G $\supset$ H $\boxed{\text{H}}$
2. G • I
_____

Once more, we make sure to pay attention to where we need to end up. Looking through the premises, we see that the 'H' that we need is on line 1—but it is all "tied up" in a conditional sentence. Somehow, then, we need to "release" this 'H.' Remember, we *cannot* conclude that 'H' is true based solely on the fact that it is the consequent of a conditional. However, if I can verify that 'G', i.e. the antecedent of this conditional sentence, is true, then I can get the 'H' out of line 1 via an application of the $\supset$**E** rule. And line 2 provides me with the resources to get 'G.' Let's complete the proof:

1. G $\supset$ H $\boxed{\text{H}}$
2. G • I
_____
3. G   •E 2
4. H $\supset$E 1, 3

_____
[6]This valid form of reasoning is also called **Modus Ponens**, which is Latin for "the way (or method) of affirming."

Here is another, somewhat longer, example:

1. X ⊃ Y   D
2. Y ⊃ ~Z
3. X
4. D ∨ Z

Approaching this in the usual way, we see that the 'D' that we need is "wrapped up" in a disjunction on line 4. What do we need in order to "release" the 'D' from this disjunction? Answer: a '~Z,' if we can get one. There is a '~Z' on line 2, but it is "tied up" in a conditional. What do we need in order to "release" the '~Z'? Answer: the antecedent of this conditional, i.e. 'Y.' Can we get this 'Y'? Well, there is a 'Y' on line 1, but it is "tied up" in another conditional sentence. However, we have the antecedent of this conditional, i.e. 'X,' by itself on line 3. At this point we can get going. Here is the completed proof:

1. X ⊃ Y   D
2. Y ⊃ ~Z
3. X
4. D ∨ Z
_____
5. Y   ⊃E 1, 3
6. ~Z   ⊃E 2, 5
7. D   ∨E 4, 6

Once more, then, our task became more manageable when we took the time to consider our goal in the proof and how we could use the resources at hand to get there.

Exercise Set 5.2

Q1. Fill in the gaps in each of the following proofs.

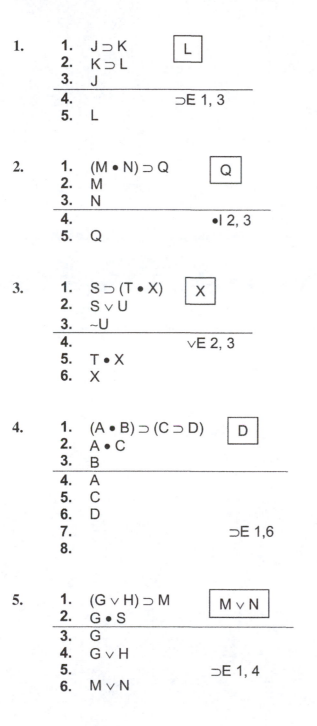

1.　　**1.** J ⊃ K　　L
　　　2. K ⊃ L
　　　3. J
　　　────────────────
　　　4. 　　　　⊃E 1, 3
　　　5. L

2.　　**1.** (M • N) ⊃ Q　　Q
　　　2. M
　　　3. N
　　　────────────────
　　　4. 　　　　•I 2, 3
　　　5. Q

3.　　**1.** S ⊃ (T • X)　　X
　　　2. S ∨ U
　　　3. ~U
　　　────────────────
　　　4. 　　　　∨E 2, 3
　　　5. T • X
　　　6. X

4.　　**1.** (A • B) ⊃ (C ⊃ D)　　D
　　　2. A • C
　　　3. B
　　　────────────────
　　　4. A
　　　5. C
　　　6. D
　　　7. 　　　　⊃E 1,6
　　　8.

5.　　**1.** (G ∨ H) ⊃ M　　M ∨ N
　　　2. G • S
　　　────────────────
　　　3. G
　　　4. G ∨ H
　　　5. 　　　　⊃E 1, 4
　　　6. M ∨ N

6.
1. (R • S) ∨ T   T
2. Q ⊃ ~(R • S)
3. Q ∨ V
4. ~V • W
_____
5. ~V
6.   ∨E 3, 5
7.   ⊃E 2, 6
8. T

7.
1. (P • Q) ⊃ (B ∨ S)   S
2. A • Q
3. B ∨ P
4 ~B
_____
5. P
6. Q
7.   •I 5, 6
8.   ⊃E 1, 7
9. S

8.
1. ~Z ⊃ ~Y   ~Y
2. ~Z ∨ ~W
3. ~~W
_____
4.   ∨E 2, 3
5. ~Y

9.
1. J • K   N ∨ (P ⊃ Q)
2. L • M
3. (L • K) ⊃ N
_____
4. L
5. K
6.   •I 4, 5
7.   ⊃E 3, 6
_____
8. N ∨ (P ⊃ Q)

10.
1. ~G ⊃ ~H   ~H
2. ~G ∨ ~I
3. ~~I • ~~K
_____
4. ~~I
5.   ∨E 2, 4
6. ~H

Q2. On a separate sheet of paper, construct a proof for each of the following valid arguments.

1. $(P \bullet Q) \supset R, P, Q \quad \therefore R$

2. $P \supset Q, Q \supset R, P \quad \therefore R$

3. $\sim A \supset \sim B, C \vee \sim A, \sim C \quad \therefore \sim B$

4. $M \vee (N \vee O), \sim M, (N \vee O) \supset (M \vee P) \quad \therefore P$

5. $\sim P \vee Q, \sim\sim P, Q \supset \sim R \quad \therefore \sim R$

6. $W \supset \sim G, (F \vee \sim G) \supset J, W \quad \therefore J$

7. $L, M, (L \bullet M) \supset \sim O, B \vee O \quad \therefore B$

8. $P \supset A, Q \supset B, P \bullet Q \quad \therefore A \bullet B$

9. $\sim X \supset \sim Y, Y \vee W, \sim V \bullet \sim X \quad \therefore W \vee X$

10. $(A \vee B) \supset (C \bullet D), (A \vee B) \vee E, \sim E \quad \therefore D$

5.3 The Conditional Introduction Inference Rule

Consider the following argument in SL:

B ⊃ G, G ⊃ M ∴ B ⊃ M

This, I hope you can see, is a valid argument. If you have any doubts, a quick run through the truth-table test should satisfy you. Note that there is no guarantee that 'B' is true, there is no guarantee that 'G' is true, and there is no guarantee that 'M' is true. Everything here is hypothetical, so to speak. How, then, can we construct a proof that will show that the argument is valid? Nothing we have in our box of inference rules to this point will do the job. What we need is an inference rule that will allow us to create conditional sentences. This rule, which we will call *Conditional Introduction* (⊃**I**), is a bit different from the inference rules we have seen so far. To see how it works, let's first consider an argument in English that follows the above argument form:

If I make this basket, then we win the game.
If we win the game, then we go to the playoffs.
_____
∴ If I make this basket, then we go to the playoffs.

Now, let's pretend that I make the basket. What happens then? Well, my making the basket, plus the first premise, entails that we win the game. And this, in turn, together with the second premise, entails that we go to the playoffs. Of course, this does not mean that we *will* win the game, or that we *will* go the playoffs. However, following this chain of reasoning, it can be seen that *if* I make the basket, *then* we go to the playoffs, i.e. the conclusion is true. Here is another way of looking at this. I imagine a scenario in which I make the basket, and within this scenario we end up going to the playoffs. There is no guarantee that anything in this scenario will *actually* happen; nevertheless, I can clearly see that *if* I make the basket *then* we go to the playoffs. The ⊃I rule will make use of this kind of reasoning, which is, for obvious reasons, sometimes called *Conditional Reasoning*, or *Conditional Proof*.

In the above argument, then, pretending that 'B' is true will eventually lead us to infer that 'M' is true, and this allows us to infer that the conditional 'B ⊃ M' is true. Let's see how this kind of reasoning works in a proof. When pretending that 'B' is true, we are in essence *assuming* that 'B' is true, and to reflect this we place this assumption on an indented line, as follows:

1. B ⊃ G   ┌─────┐
2. G ⊃ M   │ B ⊃ M │
            └─────┘
3. │ B

As an assumption, The 'B' on line 3 does not need any justification. And the fact that it is on an indented line reminds us that it is a *provisional* assumption: it will help us out in the proof, but we will end up discarding it before the end of the proof. With our assumption that 'B' is true on board, we can make some inferences:

1. B ⊃ G   ┌─────┐
2. G ⊃ M   │ B ⊃ M │
            └─────┘
3. │ B
4. │ G   ⊃E 1, 3
5. │ M   ⊃E 2, 4

The line on which each of these inferences is made is also indented: we can infer these sentences only because of our provisional assumption on line 3. In other words, the inferences made on lines 4 and 5 are valid only as a part of our "pretend" scenario. We stay on this indented line until we are done with this assumption. As a package deal, then, lines 3 through 5 represent the following: in a scenario in which 'B' is true, 'M' is also true. This, in essence, is to assert the following: 'if B, then M'—which happens to be the conditional sentence that we need to derive. At this point, therefore, we can validly write out this conditional by appealing to what goes on in this range of lines. In other words, we apply the $\supset$**I** rule:

$$
\begin{array}{lll}
\textbf{1.} & B \supset G & \boxed{B \supset M} \\
\textbf{2.} & G \supset M & \\
\textbf{3.} & \quad \big| \; B & \\
\textbf{4.} & \quad \big| \; G & \supset\text{E } 1, 3 \\
\textbf{5.} & \quad \big| \; M & \supset\text{E } 2, 4 \\
\textbf{6.} & B \supset M & \supset\text{I } 3\text{–}5
\end{array}
$$

When appealing to the $\supset$**I** rule, we refer to a *range* of lines, which we indicate by using a dash and not a comma, i.e. '3–5' instead of '3, 5.' And notice that line 6 is not indented; this is because we are no longer pretending that 'B' is true. That is, we have discarded the provisional assumption that was made in line 3. We end up with just the original assumptions as written on lines 1 and 2, and we have successfully shown that the sentence on the last line of the proof follows validly from just these assumptions.

Lines 3–5, i.e. the pretend scenario, constitutes what's called a ***sub-proof***. Picking out some key elements of this sub-proof will help us better understand how to use the $\supset$**I** rule:

- The first line of the sub-proof is identical to the antecedent of the conditional we need to derive.
- The last line of the sub-proof is identical to the consequent of the conditional that we need to derive.
- The first line *after* the sub-proof is the conditional that we need to derive.
- The $\supset$**I** rule is the justification for this first line after the sub-proof.

All of this is by design. When embarking on our game of pretend, we structure our sub-proof in such a way that we can validly infer the conditional sentence that we need. Here is the general strategy:

Strategy for Using the Conditional Introduction ($\supset$I) Rule

Scenario: I need to derive a conditional sentence, i.e. a sentence of the form '$\mathcal{P} \supset \mathcal{Q}$'

Step 1:   Assume the antecedent of this conditional, i.e. '$\mathcal{P}$.' Place this assumption on an indented line.

Step 2:   Derive the consequent of this conditional, i.e. '$\mathcal{Q}$.' All of this derivation will also be indented.

Step 3:   Discard your assumption from **Step 1** to derive the conditional '$\mathcal{P} \supset \mathcal{Q}$' by appealing to the $\supset$**I** inference rule. This line is not indented.

Step 1, here, is taken with a very specific purpose in mind: we want to derive the consequent of the conditional we need. As we make your assumption, then, it is a good idea to explicitly write down the specific sentence that we need to derive in our sub-proof. We can simply refer to this sentence as what we "want."

We are now in a position to formulate the $\supset$**I** rule:

Conditional Introduction ($\supset$I)

$$
\begin{array}{l}
\big| \; \mathcal{P} \quad \textit{want } \mathcal{Q} \\
\big| \; \mathcal{Q} \\
\mathcal{P} \supset \mathcal{Q}
\end{array}
$$

⊃**I** is an inference rule for making conditionals. The raw materials in this case, though, are not individual sentences; rather, our "input" is an entire sub-proof:

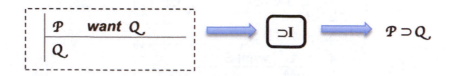

Here are two further considerations pertaining to sub-proofs (both of which also pertain to different kinds of sub-proofs that we will be getting to in a little while):

(a) You can initiate a sub-proof by provisionally assuming *any* sentence of SL—as long as you are no longer assuming this sentence at the end of the larger proof. That is, put your provisional assumption to work, but before the end of the proof make sure that you are no longer making any inferences that require it to be true.

(b) Your decision to make a provisional assumption, together with your decision on what this provisional assumption is, should be based on your goal in the proof. That is, do not assume based on what you've already got in the proof; rather, assume based on where you need to go.

This last consideration is worthy of being highlighted as a proof strategy:

Proof Strategy #3

If you ascertain that you need to make a provisional assumption, make sure that you assume based on where you need to go in the proof (and *not* based on where you are coming from).

Let's do another example. Here is the start of a proof for us to consider:

$$\begin{array}{ll} \textbf{1.} & L \supset M \\ \textbf{2.} & N \\ \textbf{3.} & (M \bullet N) \supset S \end{array} \qquad \boxed{L \supset S}$$

We need to derive the conditional 'L ⊃ S.' Following **Step 1** above, let's assume the antecedent of this conditional, i.e. 'L,' and place this on an indented line. We will also indicate that we want to derive its consequent, i.e. 'S.'

$$\begin{array}{ll} \textbf{1.} & L \supset M \\ \textbf{2.} & N \\ \textbf{3.} & (M \bullet N) \supset S \\ \textbf{4.} & \quad L \quad \text{want } S \end{array} \qquad \boxed{L \supset S}$$

Step 2 asks us to derive the consequent, 'S':

1.	L ⊃ M	⎡ L ⊃ S ⎤
2.	N	
3.	(M • N) ⊃ S	
4.	⎸ L want S	
5.	⎸ M	⊃E 1, 4
6.	⎸ M • N	•I 5, 2
7.	⎸ S	⊃E 3, 6

Our assumption that 'L' is true has allowed us to ultimately derive 'S.' The entirety of this derivation takes place at the same indentation as this provisional assumption. Now we are ready to appeal to the ⊃I rule, discard our assumption, and write out the conclusion:

1.	L ⊃ M	⎡ L ⊃ S ⎤
2.	N	
3.	(M • N) ⊃ S	
4.	⎸ L want S	
5.	⎸ M	⊃E 1, 4
6.	⎸ M • N	•I 5, 2
7.	⎸ S	⊃E 3, 6
8.	L ⊃ S	⊃I 4–7

One more example won't hurt! Here is the argument to be proven:

A ⊃ B, C ⊃ D ∴ (A • C) ⊃ (B • D)

This time let us present the complete proof, together with some annotations that explain what is going on – in "real time," so to speak:

1.	A ⊃ B	⎡ (A • C) ⊃ (B • D) ⎤	*Here we assume the antecedent of the conditional we want, i.e. everything to the left of the '⊃' in the conclusion*
2.	C ⊃ D		
3.	⎸ A • C want B • D		
4.	⎸ A	•E 3	
5.	⎸ C	•E 3	*We can now apply the other rules of inference within this scenario that assumes 'A • C'.*
6.	⎸ B	⊃E 1, 4	
7.	⎸ D	⊃E 2, 5	
8.	⎸ B • D	•I 6, 7	
9.	(A • C) ⊃ (B • D)	⊃I 3–8	*This last line concludes that if 'A • C' is true, then so is 'B • D'. We apply the ⊃I rule to justify writing out the entire conditional*

Exercise Set 5.3

Q1. Fill in the gaps in each of the following proofs. When provisionally assuming something with a view to using the ⊃I inference rule, you should also include the sentence you want to derive within the sub-proof.

1.
   1. P ⊃ Q $\boxed{P ⊃ T}$
   2. Q ⊃ S
   3. S ⊃ T
   4. | P   want T
   5. | Q
   6. | ⊃E 2, 5
   7. | ⊃E 3, 6
   8. P ⊃ T

2.
   1. J ∨ K $\boxed{\sim J ⊃ M}$
   2. K ⊃ M
   3. | want M
   4. | K
   5. | ⊃E2, 4
   6. ~J ⊃ M

3.
   1. A ⊃ B $\boxed{A ⊃ D}$
   2. B ⊃ (C • D)
   3. | A   want
   4. | B
   5. | ⊃E2, 4
   7. | D
   8. A ⊃ D

4.
   1. (G ∨ H) ⊃ L $\boxed{G ⊃ L}$
   2. | want   ⊃E1, 3
   3. | G ∨ H
   4. |
   5. G ⊃ L

5.

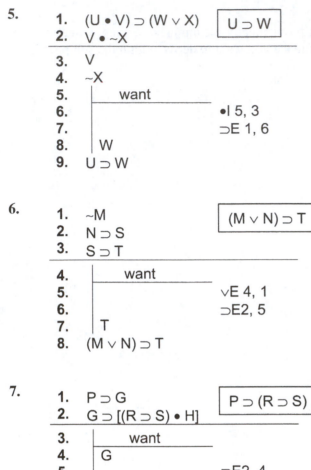

1. (U • V) ⊃ (W v X) $\boxed{\text{U} \supset \text{W}}$
2. V • ~X
3. V
4. ~X
5. | want
6. | •I 5, 3
7. | ⊃E 1, 6
8. | W
9. U ⊃ W

6.

1. ~M $\boxed{(\text{M} \vee \text{N}) \supset \text{T}}$
2. N ⊃ S
3. S ⊃ T
4. | want
5. | vE 4, 1
6. | ⊃E2, 5
7. | T
8. (M v N) ⊃ T

7.

1. P ⊃ G $\boxed{\text{P} \supset (\text{R} \supset \text{S})}$
2. G ⊃ [(R ⊃ S) • H]
3. | want
4. | G
5. | ⊃E2, 4
6. | •E 5
7.   ⊃I 3–6

8.

1. D ⊃ (T • X) $\boxed{(\text{D} \bullet \text{E}) \supset (\text{T} \bullet \text{U})}$
2. E ⊃ (U • ~Y)
3. | want
4. | D
5. | E
6. | ⊃E 1, 4
7. | ⊃E 2, 5
8. | T
9. | U
10. | •I 8, 9
11. (D • E) ⊃ (T • U)

9.

1. (O ⊃ P) ⊃ Q   ☐ Q
2. O ⊃ M
3. M ⊃ P
_____
4. | O   want P
5. | M
6. | P
7.   ⊃I 4–6
8.   ⊃E1, 7

10.

1. J ⊃ ~(K ∨ S)   ☐ J ⊃ M
2. L ∨ (K ∨ S)
3. L ⊃ M
_____
4. | want
5. | ⊃E 1, 4
6. | L
7. | M
8. J ⊃ M

Q2. On a separate piece of paper, construct a proof for each of the following valid arguments.

1. G ⊃ W, C ⊃ G   ∴ C ⊃ W
2. F ⊃ Y, Y ⊃ H   ∴ F ⊃ (Y • H)
3. (A • C) ⊃ E, A   ∴ C ⊃ E
4. S ⊃ P, P ⊃ N, N ⊃ C   ∴ S ⊃ C
5. (J ∨ K) ⊃ L   ∴ J ⊃ L
6. O ⊃ H, C ⊃ N   ∴ (O • C) ⊃ (H • N)
7. G ⊃ H   ∴ G ⊃ (G • H)
8. ~R • ~S, P ∨ (Q ∨ R), L ⊃ ~P   ∴ L ⊃ Q
9. D ∨ ~E, E ∨ ~F   ∴ ~D ⊃ ~F
10. (~A ⊃ B) ⊃ C, A ∨ B   ∴ C

5.4 The Biconditional Inference Rules

Recall that a biconditional sentence is, at bottom, two conditional sentences conjoined together. That is, a sentence of the form '$P \equiv Q$' is logically equivalent to a conjunction of the following form: '$(P \supset Q) \bullet (Q \supset P)$.' The biconditional inference rules are relatively straightforward if we remember this logical equivalence. Let's take a look at the **Biconditional Elimination** rule ($\equiv$E) first. If we are told that a sentence of the form '$P \equiv Q$' is true, what can we say about 'P,' and what can we say about 'Q'? Again, not much. We run into the same problem as we did with conditional sentences: we can't automatically know if the right-hand side *by itself* is true and we can't automatically know if the left-hand side *by itself* is true. As with conditionals, however, an extra piece of information can help break apart biconditionals. To see how this works, let's be explicit about the biconditional's component conditional sentences:

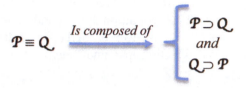

Now, if I know that '$P \equiv Q$' is true, and I *also* know that 'P' is true, then, because the conditional '$P \supset Q$' is "packed into" the biconditional, I can validly infer that 'Q' is true. Likewise, if I know that '$P \equiv Q$' is true, and I *also* know that 'Q' is true, then because the conditional '$Q \supset P$' is "packed into" the biconditional, I can validly infer that 'P' is true. Speaking loosely, given both a biconditional sentence and either side of it by itself, I can validly infer the other side of it. This reasoning, then, is the basis of the $\equiv$E inference rule:

Biconditional Elimination ($\equiv$E)

$$P \equiv Q \qquad P \equiv Q$$
$$\underline{P} \qquad\qquad \underline{Q}$$
$$\therefore Q \qquad\qquad \therefore P$$

The $\equiv$E inference rule is a rule for creating biconditionals:

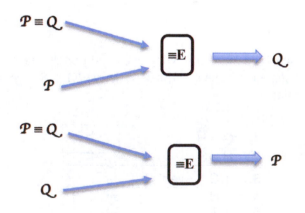

Putting just a biconditional sentence into this $\equiv$**E** machine and turning the handle will not give us any output: we need *both* a biconditional sentence *and* one side of it. Then, and only then, does turning the handle generate the output, namely the other side of the biconditional. Unlike the $\supset$**E** rule, however, the $\equiv$**E** rule goes both ways! A biconditional sentence and *either* side of it allow us to validly infer that the *other* side of it is true.

Let's do an example. Here is the start of a proof that will appeal to the $\equiv$**E** inference rule:

1. $X \equiv \sim Z$ $\boxed{X}$
2. $P \vee \sim Z$
3. $\sim P$

Looking through the premises, we see that what we need, i.e. 'X,' is "tied up" in a biconditional. As we have just discovered, though, we can break this biconditional apart and "release" the 'X' as long as we have the other side of the biconditional, i.e. '$\sim$Z.' This, however, is "tied up" in a disjunction on line 2, though line 3 provides us with the resources to break this disjunction apart and "release" the '$\sim$Z.' Here is the completed proof:

1. $X \equiv \sim Z$ $\boxed{X}$
2. $P \vee \sim Z$
3. $\sim P$
---
4. $\sim Z$ $\vee$E 2, 3
5. X $\equiv$E 1, 4

Note that, like most of the Elimination rules, the $\equiv$**E** rule requires that we refer to two line numbers when we use it in a proof.

Now on to the ***Biconditional Introduction*** inference rule ($\equiv$**I**). Here is the general idea: given that a biconditional sentence is composed of two conditional sentences, successfully deriving each of these conditional sentences means that we have effectively derived the biconditional. For example, if we know that conditionals of the form '$\boldsymbol{P} \supset \boldsymbol{Q}$' and '$\boldsymbol{Q} \supset \boldsymbol{P}$' are true, then we can validly infer that the biconditional of the form '$\boldsymbol{P} \equiv \boldsymbol{Q}$' is true. We know how to derive conditionals—we use the $\supset$**I** inference rule; so, we should be able to derive biconditionals. Let's see how this would go in an proof. Here is an argument where we need to derive a biconditional:

$G \equiv H, H \equiv S \therefore G \equiv S$

The conclusion '$G \equiv S$' is composed of the following two conditionals: '$G \supset S$,' and '$S \supset G$.' So, let's set about deriving these conditional sentences, one at a time. To derive '$G \supset S$,' we assume 'G,' derive 'S,' and then appeal to the $\supset$**I** inference rule:

1. $G \equiv H$ $\boxed{G \equiv S}$
2. $H \equiv S$
---
3. | G want S
4. | H $\equiv$E 1, 3
5. | S $\equiv$E 2, 4
6. $G \supset S$ $\supset$I 3–5

At this point, I have derived half of the biconditional, so to speak, namely the conditional from the left-hand side to the right-hand side of the biconditional. I now need to derive the conditional that goes the other way, i.e. 'S ⊃ G':

1.	G ≡ H	⟨ G ≡ S ⟩
2.	H ≡ S	
3.	G want S	
4.	H	≡E 1, 3
5.	S	≡E 2, 4
6.	G ⊃ S	⊃I 3–5
7.	S want G	
8.	H	≡E 2, 7
9.	G	≡E 1, 8
10.	S ⊃ G	⊃I 7–9

At this point, we have validly derived both conditional sentences that compose the biconditional 'G ≡ S.' Consequently, we can validly infer that this biconditional is true; we do this using the ≡**I** rule:

1.	G ≡ H	⟨ G ≡ S ⟩
2.	H ≡ S	
3.	G want S	
4.	H	≡E 1, 3
5.	S	≡E 2, 4
6.	G ⊃ S	⊃I 3–5
7.	S want G	
8.	H	≡E 2, 7
9.	G	≡E 1, 8
10.	S ⊃ G	⊃I 7–9
11.	G ≡ S	≡I 6, 10

There are a few things to note here. First of all, on line 6 we discarded the assumption we made on line 3. From this point on in the proof, then, everything that is derived based on this assumption, i.e. everything in lines 3 through 5, is out of bounds, so to speak: I cannot appeal to any sentences within this sub-proof in any further inference that I make in the proof. The 'S' that is assumed in line 7 is in this sense a different 'S' from the one that appears on line 5, and everything that appears within the second sub-proof is independent of everything that appears within the first sub-proof. Each sub-proof is a distinct game of pretend.

Here, then, is a formal statement of the ≡**I** inference rule:

Biconditional Introduction (≡I)

$$P \supset Q$$
$$Q \supset P$$
$$\overline{\qquad\qquad}$$
$$\therefore P \equiv Q$$

This is a rule for creating biconditional sentences. It requires two separate inputs, both of which are conditionals:

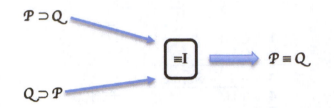

In the above example, there were two sub-proofs, one followed by another. In other cases, sub-proofs end up with their own sub-proofs—resulting in *sub-sub-proofs*. Proofs like these are said to have *nested* sub-proofs. Here is an argument that will involve one of these:

J ⊃ (K ⊃ L) ∴ K ⊃ (J ⊃ L)

The conclusion here is a conditional, so let's assume its antecedent and set about deriving its consequent:

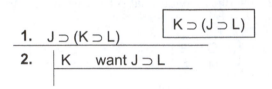

Where do we go from here? Lines 1 and 2 don't really get us anywhere. Well, as usual, we pay attention to where we are going. We have just stated that we want 'J ⊃ L'—so let's focus on deriving this conditional. We know how to derive a conditional: we assume its antecedent and derive its consequent. 'J ⊃ L' is not our *ultimate* goal in this proof—our conclusion is 'K ⊃ (J ⊃ L)'—but we need to address our immediate concerns. So, *within* the sub-proof we have already begun on line 2, let's assume 'J' and derive 'L':

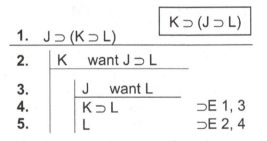

Line 3 has another provisional assumption, and because it occurs within a sub-proof it is further indented. Lines 3 through 5 show us that based on our assumption that 'J' is true (on line 3), we can derive 'L.' And this allows us to write down the corresponding conditional sentence on line 6, using the ⊃**I** rule:

1.   J ⊃ (K ⊃ L)
2. | K   want J ⊃ L
3. | | J   want L
4. | | K ⊃ L   ⊃E 1, 3
5. | | L   ⊃E 2, 4
6. | J ⊃ L   ⊃I 3–5

The nested proof in lines 3–5 has now done its job and provided us with 'J ⊃ L.' Line 6 is still indented because the 'J ⊃ L' depends on the provisional assumption made on line 2, i.e. 'K.' Now, we can derive our ultimate goal, i.e. the conclusion 'K ⊃ (J ⊃ L)':

1.	J ⊃ (K ⊃ L)	
2.	K want J ⊃ L	
3.	J want L	
4.	K ⊃ L	⊃E 1, 3
5.	L	⊃E 2, 4
6.	J ⊃ L	⊃I 3–5
7.	K ⊃ (J ⊃ L)	⊃I 2–6

Note that on line 6 we discarded the assumption (on line 3) that 'J' is true; and on line 7 we discarded the assumption (on line 2) that 'K' is true. We end up then with just the original assumption as written on line 1, so we have successfully shown that the sentence on this last line of the proof follows validly from this one assumption.

Proofs with nested sub-proofs can look a bit complicated, but there is nothing too new going on. Every step along the way we just kept track of where we needed to go, and then assumed accordingly. When making the provisional assumption on line 2, for example, we explicitly stated what we wanted, namely 'J ⊃ L.' At that point, deriving 'J ⊃ L' became our immediate goal and we turned all our attention to doing this, in the full knowledge that successfully deriving this sentence would help us get to our ultimate goal, i.e. the conclusion.

In a sense, a nested proof is like a game of pretend within another game of pretend. A couple of analogies come to mind. For example, a movie can be viewed as a game of pretend. If a movie has the making of a movie as part of its plot, then what you have is a game of pretend within a game of pretend! Or, consider the movie *Inception*, in which we are asked to consider the possibility of a dream within a dream. In fact, at one point in the movie, the nesting of dreams goes five-deep: there is a dream within a dream within a dream within a dream within a dream! Luckily, none of the proofs we encounter in this book will have this many nested proofs.

Exercise Set 5.4

Q1. Fill in the gaps in each of the following proofs. Remember, when provisionally assuming something with a view to using the ⊃**I** inference rule, you should also include the sentence you want to derive within the sub-proof.

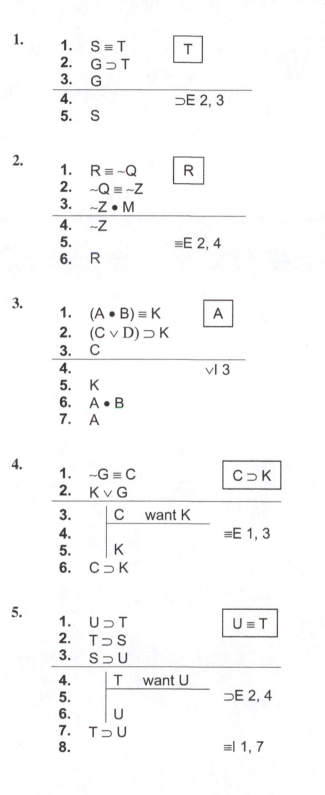

1.
1. S ≡ T   T
2. G ⊃ T
3. G
——————————
4.   ⊃E 2, 3
5. S

2.
1. R ≡ ~Q   R
2. ~Q ≡ ~Z
3. ~Z • M
——————————
4. ~Z
5.   ≡E 2, 4
6. R

3.
1. (A • B) ≡ K   A
2. (C ∨ D) ⊃ K
3. C
——————————
4.   ∨I 3
5. K
6. A • B
7. A

4.
1. ~G ≡ C   C ⊃ K
2. K ∨ G
——————————
3. │ C   want K
4. │   ≡E 1, 3
5. │ K
6. C ⊃ K

5.
1. U ⊃ T   U ≡ T
2. T ⊃ S
3. S ⊃ U
——————————
4. │ T   want U
5. │   ⊃E 2, 4
6. │ U
7. T ⊃ U
8.   ≡I 1, 7

6.

1. G ∨ H | ~G ≡ H |
2. H ⊃ (~F • ~G)
─────────────────────────────
3. | ~G want H
4. | H
5.   ⊃I 3–4
6. | H   want ~G
7. | ~F • ~G
8.   •E 7
9. H ⊃ ~G
10.   ≡I 5, 9

7.

1. ~O ≡ ~M | ~M ≡ ~N |
2. F ∨ O
3. F ≡ ~N
4. F ⊃ ~M
─────────────────────────────
5. | ~M   want ~N
6. | ~O
7.   ∨E 2, 6
8. | ~N
9. ~M ⊃ ~N
10. | ~N   want ~M
11. | F
12. | ~M
13.   ⊃I 10–12
14. ~M ≡ ~N

8.

                                  | (O • K) ⊃ (P ⊃ L) |
1. P ⊃ [(O • K) ⊃ L]
─────────────────────────────
2. | O • K   want
3. | | P   want
4. | | [(O • K) ⊃ L   ⊃E 2, 4
5. | | L
6. | ⊃I 3–5
7. (O • K) ⊃ (P ⊃ L)

9.

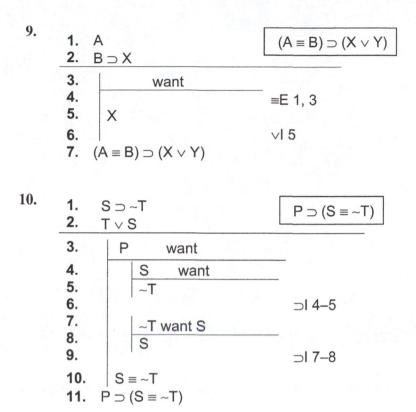

1. A
2. B ⊃ X

$(A \equiv B) \supset (X \vee Y)$

3. | want
4. |
      ≡E 1, 3
5. | X
6. |
      ∨I 5
7. (A ≡ B) ⊃ (X ∨ Y)

10.

1. S ⊃ ~T
2. T ∨ S

$P \supset (S \equiv \sim T)$

3. | P   want
4. | | S   want
5. | | ~T
6. |
      ⊃I 4–5
7. | | ~T want S
8. | | S
9. |
      ⊃I 7–8
10. | S ≡ ~T
11. P ⊃ (S ≡ ~T)

Q2. On a separate piece of paper, construct a proof for each of the following valid arguments.

1. I ⊃ (B • J) ∴ (I ⊃ B) • (I ⊃ J)

2. L ⊃ M, (N ⊃ O) • (M ⊃ N) ∴ L ⊃ O

3. P ⊃ Q, R ⊃ S ∴ (P • R) ⊃ (Q • S)

4. A ≡ ~B, ~B ∴ A ∨ C

5. J ≡ A, K ≡ B ∴ (K • J) ≡ (A • B)

6. C ⊃ L, L ⊃ F, F ⊃ C ∴ C ≡ F

7. T ∨ (X ≡ Y), ~T ∨ ~S, ~~S • X ∴ Y

8. (~F ≡ G) ⊃ B, F ∨ Y, Y ≡ G, Y ⊃ ~F ∴ B

9. F ⊃ (D • M) ∴ D ⊃ (F ⊃ M)

10. T ⊃ [U ⊃ (W ⊃ X)] ∴ W ⊃ [U ⊃ (T ⊃ X)]

5.5 The Negation Inference Rules

At this point, we have developed Introduction and Elimination rules for four of the five sentence operators of SL. Let us turn now to the one remaining kind of sentence, i.e. the negation. We need an Introduction rule that will enable us to derive negations; and we need an Elimination rule that will enable us to "break apart" negations. The good news is that both rules are, at bottom, just different applications of the same kind of inference: ***Reductio ad Absurdum***. (The phrase is Latin for "reduction to absurdity.") This form of reasoning has a long history in mathematics and logic, and perhaps you have encountered it before. Let's look at the general idea behind it before integrating it into our natural deduction system.

So far, we have been able to navigate a ***direct*** path from an argument's premises all the way to the argument's conclusion. If, for example, we need to show that a sentence 'A' follows from a set of premises, we try to show how it can be derived from the premises via an application of the inference rules. Conceivably, however, there is alternative way of showing that one sentence follows validly from some other sentences. We could, for example, proceed as follows:

- Show that, based on my premises, the sentence '~A' is false.
- Recognize that the fact that '~A' is false logically entails that 'A' is true.

Why does '~A' being false logically entail that 'A' is true? Well, recall that we assumed the Principle of Bivalence in Chapter 1. This principle states that every sentence in the logical sense is either true or false. In SL terms, this means that for a sentence of SL like 'A,' there are only two options: either 'A' is true or 'A' is false, which is the same as saying that either 'A' is true or '~A' is true, i.e. 'A ∨ ~A.' Consequently, showing that '~A' is false is sufficient to show that 'A' is true. (Notice how the ∨E rule comes into play here as well: if 'A ∨ ~A' is true, and '~~A' is true, we can validly infer that 'A' is true). All of this amounts to an ***indirect*** approach to proving what we need to prove: we indirectly show that 'A' is true by directly showing that its negation is false. This is why this way of reasoning is sometimes referred to as ***Indirect Proof***.

Let us see how this might work in the context of a proof in our natural deduction system. Consider the following valid argument:

~B ∨ A, B ∴ A

This *looks* like we will need a straightforward application of the ∨E rule, but the premises do not map onto the ∨E rule exactly. (We encountered a similar situation earlier in the chapter). So, at this point, there is nothing we can do to *directly* show that the conclusion follows from the premises. Let's see if there is an *indirect* alternative. This would involve the following: proving that, given these premises, '~A' is false, thus showing that 'A' is true. But how can I show that '~A' is false? In SL, we have moved away from the content of sentences, so how can we show that *anything* is false? There is one type of sentence that is false solely on the basis of its logical form, however: a logical contradiction. Consequently, to show that '~A' is a logical contradiction would be to show that it is false. Furthermore, to show that taking our premises and '~A' to be true *involves us* in a contradiction, or *leads directly to* a contradiction, would be enough to show us that '~A' is false. In the context of a proof for the above argument, then, we make the provisional assumption that '~A' is true, and then derive a contradiction from this assumption. Doing this allows us to infer that 'A' is true. Let's work through this in the proof:

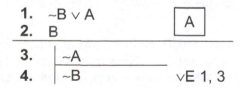

1.	~B ∨ A	A
2.	B	
3.	~A	
4.	~B	∨E 1, 3

In line 3, we provisionally assume that '~A' is true. And by line 4, we can notice that something weird is going on. Our assumption that 'A' is true leads us, via just one more valid inference, to '~B' being true. However, line 2 states that 'B' is true. In other words, we have the makings of an obvious logical contradiction, i.e. 'B • ~B.' It is our assumption on line 3 that '~A' is true that leads us to this contradictory state of affairs; consequently, '~A' has to be false. And if '~A' is false, then 'A,' the argument's conclusion, must be true. How do we record all this in the proof? It is useful to make it explicit that our provisional assumption leads to a contradiction, and we can do this here by rewriting the sentence that is on line 2 right after line 5. The fact that we can validly rewrite any sentence at any point in a proof is, in fact, a valid inference rule in its own right, called ***Reiteration*** (**R**). We can formulate this rule as follows:

Reiteration (R)

The Reiteration rule doesn't generate any new sentence; its output is identical to its input, so to speak:

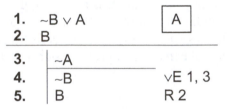

Using this rule in our proof, then, allows us to make explicit the fact that the provisional assumption made on line 3, i.e. '~A,' leads to a contradiction:

1.	~B ∨ A	A
2.	B	
3.	~A	
4.	~B	∨E 1, 3
5.	B	R 2

At this point, we can implement a new rule, ***Negation Elimination*** (**~E**). Lines 4 and 5 together show us that our provisional assumption on line 3 is false. In fact, the whole sub-proof from lines 3 through 5 is a dead end—which is exactly what we wanted it to be! Consequently, we can conclude that the non-negated version of our provisional assumption is true:

1.	~B ∨ A	A
2.	~B	
3.	~A	
4.	~B	∨E 1, 3
5.	B	R 2
6.	A	~E 4–6

Like in earlier proofs that involved sub-proofs, on line 6 we have discarded the provisional assumption we made on line 3. So, we have shown that 'A' validly follows from the original premises on lines 1 and 2.

Of course, we assumed '~A' on line 3 for a specific purpose: to show that it leads to a contradiction, and is therefore false. When we have such a purpose in mind, it is a good idea to take note of it. To do this, we will include the words "for reductio" every time we assume a sentence with the intention of deriving a contradiction from it.

Here, then, is a more formal presentation of the ~**E** rule appealed to on line 7 of the above proof:

Negation Elimination (~E)

$$
\begin{array}{|l}
\sim\!\mathcal{P} \quad \textit{for reductio} \\
\mathcal{Q} \\
\sim\!\mathcal{Q}
\end{array}
$$
$\therefore \mathcal{P}$

This is a rule for "breaking down" negations, or showing that the non-negated version of a sentence is true: we eliminate the '~'from a provisional assumption. Like with the ⊃**I** rule, however, the raw materials are not individual sentences; rather, our input is an entire sub-proof:

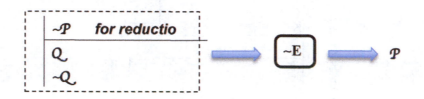

Intuitively, of course, contradictions are weird: How can something both be and not be the case at the same time? But a logician's aversion to contradictions goes deeper. Recall that in Chapter 1 we assumed the Principle of Non-Contradiction, which states that no sentence in the logical sense is both true and false. And truth tables bear this out, of course: any sentence of the form '$\mathcal{P} \cdot \sim\!\mathcal{P}$' will be necessarily false. And who wants to hang out with necessarily false sentences?! More crucial, perhaps, is the fact that if we allowed for logical contradictions in our natural deduction system, we would be able to prove that *every* sentence is true. And this, of course, is absurd—*some* sentences are false, right?! It is relatively straightforward to show how contradictions cause all this trouble. Allow, for the time being, that the following contradiction is true: 'A • ~A.' Now, let's prove that the sentence 'B' is true:

$\boxed{\text{B}}$

1.	A • ~A	
2.	A	•E 1
3.	~A	•E 1
4.	A ∨ B	∨I 2
5.	B	∨E 3, 4

All very straightforward. However, based on the same assumption, we can also prove that '~B' is true:

$\boxed{\text{~B}}$

1.	A • ~A	
2.	A	•E 1
3.	~A	•E 1
4.	A ∨ ~B	∨I 2
5.	~B	∨E 3, 4

Both proofs are legitimate. And, clearly, we could do the same thing for *any* sentence of SL. But our proof system isn't going to be of much use to us if it allows us to prove that everything is true! Consequently, we just cannot allow contradictions into the system. And if some assumption or other in a proof leads us to a contradiction, then this assumption cannot be allowed to stand!

The ***Negation Introduction*** rule (~**I**) involves the same kind of reasoning as in the ~**E** rule. Let's work through an example to illustrate this. Consider the following argument:

J ⊃ K, ~K ∴ ~J

As it stands, there is no direct route to the conclusion open to us, so let's see if we can reason indirectly to the conclusion. In our first example above, we assumed the negation of the conclusion and derived a contradiction, thus showing that the conclusion is true. In this case, we will assume the non-negated version of the conclusion and derive a contradiction, thus showing that the conclusion is true.

1.	J ⊃ K		~J
2.	~K		
3.	J	for reductio	
4.	K	⊃E 1, 3	
5.	~K	R 2	
6.	~J	~E 3–5	

Again, line 5 is simply a reiteration of line 2 that makes the contradiction more explicit. And, in this case, what we conclude has one more '~' than what we assumed *for reductio*, so we use the ~**I** rule rather than the ~**E** rule. As you can see, though, the basic setup is the same in each case: show that the opposite of what you need leads to a contradiction.

Here is a more formal statement of the ~**I** rule:

Negation Introduction (~I)

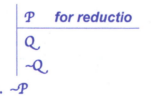

This rule is a negation creator, with the input again being an entire sub-proof rather than individual sentences:

When should you make use of these Negation rules? Typically, you will use them when you can see no way of *directly* going from the premises to the conclusion. That is, when you get stuck in a proof, instead of just walking away, try assuming the opposite of what you need and hope for the worst! If you assume something and things go badly wrong based on that assumption, i.e. you end up with a contradiction, then that's awesome—it means that the opposite of what you assumed must be true. Here is the general strategy:

Using the ~E and ~I Inference Rules

Scenario: You can see no way to directly derive what you need in a proof.

Step 1:   Assume the opposite of what you need. That is, assume the negation of what you need or the non-negated version of what you need.

Step 2:   Derive a contradiction. Make sure that the last two lines of the sub-proof directly contradict each other, i.e. one of them is the negation of the other.

Step 3:   Use either the ~**I** rule or the ~**E** rule:
- If the first line after the sub-proof contains one more '~' than the provisional assumption you made at the start of the sub-proof, then use the ~**I** rule.
- If the first line after the sub-proof contains one fewer '~' than the provisional assumption you made at the start of the sub-proof, then use the ~**E** rule.

Let's look at another example. Here is the start of a proof:

1. P ⊃ Q | ~(P • ~Q)

Clearly, there is no way to go directly from the one premise to the conclusion. Consequently, let's try to get there indirectly. **Step 1** tells us to assume the opposite of what we need. To do this, it's very important to be aware of the main operator. The conclusion is a negation—so let's assume its non-negated version, i.e. the entirety of the conjunction inside the parentheses:

1. P ⊃ Q | ~(P • ~Q)

2. | P • ~Q   for reductio

Step 2 tells me to go find a contradiction based on this provisional assumption. It is convenient to have a conjunction as an assumption, because you can straightaway use the •**E** rule. And in this case, this leads to an opportunity to use the ⊃**E** rule to get 'Q':

1. P ⊃ Q | ~(P • ~Q)

2. | P • ~Q   for reductio
3. | P   •E 2
4. | Q   ⊃E 1, 3

Remember, once you assume something *for reductio*, you should be constantly on the lookout for a contradiction. In this instance, our two contradictory sentences will be 'Q' and '~Q.' Here is the completed proof:

1. P ⊃ Q   ~(P • ~Q)

2. │ P • ~Q   for reductio
3. │ P   •E 2
4. │ Q   ⊃E 1, 3
5. │ ~Q   •E 2
6. ~(P • ~Q)   ~I 2–5

Once I see that my assumption on line 2 leads me to a contradiction, I can follow **Step 3** and write down the negation of that assumption—the *entire* assumption—using the **~I** rule.

As I'm sure you've discovered already, in logic practice makes perfect. So, let's do two more examples before you work your way through the exercise set at the end of this section. Here is the first one:

1. ~(X • Y)   Z
2. ~Z ⊃ Y
3. X

Again, there is no direct path from the premises to the conclusion, so let's see how far we can get by assuming the opposite of the conclusion:

1. ~(X • Y)   Z
2. ~Z ⊃ Y
3. X

4. │ ~Z   for reductio
5. │ Y   ⊃E 2, 4

But now what? Where is our contradiction going to come from? One thing to remember is that the contradiction does not have to take the form of an atomic sentence together with the negation of that atomic sentence. *Any* sentence of SL—either atomic or compound—together with its negation will do the job just as well. It is also worth noting that if one of your premises is a negation, very often it ends up being one half of the contradiction you need. In this case, the sentence on line 1 is a negation. Do I have the resources to generate the non-negated version of it? Yes! Take a look:

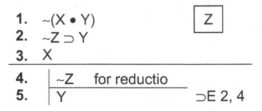

1. ~(X • Y)   Z
2. ~Z ⊃ Y
3. X

4. │ ~Z   for reductio
5. │ Y   ⊃E 2, 4
6. │ X • Y   •I 3, 5
7. │ ~(X • Y)   R 1

Lines 6 and 7 contradict each other, so now I can use ~**E** to get the conclusion:

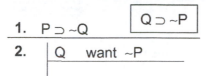

One last example involves nested sub-proofs. Consider the following valid argument:

P ⊃ ~Q ∴ Q ⊃ ~P

The conclusion here is a conditional sentence, so we will be using the ⊃**I** rule. Let's start that process:

```
                        ┌─────────┐
1.  P ⊃ ~Q              │ Q ⊃ ~P  │
                        └─────────┘
2.  │ Q    want ~P
    │
```

But now what? How can our original assumption on line 1, together with our provisional assumption on line 2, get us to '~P'? We're stuck. Luckily, however, we have a strategy for when we are stuck! So, let's assume the opposite of what we need and see where that takes us:

```
                        ┌─────────┐
1.  P ⊃ ~Q              │ Q ⊃ ~P  │
                        └─────────┘
2.  │ Q      want ~P
    │
3.  │ │ P    for reductio
4.  │ │ ~Q              ⊃E 1, 3
5.  │ │ Q               R 2
```

So, our assumption that 'P' is true in our innermost sub-proof leads to a contradiction. (Note that every sentence we have written down before this sub-sub-proof is one that we can use within this sub-sub-proof— even if, like the 'Q' on line 2, it is also a provisional assumption). This means that we have shown that '~P' is true, though we still write this down on an indented line to illustrate that it is true based on our assumption on line 2 that 'Q' is true on line 2:

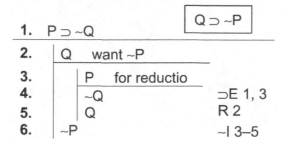

And, at this point, I have shown that if 'Q' is true, so is '~P':

1.	P ⊃ ~Q		
2.	Q want ~P		
3.		P for reductio	
4.		~Q	⊃E 1, 3
5.		Q	R 2
6.	~P		~I 3–5
7.	Q ⊃ ~P		⊃I 2–6

Exercise Set 5.5

Q1. Fill in the gaps in each of the following proofs.

1.

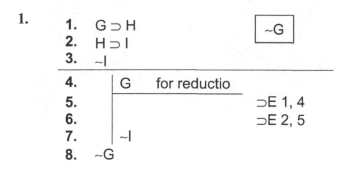

1.	G ⊃ H	~G
2.	H ⊃ I	
3.	~I	
4.	G for reductio	
5.		⊃E 1, 4
6.		⊃E 2, 5
7.	~I	
8.	~G	

2.

1.	A	~~A
2.	~A for reductio	
3.		R 1
4.	~~A	

3.

1.	F ∨ T	F
2.	T ⊃ ~C	
3.	C • D	
4.	~F for reductio	
5.		∨E 1, 4
6.	C	
7.		⊃E 2, 5
8.	F	

4.

1.	~X ⊃ ~Y	X
2.	Y	
3.	for reductio	
4.	~Y	
5.		R 2
6.	X	

5.

1.	N ⊃ ~X	~N • ~C
2.	X	
3.	~N ⊃ ~C	
4.	| N for reductio	
5.	|	⊃E 1, 4
6.	|	R 2
7.	~N	
8.		⊃E 3, 7
9.	~N • ~C	

6.

1.	~(L ∨ M)	~M
2.	| for reductio	
3.	| L ∨ M	
4.	|	R 1
5.	~(L ∨ M)	

7.

1.	J ⊃ (T • S)	~(J • K)
2.	K ⊃ ~(T • S)	
3.	| for reductio	
4.	| J	
5.	| K	
6.	|	⊃E 1, 4
7.	|	⊃E 2, 5
8.	~ (J • K)	

8.

1.	S ∨ U	~W
2.	~S	
3.	~(U • W)	
4.	U	
5.	| for reductio	
6.	|	•I 4, 5
7.	| ~(U • W)	
8.	W	

9.

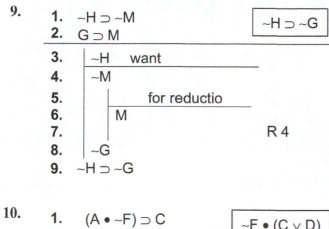

1. ~H ⊃ ~M
2. G ⊃ M   ~H ⊃ ~G
3. | ~H   want
4. | ~M
5. | | for reductio
6. | | M
7. | | R 4
8. | ~G
9. ~H ⊃ ~G

10.

1. (A • ~F) ⊃ C
2. A   ~F • (C ∨ D)
3. ~(F ∨ S)
4. | for reductio
5. | F ∨ S
6. | R 3
7. ~F
8.   •I 2, 5
9. C
10. C ∨ D
11. ~F • (C ∨ D)

Q2. On a separate piece of paper, construct a proof for each of the following valid arguments.

1. ~S ⊃ ~A, ~A ⊃ G, ~G ⊃ ~S   ∴ G

2. ~(D • E), E   ∴ ~D

3. A ⊃ (E ≡ S), E • ~S   ∴ ~A

4. T ⊃ U, ~(U • C)   ∴ ~(T • C)

5. ~J • ~K   ∴ ~(J • K)

6. ~H ⊃ I   ∴ ~I ⊃ H

7. S ⊃ B, ~~S   ∴ B

8. ~(R • S)   ∴ R ⊃ ~S

9. N ⊃ (O ⊃ P)   ∴ O ⊃ (~P ⊃ ~N)

10. ~(N • ~B), ~(B • ~O)   ∴ ~(N • ~O)

Chapter 6

Sentential Logic Proofs: Derived Rules and Substitution Rules

So far, our natural deduction system has eleven valid inference rules on board: two for each sentence operator, plus the Reiteration rule. We can call these eleven rules the **Basic Inference Rules**. Logicians have proven that the correct application of these rules enables us to prove *only* valid arguments of Sentential Logic (SL). That is, it is not possible, using these rules, to construct a proof for an invalid argument. Because of this, logicians refer to a natural deduction system like ours as **Sound**.[1] We will not consider the detailed proof of the soundness of our natural deduction system—this is beyond the scope of the text—but we can easily convince ourselves that our system does indeed have this property. Using truth tables, it can be shown that each inference rule describes a valid inference. So, if we insist on each line in a proof being either an assumption or derived via one of the inference rules, validity will always be guaranteed.

It also turns out that *every* valid argument in SL is provable using the basic inference rules. Because of this, logicians refer to a natural deduction system like ours as **Complete**. Proving the completeness of our natural deduction system is complete is considerably more complicated than proving its soundness, but it has been proved. The proof is beyond the scope of this text.

Taken together, then, the basic inference rules provide us with a sound and complete natural deduction system. In other words, they allow us to prove *all and only valid arguments*. Consequently, if we can construct a proof by appealing correctly to these inference rules, we can rest assured that the argument is valid. But what if we try, and fail, to construct a proof for an argument? In this case, there are two possibilities:

(A) There is no proof available, i.e. the argument is invalid.
(B) There is a proof available, but we just haven't found it yet.

To eliminate possibility **(A)**, we can always perform a truth-table test for validity. If we find that the argument is invalid, then we can stop looking for a proof: the soundness of the system dictates that it will be impossible to construct one. This, in fact, suggests another proof strategy:

Proof Strategy #4

If you are stuck, then use the truth-table test to confirm that the argument you are trying to prove is valid. If you discover that the argument is invalid, then stop—it will not be possible to construct a proof for that argument.

If we find that the argument is valid, however, then we will be forced to admit that possibility **(B)** obtains. The completeness of the system tells us that there must be a proof available, so we must decide how much effort we are going to put into finding this proof. If we don't manage to construct a proof on our first attempt, then, . . . well, we should keep trying! It can be a good idea to set the proof aside for a while—or even sleep on it—but we should be willing to give it at least a few honest attempts. The good news is that most of the valid

---

[1]This notion of soundness, which describes a property of our natural deduction system, is very different from the earlier notion of soundness we encountered in Chapter 1, which pertains to individual arguments.

arguments in this book have proofs with fewer than 15 lines, though some of the more challenging ones have over 20 lines.

Let us now make things a little bit more convenient by introducing some shortcuts. There are two different types of shortcuts that we will take on board. ***Derived Inference Rules*** will reflect further valid argument forms that we will allow ourselves to appeal to in a proof. ***Substitution Rules*** will enable us to replace sentences in a proof with logically equivalent sentences. It is important to remember that such shortcuts will not enable us to prove anything new. Think of the inference rules as a box of tools. The basic inference rules are a set of *hand* tools: we can construct anything we want to construct, as long as we have enough time and space to do so. However, it would be convenient to have some *power* tools available—we would then be able to construct things more efficiently. This is how we ought to think of the derived rules and the substitution rules. These latter don't allow us to construct any proofs that cannot be constructed using the basic inference rules; however, they help us to construct proofs more efficiently.

6.1 Derived Inference Rules

In principle, we could add an infinite number of valid inference rules to our list. However, we will limit ourselves to just three, each of which reflects a common valid form of reasoning that does not appear on the list of basic inference rules. Let us consider these three rules in turn.

Modus Tollens

So far, we have used the ⊃**E** inference rule to "break up" conditional sentences in a proof. We also referred to this valid form of reasoning as *Modus Ponens*, which as we saw is Latin for "the way (or method) of affirming." *Modus Tollens* is Latin for "the way (or method) of denying" and can be stated as follows:

Modus Tollens (MT)

$$P \supset Q$$
$$\sim Q$$
$$\therefore \sim P$$

That is, if I have a conditional sentence and the negation of its consequent, then I can validly infer the negation of its antecedent. It is another way to get something out of a conditional sentence:

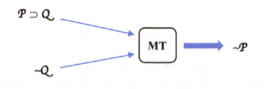

Note that a conditional sentence together with the negation of its antecedent does *not* entail the negation of the consequent. As always, we have to be careful when dealing with conditionals!

We have already proven that this inference is valid, using the ~**I** rule. From this point on, though, we can take it as a given that the inference is a valid one, and appeal to it in a proof. So, let's do that in an example. Here is a setup for us to consider:

1. M ⊃ N   ~M
2. L • ~N

Using the basic inference rules, there is no way to go directly from the premises to the conclusion. However, the **MT** rule will enable us to take a direct route. Notice that the conclusion is the negation of the antecedent of the conditional in line 1. Our new rule tells us that we can write out the negation of a conditional's antecedent whenever we have the negation of that conditional's consequent. In this case, we need '~N,' which we have the resources to get—it's part of the conjunction in line 2. Here is the completed proof:

> **1.** M ⊃ N $\boxed{\text{~M}}$
> **2.** L • ~N
> ─────────────
> **3.** ~N   •E 2
> **4.** ~M   MT 1, 3

When using the ⊃**E** rule, the idea was that when you have a conditional sentence, always be on the lookout for, or try to generate, the antecedent on a separate line. With **MT**, you can use a similar strategy: when you have a conditional, always be on the lookout for, or try to generate, the negation of the consequent on a separate line.

Hypothetical Syllogism

Syllogism is an old word for an argument that has two premises. A *hypothetical* is an exploration of a "what-if" scenario—basically, a conditional sentence. Consequently, a hypothetical syllogism will involve two premises and conditionals:

Hypothetical Syllogism (HS)

$$\mathcal{P} \supset \mathcal{Q}$$
$$\underline{\mathcal{Q} \supset \mathcal{R}}$$
$$\therefore \mathcal{P} \supset \mathcal{R}$$

This is another way of deriving a conditional sentence, one that doesn't depend on the construction of a sub-proof. Of course, we need the right pair of conditional sentences to generate the output we want with this rule:

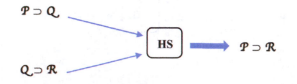

This common way of reasoning is also sometimes known as *chain* reasoning. Let's use it in a proof. Here is the start of a proof:

> **1.** A ⊃ ~B $\boxed{\text{A} \supset \text{~(D • E)}}$
> **2.** ~B ⊃ C
> **3.** C ⊃ ~(D • E)
> ──────────────

With just the basic inference rules on board, we would assume 'A' and try to derive '~(D • E).' The proof is a lot more straightforward with the **HS** rule on board, however. Notice that each component of the conditional sentence that we need is present in the premises: 'A' is the antecedent of the conditional in line 1, and '~(D • E)' is the consequent of the conditional in line 3. (As with all the inference rules, the **HS** rule applies to atomic and compound sentences). Furthermore, we can trace a "chain" between the former and the latter, meaning that our new rule is applicable. Here is the full proof:

1.	A ⊃ ~B	$\boxed{A ⊃ ~(D • E)}$
2.	~B ⊃ C	
3.	C ⊃ ~(D • E)	
4.	A ⊃ C	HS 1, 2
5.	A ⊃ ~(D • E)	HS 4, 3

In general, whenever you have some conditionals, always check to see if you can map them onto the **HS** rule.

Constructive Dilemma

Let's write this derived rule out straightaway. It captures a very common way of reasoning:

Constructive Dilemma (CD)

$$\mathcal{P} \vee \mathcal{Q}$$
$$\mathcal{P} \supset \mathcal{R}$$
$$\underline{\mathcal{Q} \supset \mathcal{S}}$$
$$\therefore \mathcal{R} \vee \mathcal{S}$$

This is the only inference rule we will encounter that requires three "inputs" to generate an "output":

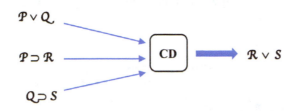

A moment's reflection should convince you that the rule is valid, though as always you can double-check via a truth-table test. Let's use it in an example. Consider the following argument:

X ⊃ A, Y ⊃ B ∴ (X ∨ Y) ⊃ (A ∨ B)

To get started, we notice that the conclusion is a conditional sentence, so we can set up a conditional proof:

1.   X ⊃ A $(X \vee Y) \supset (A \vee B)$
2.   Y ⊃ B
_____
3. | X ∨ Y want A ∨ B

With just the basic inference rules we would then construct the following proof:

1.   X ⊃ A $(X \vee Y) \supset (A \vee B)$
2.   Y ⊃ B
_____
3. | X ∨ Y   want A ∨ B
4. | | ~(A ∨ B)   for reductio
5. | | | X   for reductio
6. | | | A   ⊃E 1, 5
7. | | | A ∨ B   ∨I 6
8. | | | ~(A ∨ B)   R 4
9. | | ~X   ~I 5–8
10. | | Y   ∨E 3, 9
11. | | B   ⊃E 2, 10
12. | | A ∨ B   ∨I 11
13. | | ~(A ∨ B)   R 4
14. | A ∨ B   ~E 4–13
15. (X ∨ Y) ⊃ (A ∨ B)   ⊃I 3–14

This, as I'm sure you will agree, is a pretty complicated proof! The **CD** rule enables us to simplify things a lot:

1.	X ⊃ A	(X ∨ Y) ⊃ (A ∨ B)
2.	Y ⊃ B	
3.	X ∨ Y want A ∨ B	
4.	A ∨ B	CD 1, 2, 3
5.	(X ∨ Y) ⊃ (A ∨ B)	⊃I 3–4

So, the **CD** rule saves us ten lines! We didn't *need* to use the derived rule to construct a proof for the argument, but it clearly makes things a lot more convenient. The same is true for all the derived rules. If, for example, you are not particularly fond of having to construct sub-proofs, (or sub-sub-proofs, etc.), then the availability of these three derived rules reduces the number of times you will have to do this in a proof. Though note that it does *not* eliminate the need to do this. The number of sub-proofs required will be reduced even more when we take on board the substitution rules that are covered in the next section.

Exercise Set 6.1

Q1. Fill in the gaps in each of the following proofs. Remember, except for assumption lines, each line of a proof should have three elements: the line number, a sentence of Sentential Logic that is validly derived from earlier sentences in the proof, and a record of the inference rule that is being used to derive that sentence together with the line numbers of the proof to which the inference rule is being applied.

1.
1. T ⊃ H   ~T
2. H ⊃ L
3. ~L
_____
4.   MT 2, 3
5. ~T

2.
1. G ⊃ (H • B)   M
2. (H • B) ⊃ M
3. G • V
_____
4.   HS 1, 2
5.   •E 3
6. M

3.
1. (A ⊃ F) • (A ∨ N)   F ∨ G
2. N ⊃ G
_____
3.   •E 1
4.   •E 1
5. F ∨ G

4.
1. (L ⊃ M) • (M ⊃ N)   L ⊃ P
2. (N ⊃ O) • (O ⊃ P)
_____
3.   •E 1
4.   •E 1
5. L ⊃ N
6.   •E 2
7. N ⊃ P
8. L ⊃ P

5.

1.	T ⊃ ~H	~T
2.	~~H • ~~D	
3.		•E 2
4.	~T	

6.

1.	D ∨ E	X ∨ Y
2.	D ⊃ J	
3.	J ⊃ X	
4.	E ⊃ Y	
5.		HS 2, 3
6.	X ∨ Y	

7.

1.	F ⊃ G	H • O
2.	M ⊃ N	
3.	~G • ~N	
4.	~F ⊃ H	
5.	~M ⊃ O	
6.		•E 3
7.		•E 3
8.		MT 2, 6
9.	~F	
10.		⊃E 5, 9
11.	H	
12.	H • O	

8.

1.	~(W • E) ∨ ~(Y ∨ X)	A
2.	~(Y ∨ X) ⊃ J	
3.	J ⊃ A	
4.	~(W • E) ⊃ B	
5.	~B	
6.		HS 2, 3
7.	A ∨ B	
8.	A	

9.

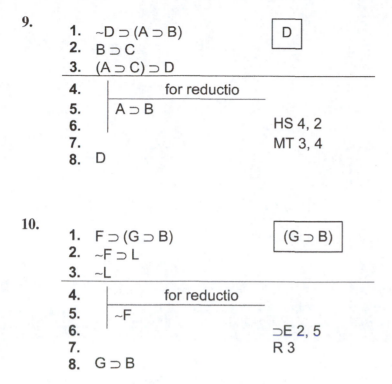

1. ~D ⊃ (A ⊃ B)   D
2. B ⊃ C
3. (A ⊃ C) ⊃ D
4. | for reductio
5. | A ⊃ B
6. | HS 4, 2
7. | MT 3, 4
8. D

10.

1. F ⊃ (G ⊃ B)   (G ⊃ B)
2. ~F ⊃ L
3. ~L
4. | for reductio
5. | ~F
6. | ⊃E 2, 5
7. | R 3
8. G ⊃ B

Q2. On a separate piece of paper, construct a proof for each of the following valid arguments. Try to make use of the three derived rules we have just introduced.

1. A ⊃ B, B ⊃ T, T ⊃ W   ∴ A ⊃ W

2. (H ⊃ B) • ~B   ∴ ~H

3. X ⊃ Y, (X ⊃ Z) ⊃ ~A, Y ⊃ Z, A ∨ B   ∴ B

4. A ⊃ J, ~C, J ⊃ C   ∴ ~A • ~J

5. R ⊃ C, L ⊃ C   ∴ (R ∨ L) ⊃ C

6. ~A, B ⊃ A, B ∨ ~C   ∴ ~C

7. K ⊃ L, ~M, L ⊃ M   ∴ ~K • ~L

8. (E • F) ⊃ G, E • ~G   ∴ ~F

9. S ⊃ T, S ∨ U, ~T, ~(U • W)   ∴ ~W

10. A ⊃ F, ~A ⊃ F   ∴ F

6.2 Substitution Rules[2]

The basic idea behind the Substitution Rules is quite simple: we list some pairs of logically equivalent sentence forms; then, when constructing a proof, we allow ourselves to substitute a sentence matching one of these forms with a sentence that is logically equivalent. As a result, the substitution rules allow us to "rearrange" the sentences we already have so that we can more readily apply the basic and derived inference rules. Most of the substitution rules we take on board describe fairly obvious logical equivalences, though, as before, we can always use truth tables to confirm this. Let us introduce each rule, beginning with one of the more easily understood rules, **Commutivity**:

Commutivity (Comm)

$$(\mathcal{P} \bullet \mathcal{Q}) \Leftrightarrow (\mathcal{Q} \bullet \mathcal{P})$$

$$(\mathcal{P} \vee \mathcal{Q}) \Leftrightarrow (\mathcal{Q} \vee \mathcal{P})$$

$$(\mathcal{P} \equiv \mathcal{Q}) \Leftrightarrow (\mathcal{Q} \equiv \mathcal{P})$$

The double arrow here, i.e. the '$\Leftrightarrow$,' is *not* a logical operator. It indicates that any sentence of the form that is to the left of it is logically equivalent to a sentence of the form to the right of it. And, of course, logical equivalence goes both ways: a sentence of the form that is to the right of '$\Leftrightarrow$' is logically equivalent to a sentence of the form that is to the left of it. What the **Comm** rule shows is that the order doesn't matter for sentences that have either the '$\bullet$,' the '$\vee$,' or the '$\equiv$' as the main operator. The **Comm** rule does not apply to the '$\supset$,' of course, where the order most definitely *does* matter: you should *never* swap the antecedent and the consequent of a conditional and assume that the result is a logically equivalent sentence!

Each of the following is an instance of the **Comm** rule:

A $\bullet$ B	$\Longleftrightarrow$	B $\bullet$ A
G $\vee$ (H $\bullet$ S)	$\Longleftrightarrow$	(H $\bullet$ S) $\vee$ G
M $\equiv$ L	$\Longleftrightarrow$	L $\equiv$ M
X $\bullet$ (Y $\equiv$ Z)	$\Longleftrightarrow$	(Y $\equiv$ Z) $\bullet$ X
(C $\supset$ D) $\vee$ (E $\supset$ F)	$\Longleftrightarrow$	(E $\supset$ F) $\vee$ (C $\supset$ D)

As should be clear from some of these example, this rule, like all the rules in our natural deduction system, is articulated using sentence variables. Let's see how we can use the **Comm** rule in proof. Consider the following setup:

> **1.** (S $\vee$ T) $\supset$ U $\boxed{\text{U}}$
> **2.** T $\vee$ S

It looks like lines 1 and 2 here map on to the $\supset$**E** rule, so we might be tempted to go straight to the conclusion on line 3. However, the sentence on line 2, 'T $\vee$ S,' is not identical to the antecedent of the conditional on line 1, 'S $\vee$ T.' Sure, it's obvious that these two sentences are logically equivalent, but when you judge that this is the case, you are making an inference—and, as we have emphasized a few times already, we need to

---

[2]Substitution Rules are also sometimes referred to as ***Replacement Rules***, or ***Equivalence Rules***.

record *every* inference that we make in a proof. Consequently, before appealing to the ⊃E rule, we need to make everything line up exactly right—and we can use the **Comm** rule to do this. Here is the completed proof:

1.	(S ∨ T) ⊃ U	U
2.	T ∨ S	
3.	S ∨ T	Comm 2
4.	U	⊃E 1, 3

On line 2, we simply replace one sentence of the proof with another, logically equivalent sentence, as provided by the **Comm** rule. All the substitution rules work like this: in the context of the proof at hand, we remove a sentence and replace it with a logically equivalent sentence.

Like the derived inference rules, the substitution rules are shortcuts. And, also like the derived inference rules, the substitution rules do not allow you to prove anything that cannot be proven by appealing to the basic inference rules only. However, there is one way in which the substitution rules are very unlike the derived inference rules (and the basic inference rules): we can apply them to *parts* of lines. That is, when we see that a *part* of a sentence on a proof line is, according to one of the substitution rules, logically equivalent to some other sentence, then we can replace *that part* of the line with the logically equivalent sentence. For example, the above proof could also have been completed in the following way:

1.	(S ∨ T) ⊃ U	U
2.	T ∨ S	
3.	(T ∨ S) ⊃ U	Comm 1
4.	U	⊃E 3, 2

Do you see the difference? Instead of applying the **Comm** rule to line 2, we applied it to the antecedent of the conditional on line 1, with everything else on line 1 remaining the same. This enabled us to apply the ⊃E rule on line 4.

The next substitution rule we will look at allows us to either add or subtract two negations to a sentence in a proof:

Double Negation (DN)

$$\mathcal{P} \Leftrightarrow \sim\sim\mathcal{P}$$

Again, this is obviously a valid rule. Here are some instances of the **DN** rule:

A	⟷	~~A
~B	⟷	~~~B
~~X	⟷	X
~~(G • H)	⟷	G • H
M ⊃ (N • O)	⟷	~~[M ⊃ (N • O)]

Let's use the **DN** rule in a proof. Consider the following setup, for example:

$$
\begin{array}{ll}
\textbf{1.} & \text{F} \supset \text{\raise.17ex\hbox{$\scriptstyle\sim$}}\text{G} \quad \boxed{\text{\raise.17ex\hbox{$\scriptstyle\sim$}}\text{F}} \\
\textbf{2.} & \text{G} \\
\hline
\end{array}
$$

At first glance, lines 1 and 2 look like they align with the **MT** rule. On further inspection, though, it is not an exact match. The **MT** rule tells us that if we have a conditional sentence together with the negation of its consequent, then we can validly infer the negation of the conditional's antecedent. The consequent of the conditional on line 1 is '~G,' and the negation of this is '~~G.' But this is *not* what we have on line 2: 'G' and '~~G' are different sentences of SL. Yes, it is obvious that these two sentences are logically equivalent; and for many students, the **DN** rule is *so* obvious that they think it is not necessary to record in the proof. Again, though, to judge that the two sentences are logically equivalent is to make an inference, and so we need to record this in our proof. Up to this point, our only way forward in this proof would have been to use the ~**I** rule: we would assume 'F' and derive a contradiction. Now, however, we can use the **DN** rule, which enables us to apply the **MT** rule:

$$
\begin{array}{lll}
\textbf{1.} & \text{F} \supset \text{\raise.17ex\hbox{$\scriptstyle\sim$}}\text{G} \quad \boxed{\text{\raise.17ex\hbox{$\scriptstyle\sim$}}\text{F}} \\
\textbf{2.} & \text{G} \\
\hline
\textbf{3.} & \text{\raise.17ex\hbox{$\scriptstyle\sim$}}\text{\raise.17ex\hbox{$\scriptstyle\sim$}}\text{G} & \text{DN 2} \\
\textbf{4.} & \text{\raise.17ex\hbox{$\scriptstyle\sim$}}\text{F} & \text{MT 1, 3}
\end{array}
$$

What we did here is typical of how we use the substitution rules: we used the **DN** rule to set up an application of one of the inference rules. Let's formulate this approach as a proof strategy:

Proof Strategy #5

Try to use the substitution rules to allow for an application of the inference rules (both basic and derived)

The next substitution rule is named after the English logician, Augustus De Morgan (1806–1871). It is typically listed as a pair of logically equivalent sentence forms:

De Morgan's (DeM)

$$\sim(\mathcal{P} \bullet \mathcal{Q}) \Leftrightarrow (\sim\mathcal{P} \vee \sim\mathcal{Q})$$

$$\sim(\mathcal{P} \vee \mathcal{Q}) \Leftrightarrow (\sim\mathcal{P} \bullet \sim\mathcal{Q})$$

We have already come across something like this rule before. Recall from Chapter 2 that a "neither-nor" sentence can be translated into SL in two ways. For example, "neither A nor B" can be symbolized as '~(A ∨ B)' or as '~A • ~B.' The second of the above pair of logically equivalent sentence forms basically captures this. In a similar fashion, the first of the above pairs reflects our earlier understanding that a "not-both" sentence can be symbolized as a disjunction of two negations.

The following are instances of the **DeM** rule:

~A • ~B	⬌	~(A ∨ B)
~(X ∨ Y)	⬌	~X • ~Y
~(~G • H)	⬌	~~G ∨ ~H
~M ∨ ~~N	⬌	~(M • ~N)
~[J • (K ⊃ L)]	⬌	~J ∨ ~(K ⊃ L)

Like the other substitution rules, the **DeM** rule can be very useful for rearranging sentences so that they line up better with the inference rules. Consider the following:

> 1. A ⊃ (B • C)   [~A]
> 2. ~B

Up to this point, our strategy here would have been to assume 'A' *for reductio* and then derive the conclusion indirectly. With the **DeM** rule on board, however, a little reflection reveals a more direct route to the conclusion. Notice that the conclusion is the negation of the antecedent of the conditional in line 1, which means that if we can get the negation of the conditional's consequent, then an application of the **MT** rule will provide us with the conclusion. So, can we get the negation of the consequent, i.e. '~(B • C)'? Well, this sentence is equivalent, via the **DeM** rule, to the following: '~B ∨ ~C.' And the '~B' on line 2 can provide us with this sentence, as long as we remember our old friend, the ∨I inference rule. Here is the complete proof:

> 1. A ⊃ (B • C)   [~A]
> 2. ~B
> 3. ~B ∨ ~C   ∨I 2
> 4. ~(B • C)   DeM 3
> 5. ~A   MT 1, 4

Using the **DeM** rule on line 4 allowed us to use the **MT** rule. Again, this is typical of all the substitution rules: we use them to get sentences to map onto the basic and derived inference rules.

Our next substitution rule is the ***Material Conditional*** rule (**MC**). In Chapter 3, we used the phrase *Material Conditional* to refer to our interpretation of horseshoe sentences. The **MC** substitution rule uses this interpretation of conditional sentences to allow us to turn a conditional sentence into a disjunction (and vice versa) in a proof:

Material Conditional (MC)

$$(\mathcal{P} \supset \mathcal{Q}) \Leftrightarrow (\sim\mathcal{P} \vee \mathcal{Q})$$
$$(\mathcal{P} \vee \mathcal{Q}) \Leftrightarrow (\sim\mathcal{P} \supset \mathcal{Q})$$

For many, this is the least intuitively obvious of the substitution rules. As with all the rules, however, it is a straightforward matter to use truth tables to check that what we have described in the rule are, indeed, logically equivalent sentence forms. Here are some instances of the **MC** rule:

A ⊃ B	⟷	~A ∨ B
X ∨ Y	⟷	~X ⊃ Y
~G ⊃ ~H	⟷	G ∨ ~H
~M ∨ ~N	⟷	M ⊃ ~N
(J ∨ K) ⊃ (L • M)	⟷	~(J ∨ K) ∨ (L • M)

Let's use this new substitution rule in a proof. Here is the setup:

1. A ⊃ B | A ⊃ C |
2. C ∨ ~B

Up to this point, our approach would have been to assume the antecedent of the conditional we need, i.e. 'A,' and then try to derive the consequent, i.e. 'C,' which would give us what we need via an application of the ⊃I rule. But let's try a different approach here. Notice that the conditional on line 1 has the same antecedent as the conclusion. We can also see that the disjunction on line 2 involves the consequent of the conditional on line 1, together with the consequent of the conclusion. All this suggests that an opportunity to apply the **HS** rule might be lurking! Let's try to line things up in the right way. The **MC** rule allows us to change certain disjunctions into conditionals; if we are lucky, using this rule on the disjunction on line 2 will give us a conditional that will allow us to use the **HS** rule. And this is exactly what transpires, though we do have to use the **Comm** rule as well. Here is the complete proof:

1. A ⊃ B | A ⊃ C |
2. C ∨ ~B
3. ~B ∨ C   Comm 2
4. B ⊃ C   MC 3
5. A ⊃ C   HS 1, 4

This way of constructing the proof might not be evident right off the bat, of course. With practice, however, you will begin to see how using the substitution rules can really help you out. Also, when trying to construct a proof, you might find yourself trying out things that don't quite work. This is fine, and normal. In fact, it is recommended that you try different approaches even if you are not sure they will get you all the way to the conclusion. The *worst* thing to do is to give up just because you can't visualize the entire proof. So, feel free to tinker with the substitution rules: transform conditionals into disjunctions, for example, and see if that works. If it doesn't, then try something else. It is a good idea to use a pencil—otherwise, things can get messy fairly quickly! Let's elevate this trial-and-error approach to a proof strategy:

Proof Strategy #6

When constructing a proof, don't be afraid to try something out even if you are not sure it will work.

Our final substitution rule for SL proofs—*Material Equivalence* (**Equiv**) —is one that allows us to more efficiently deal with biconditionals in proofs. This rule appeals to our understanding of biconditionals as being constituted by two conditional sentences. Here is a statement of the rule:

Material Equivalence (Equiv)

$$(\mathcal{P} \equiv \mathcal{Q}) \Leftrightarrow [(\mathcal{P} \supset \mathcal{Q}) \bullet (\mathcal{Q} \supset \mathcal{P})]$$

Here are some instances of the **Equiv** rule:

A ≡ B	⟺	(A ⊃ B) • (B ⊃ A)
(C ⊃ D) • (D ⊃ C)	⟺	C ≡ D
X ≡ (Y ∨ Z)	⟺	[X ⊃ (Y ∨ Z)] • [(Y ∨ Z) ⊃ X]
(~G ⊃ H) • (H ⊃ ~G)	⟺	~G ≡ H

And here is an example of how we can use the **Equiv** rule in a proof:

1.	J ≡ T	~T
2.	~J	
3.	(J ⊃ T) • (T ⊃ J)	Equiv 2
4.	T ⊃ J	•E 3
5.	~T	MT 4, 2

As before, we used a substitution rule to generate the conditions under which we can apply the inference rules.

And that is the end of the rules for constructing SL proofs in our natural deduction system. As mentioned, we could introduce more pairs of logically equivalent sentences, and we could allow ourselves to appeal to more valid forms of inferences. However, doing either or both of these would run the risk of having a list of rules that is too unwieldy. Consequently, we will stop here and work with what we have. However, let's do a few more examples. Consider this setup:

1.	~S ⊃ ~T	T ⊃ U
2.	~U ⊃ ~S	

This argument kind of looks like it is appealing to the **HS** rule—except that things are the wrong way around, and with negations. The substitution rules are good for getting things the right way around—so let's see if there's anything they can do to help in this case. Again, some trial and error may be required (remember to use that pencil!), but eventually we can line things up in the right way. Here is the completed proof:

1.	~S ⊃ ~T	T ⊃ U
2.	~U ⊃ ~S	
3.	S ∨ ~T	MC 2
4.	~T ∨ S	Comm 3
5.	T ⊃ S	MC 4
6.	U ∨ ~S	MC 2
7.	~S ∨ U	Comm 6
8.	S ⊃ U	MC 7
9.	T ⊃ U	HS 5, 8

Here is another example, already under way:

1.	A ⊃ B	~C ∨ ~D
2.	B ⊃ ~C	
3.	C ⊃ (D ⊃ A)	
4.	A ⊃ ~C	HS 1, 2

After making use of the **HS** rule on line 4, it looks like we will need to derive the conclusion indirectly. But, what should we assume *for reductio*? Well, notice that the conclusion, as a disjunction of two negations, maps onto the **DeM** rule: '~C ∨ ~D' is logically equivalent to '~(C • D).' If we can derive this latter sentence, then one more line will give us the conclusion. So, let's make '~(C • D)' our goal. To arrive at this indirectly would mean assuming 'C • D' —and assuming a conjunction is always a plus, given that you can immediately use the •**E** rule to get things moving. Here is the completed proof:

1.	A ⊃ B	~C ∨ ~D
2.	B ⊃ ~C	
3.	C ⊃ (D ⊃ A)	
4.	A ⊃ ~C	HS 1, 2
5.	C • D for reductio	
6.	C	•E 5
7.	D	•E 5
8.	D ⊃ A	⊃E 3, 6
9.	A	⊃E 8, 7
10.	~C	⊃E 4, 9
11.	C	R 6
12.	~(C • D)	~I 5–11
13.	~C ∨ ~D	DeM 12

As you can see, our understanding that the conclusion is logically equivalent to a more readily attainable sentence made things a lot easier. This is worth articulating as a proof strategy:

Proof Strategy #7

If you cannot see how to get to your goal, try substituting your goal with a logically equivalent sentence and see if you can derive that sentence.

And the rest is up to you! There is no substitute for practice, so make sure to work your way through all of the proofs in the following exercise set. Note that I have also included here are some questions that ask you to translate arguments and then construct a proof for them. For these questions, be sure to get the translation right—otherwise you might end up trying to construct a proof for an invalid argument!

Exercise Set 6.2

Q1. For each of the following sentences of SL, use at least one substitution rule and write down a logically equivalent sentence. The first one is done for you.

	This sentence . . .	. . . is logically equivalent to this sentence . . .	. . . using this substitution rule . . .
1.	~J • ~K	~(J ∨ K)	DeM
2.	~~X		
3.	~M ≡ ~N		
4.	A ∨ B		
5.	~G ∨ H		
6.	~~~(P ∨ L)		
7.	~~C • ~~D		
8.	O ⊃ ~T		
9.	(S ∨ R) ∨ (T ∨ U)		
10.	~Z ⊃ (L • V)		
11.	~~(I • ~K)		
12.	~~F ∨ ~~P		
13.	(S ≡ T) ≡ (U ≡ V)		
14.	(A ∨ ~G) ⊃ D		
15.	~(R ⊃ S) ∨ Q		

Q2. Fill in the gaps in each of the following proofs.

1.
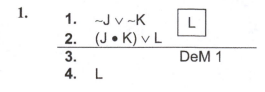
    1. ~J ∨ ~K   ⬚ L
    2. (J • K) ∨ L
    3.   DeM 1
    4. L

2.
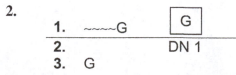
    1. ~~~~G   ⬚ G
    2.   DN 1
    3. G

3.
    1. H ∨ S   ⬚ T ⊃ S
    2. T ⊃ ~H
    3. ~H ⊃ S
    4. T ⊃ S

4.
1. ~X ⊃ ~Y $\boxed{X}$
2. ~Y ⊃ ~Z
3. Z
———————————————————
4. _____ DN 3
5. ~~Y
6. _____ MT 1, 5
7. X

5.
1. S ⊃ ~T $\boxed{\sim T}$
2. ~(~S ∨ C)
———————————————————
3. _____ DeM 2
4. ~~S
5. _____ DN 4
6. ~T

6.
1. ~D ≡ ~E $\boxed{E}$
2. D
———————————————————
3. _____ Equiv 1
4. ~E ⊃ ~D
5. ~~D
6. _____ MT 4, 5
7. E

7.
1. O ⊃ (M • N) $\boxed{\sim O}$
2. ~N
———————————————————
3. ~N ∨ ~M
4. _____ DeM 3
5. ~O

8.
1. (A ∨ U) ≡ ~R $\boxed{\sim U}$
2. ~(~R ∨ A)
———————————————————
3. ~~R • ~A
4. _____ •E 3
5. (A ∨ U) ⊃ ~R   Equiv 1
6. ~(A ∨ U)
7. _____ DeM 6
8. ~U

9.

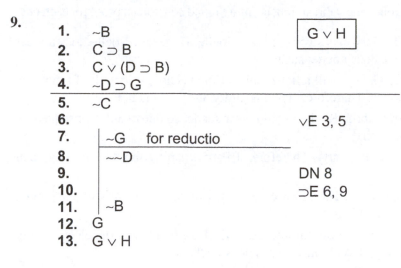

1.	~B	G ∨ H
2.	C ⊃ B	
3.	C ∨ (D ⊃ B)	
4.	~D ⊃ G	
5.	~C	
6.		∨E 3, 5
7.		~G for reductio	
8.		~~D	
9.			DN 8
10.			⊃E 6, 9
11.		~B	
12.	G	
13.	G ∨ H	

10.

1.	D ⊃ C	D ⊃ ~S
2.	~(C • S)	
3.		want ~S	
4.			⊃E 1, 3
5.		~C ∨ ~S	
6.			DN 4
7.		~S	
8.	D ⊃ ~S	

Q3. On a separate sheet of paper, construct a proof for each of the following valid arguments.

1. ~C ∨ H   ∴ ~(C • ~H)
2. P ∨ ~Q   ∴ ~(~P • Q)
3. ~(I • ~J), ~J   ∴ ~I
4. (X ∨ Y) ⊃ Z, ~Z   ∴ ~X
5. ~(N • O), N, O ∨ P   ∴ P
6. (A • B) ⊃ C, A • ~C   ∴ ~B
7. (P • Q) ∨ S, ~(Q • P)   ∴ S
8. (R • S) ≡ (G • H), R ⊃ S, H ⊃ G   ∴ R ≡ H
9. (E ∨ F) ⊃ G, ~H ⊃ F, ~G   ∴ H
10. A ⊃ (B • C), ~(A ⊃ D)   ∴ B
11. A ~(A ∨ E)   ∴ A ⊃ F
12. X ⊃ (Y • Z), ~(X ⊃ W)   ∴ Y
13. (~A ⊃ ~C) ⊃ (Q • ~W)   ∴ ~W ∨ C
14. S ≡ ~T   ∴ ~(S ≡ T)
15. [C ⊃ (D ⊃ C)] ⊃ E   ∴ E

Q4. On a separate sheet of paper, translate the following valid arguments into SL and construct a proof for each one.

1. If George eats sushi, so does Mary. If Mary eats sushi, so does Noelle. However, Noelle does not eat sushi. So, we can conclude that George does not eat sushi.

2. If either Ellen or Francis is guilty, then George will tell the police. Helen is not guilty only if Francis is guilty. But George will not tell the police. Therefore, Helen is guilty and Ellen is not guilty.

3. If Paul wears suede, so does Juan. And if both Raul and Said wear suede, so does Paul. Consequently, Said wears suede only if Juan does as well.

4. Neither Salvador nor Juanita is going to the party. Therefore, if Patrick isn't going to the party, then Salvador isn't.

5. Iran will not go to war with the United States. Therefore, either Iran will not go to war with the United States or Australia will go to war with the United States.

6. William will win the election only if there is a big turnout. And, Zachary won't win the election only if there isn't a big turnout. Consequently, if William wins, so does Zachary.

6.3 Tautologies and Contradictions

Consider the following argument:

G ∴ H ∨ ~H

One of our proof strategies (#2) tells us that when the conclusion of an argument has a component that is nowhere to be found in the premises, then it is likely that we will appeal to the ∨I rule at some point. However, the situation here is more extreme: the conclusion has *nothing* in common with the premises. A truth-table test, however, shows that the argument is valid:

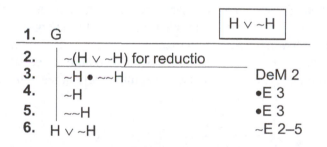

So, what should we do? Well, when we are stuck, we are encouraged to assume the opposite of what we need and see if we can derive a contradiction. So, let's try that:

		H ∨ ~H
1.	G	
2.	~(H ∨ ~H) for reductio	
3.	~H • ~~H	DeM 2
4.	~H	•E 3
5.	~~H	•E 3
6.	H ∨ ~H	~E 2–5

This is a legitimate proof—take the time to convince yourself of this. Notice that we did not appeal to the premise even once in the proof! This means that we could have constructed this proof if the premises were different—or even if there were no premises at all! What is going on? There is a straightforward explanation, as it turns out. The conclusion of this argument is a tautology, i.e. a sentence that, based on its form alone, is necessarily true. And if an argument's conclusion is necessarily true, then that argument is automatically valid: there will *never* be a case in which all the premises are true and the conclusion is false. A proof for such an argument doesn't really require us to show how you *derive* the conclusion *from* the premises. Rather, we can deal with just the conclusion and show that it has to be true regardless of what the premises are. Often, this will involve an indirect proof like the one we have just constructed. At other times, using the ⊃I rule is appropriate. Here, for example, is a proof that shows that the sentence 'H ⊃ (K ⊃ H)' is a tautology:

		H ⊃ (K ⊃ H)
1.	H want K ⊃ H	
2.	K want H	
3.	H	R 1
4.	K ⊃ H	⊃I 2–3
5.	H ⊃ (K ⊃ H)	⊃I 1–4

Notice that we didn't include any premises here at all. Whenever we can construct a legitimate proof that has no premises, then the sentence we have proven is a tautology.

Is there a corresponding way to show that a sentence is a logical contradiction? Well, recall that the negation of a tautology is a logical contradiction: if a sentence is necessarily true, then the negation of that sentence is necessarily false. Likewise, the negation of a logical contradiction is a tautology. This suggests the following way of showing that a sentence is a contradiction: show that its negation is a tautology. For example, consider the following sentence:

~(S ⊃ S)

This, unsurprisingly, is a contradiction. Let's prove that this is the case by showing that its negation is a tautology:

1.	S want S	
2.	S	R 1
3.	S ⊃ S	⊃I 1-2
4.	~~(S ⊃ S)	DN 3

The sentence '~~(P ⊃ P)' can be derived without appeal to any premises, which means that it is a tautology. And this means that the sentence '~(P ⊃ P)' is a contradiction.

There is an alternative method for showing that a sentence is a contradiction. Recall how the Negation inference rules, i.e. ~**I** and ~**E**, work. In the context of constructing a proof for an argument, deriving a sentence '$\mathcal{P}$,' and its negation '~$\mathcal{P}$,' from a provisional assumption together with the original premises of the argument, tells us that the provisional assumption is a contradiction. This suggests that, if we can derive a sentence '$\mathcal{P}$' and its negation '~$\mathcal{P}$' from just one sentence, i.e. without also appealing to any other sentence, then that sentence is a contradiction. Let's try this out on the above sentence:

1.	~(S ⊃ S)	
2.	~(~S ∨ S)	MC 1
3.	~~S • ~S	DeM 2
4.	~S	•E 3
5.	~~S	•E 3

As you can see, it is possible to generate a contradiction of the form '$\mathcal{P}$ • ~$\mathcal{P}$' from the sentence '~(S ⊃ S).' We can conclude, then, that the sentence '~(S ⊃ S)' is a contradiction.

This also suggests an alternative way of showing that a sentence is a tautology: show that a contradiction can be derived from its negation. In each case, which method should we use? Answer: it's your choice! In some cases, the methods don't diverge all that much anyway – constructing a proof for a sentence, without appealing to any premises, often involves deriving a contradiction from its negation, as in the first example above. In other cases, one way will clearly be more straightforward than the other.

Let's summarize:

Using the Natural Deduction System to show that a sentence '𝒫' is a tautology:
Either *(a)* Construct a proof for '𝒫' that does not appeal to any premises, or *(b)* show that you can derive a contradiction of the form '𝒫 • ~𝒫' from '~𝒫.'

Using the Natural Deduction System to show that a sentence '𝒫' is a contradiction:
Either *(a)* Construct a proof for '~𝒫' that does not appeal to any premises, or *(b)* show that you can derive a contradiction of the form '𝒫 • ~𝒫' from '𝒫.'

Exercise Set 6.3

Q1. On a separate piece of paper, construct a proof that shows that each of the following sentences of SL is a **TAUTOLOGY**.

1. ~(P • ~P)
2. F ⊃ (F ∨ G)
3. P ⊃ P
4. (P ≡ P)
5. (A ⊃ B) ⊃ (~B ⊃ ~A)
6. S ⊃ [(V • ~V) ⊃ W]
7. (M ⊃ N) ∨ ~(M ⊃ N)
8. G ⊃ [(~B ⊃ ~G) ⊃ B]

Q2. On a separate piece of paper, construct a proof that shows that each of the following sentences of Sentential Logic is a **CONTRADICTION**.

1. ~(P ∨ ~P)
2. ~[S ⊃ (T ⊃ S)]
3. (J ⊃ K) • ~(~K ⊃ ~J)
4. ~(~A • ~B) • ~(A ∨ B)
5. ~[(~S ⊃ T) ≡ (S ∨ T)]
6. ~[(D ⊃ D) ∨ (D ⊃ E)]
7. ~[~(M ∨ N) ⊃ (~M • ~N)]
8. ~{A ⊃ [(A ⊃ B) ⊃ B]}

Proof Strategies

The Basic Requirement of Proof Construction

When constructing a proof, record every inference that you make. Each inference must be an instance of one of the valid inference rules that we are using in our natural deduction system.

Proof Strategy #1

When constructing a proof, always keep in mind where you are going. If the argument is valid, then the sentences you already have will provide you with the resources to get there. Scan these sentences to see if they map onto any of the inference rules.

Proof Strategy #2

If your goal in a proof includes a component that is nowhere to be found in the premises, then it is likely that at some point you will have to use the ∨I rule. Look for an opportunity to do this.

Proof Strategy #3

If you ascertain that you need to make a provisional assumption, make sure that you assume based on where you need to go in the proof (and *not* based on where you are coming from).

Proof Strategy #4

If you are stuck, then use the truth-table test to confirm that the argument you are trying to prove is valid. If you discover that the argument is invalid, then stop—it will not be possible to construct a proof for that argument.

Proof Strategy #5

Try to use the substitution rules to allow for an application of the inference rules (both basic and derived).

Proof Strategy #6

When constructing a proof, don't be afraid to try something out even if you are not sure it will work.

Proof Strategy #7

If you cannot see how to get to your goal, try substituting your goal with a logically equivalent sentence and see if you can derive that sentence.

Chapter 7
Predicate Logic: Sentences

Consider the following argument:

> All dogs are mammals.
> Ollie is a dog.
>
> ———————
>
> Therefore, Ollie is a mammal.

This argument is obviously valid. If we translate the argument into Sentential Logic (SL) and then try to show that it is valid via a truth-table, however, we run into a problem. First, here is a symbolization key:

D: All dogs are mammals.
O: Ollie is a dog.
M: Ollie is a mammal.

And here is the translation:

D, O ∴ M

This certainly doesn't look valid. Here is a brief truth table showing that it is possible for all the premises to be true and the conclusion false:

D	O	M	D	O	∴ M
F	T	T	T	T	F

There is also clearly no proof available. What has gone wrong? Two possibilities present themselves. Here is the first one:

(A) SL adequately captures the logical form of the argument, but this is not sufficient to correctly evaluate the argument for validity.

In Chapter 3, we began to understand the validity of an argument in terms of the logical form of the argument. We developed the formal language of SL in order to capture an argument's logical form, with a view to evaluating an argument for validity once we had done this. It would be surprising, then, if by using SL we succeed in capturing the logical form of an argument, but then cannot successfully check the argument for validity.

Here is the other option:

(B) SL does *not* adequately capture the logical form of the argument, so translating the argument into SL does not enable us to evaluate it for validity.

The SL translation of the argument does seem to be missing something: there are just three atomic sentences, with no evident connection between them. However, the parts of the sentences in the original English argument clearly *are* connected in some way, which we can represent as follows:

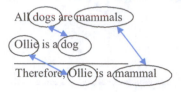

This connection between the parts of the argument's sentences is not at all evident in our attempt to capture the argument's form in SL. In cases like this, you might expect that our formal logical language would be able to "dive into" the parts of the sentences in a way that will highlight such connections, but SL clearly does not have the resources to do this. In this chapter, then, we will describe another formal logical language—***Predicate Logic (PL)***[1]—that provides us with these resources. PL should be viewed as an *extension* of SL, and not a replacement. The apparatus that SL provides is obviously useful for evaluating many kinds of arguments, so we will not be discarding all that we have learned in the last few chapters. In particular, the five sentence operators will be retained: the '•,' the '∨,' the '~,' the '⊃,' and the '≡.' Furthermore, nothing in PL will render the inference rules of our natural deduction system invalid. PL will simply help us to do something more than what SL enables us to do, namely, represent connections between the parts of sentences and arguments.

As an analogy, think of the moment in the history of science when physicists and chemists realized that atoms, which were understood to be the basic building blocks of physical reality, actually have an internal structure. The concept of an atom didn't disappear, and it remains legitimate in physics and chemistry. However, scientists appreciated the need for something more: a way of understanding what goes on *inside* an atom. Ultimately, scientists can better understand how atoms interact if they more fully understand how the parts of an atom interact with the parts of another atom. In PL, then, we are simply "cranking up" the logical microscope, so to speak, so that we are not just dealing with atoms, i.e. the atomic sentences, but also with *subatomic* particles, i.e. the *parts* of atomic sentences. Doing this will enable us to better understand how the parts of different sentences interact with each other in an argument.

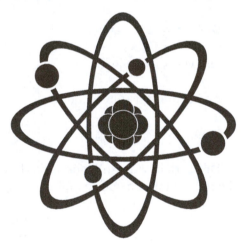

---

[1]What we call ***Predicate Logic*** in this book, logicians have also referred to as the ***Logic of Quantifiers***, ***Quantified Logic***, and ***Quantificational Logic***.

7.1 The Building Blocks of Predicate Logic[2]

Predicate Logic, like Sentential Logic, has a vocabulary, i.e. a list of the symbols that are used to construct sentences of the language. Here it is:

> Individual constants: a, b, c, . . . w
> Individual variables: x, y, z
> Predicates: A, B, C, . . . Z
> Sentence Operators: •, ∨, ~, ⊃, ≡
> Quantifiers Symbols: ∀, ∃
> The identity operator: =
> Grouping symbols: ( )

Obviously, there are some unfamiliar elements here, so let's work through those. We can begin by considering one of the sentences from the above argument:

Ollie is a dog.

This is an atomic sentence—it cannot be broken down into parts that are themselves sentences. Accordingly, in SL, it is translated by a single capital letter:

O

As noted, however, this translation misses out on the internal structure of the sentence. So, let's try to represent this structure. Appealing to concepts from high-school grammar, the sentence can be broken down as follows:

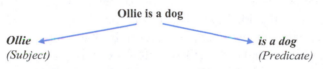

Ollie is a dog

Ollie   *is a dog*
(Subject)   *(Predicate)*

The *subject* of this sentence, i.e. what the sentence is about, is the entity picked out by the word "Ollie." Words like "Ollie" are proper names, and they refer to, or "pick out," just one single entity. In PL, ***individual constants*** serve the same purpose as proper names do in English. (A constant is also called a ***singular term*** because it refers to just one single entity, though using a constant is not the only way to refer to a single entity in PL – we will introduce another way of doing so later in the chapter). As indicated above constants are lower-case letters from 'a' through to 'w.' So, let's use the lower-case 'o' to symbolize the word "Ollie" in the above sentence. This is our first symbolization in PL, though it does not qualify as a sentence, of course—it is just *part* of a sentence.

The *predicate* part of the above sentence, i.e. the phrase "is a dog," picks out what the sentence is *saying about* the subject of the sentence. In PL, predicates are symbolized by upper-case letters from 'A' to 'Z.' In this example, let's use an upper-case 'D' to symbolize the phrase "is a dog." In SL, an upper-case letter by itself symbolizes an atomic sentence, but this is not the case in PL. 'D' here is just a *part* of a sentence.

At this point, then, we are in a position to offer our first PL translation of an English sentence. The English sentence "Ollie is a dog" is translated into PL as follows:

Do

This is what is called a ***singular sentence***, in that it is making an assertion about one specific entity: the predicate picked out by 'D' is being attributed to the entity referred to by the individual constant 'o.'

---

[2]The formal system of Predicate Logic presented here can be traced back to the work of German mathematician, Gottlob Frege (1848-1925). In 1879, Frege published his *Begriffsschrift* ("Concept Language"), which contained most of the elements of Predicate Logic that you will encounter here. The notation that Frege used for this system was very non-intuitive, however; the notation that is most widely used today (including in this text) was popularized by English philosopher, Bertrand Russell (1872-1970).

There are two features of this translation that you might not have expected. First of all, the part of this translation that corresponds to the English proper name "Ollie," i.e. the constant 'o,' is in lower-case, whereas the part of the translation that corresponds to the predicate "is a dog," i.e. 'D,' is in upper-case. This is the opposite of what happens in English, in which proper names are capitalized. A second surprising feature of the translation, perhaps, is the order in which the parts of the sentence appear: the predicate part of the sentence comes first, with the constant appearing after this. Again, this is the opposite of how things are typically done in English, where the name comes first, followed by the predicate. But these features of the translation are surprising to us only because we are familiar with the conventions of the English language. Other natural languages line up better with the translation. In Irish Gaelic, for example, the above sentence is translated as follows:

Is madra é Ollie

Here, the predicate part of the sentence comes *before* the subject part, just like in the PL translation of the sentence. There is nothing about language in general that insists that the subject comes first in a sentence, with the predicate coming after it. Likewise, there is nothing about language in general that insists that proper names are capitalized. And, just like we've gotten used to the conventions of the English language, we're just going to have to get used to the conventions of the language of PL.

Here is another example:

Alice is tall.

Let's try to outline a symbolization key for this sentence. Here is a first version of this:

T__: __ is tall.
a: Alice

As before, a lower-case letter will symbolize the English name of the sentence. (Another convention: constants are listed last in PL symbolization keys). The upper-case 'T' will symbolize the predicate part of the sentence. The way it is written here suggests that predicates in PL have gaps, and this is a good way to think about it. These gaps, or placeholders, need to be "filled" before we end up with a complete sentence. In PL, we use the individual variable letters 'x,' 'y,' and 'z' to represent the fact that there is a gap. So, our symbolization key ends up looking like this:

Tx: x is tall.
a: Alice

Note that the 'Tx' here merely describes the predicate, and so is not a complete sentence of PL. We can call it a ***predicate expression***. To get a complete sentence, we can replace the variable with an individual constant, like the one listed in the symbolization key:

Ta

This sentence of PL says that the predicate symbolized by 'T' is attributed to the entity picked out by the individual constant letter 'a.' This might sound a bit awkward, though; we can just read it as "a is T," or "Ta."

In PL, then, we can generate sentences simply by combining predicate letters with individual constant letters. We can also generate truth-functional combinations of such sentences. Consider the following, for example:

Both Alice and Bob are tall.

To translate this, we need to extend the above symbolization key, so that we have an individual constant letter for the proper name "Bob":

Tx: x is tall.
a: Alice
b: Bob

Now, to say that both Alice and Bob are tall is, in essence, to say that the predicate "is tall" applies to both Alice and Bob. In PL, we can capture this as follows:

Ta • Tb

As we have already mentioned, PL is an extension of SL, so we represent a claim that two things are both true as a conjunction. Two other candidate translations might suggest themselves, though, and it is important to see how they are *incorrect* translations:

Tab   **INCORRECT!**

Ta•b

At first glance, these may *look* like they capture what is going on in the English sentence, but something is amiss in each case. As indicated, the predicate expression 'Tx' has a gap, but this gap is large enough, so to speak, for just *one* individual constant letter. It is what is called a **one-place**, or **monadic**, predicate. 'Tab' is an attempt to fill this one-place gap with two constant letters, and there just isn't enough room for them both! Consequently, the first candidate translation is incorrect. The second candidate translation tries to squeeze even more stuff into the predicate expression's gap, so it too is incorrect. Note, also, that the conjunction symbol, i.e. the '•,' is a *sentence* operator, whereas in this second attempted translation, it operates on two *constants* and not on two sentences. Both 'Ta' and 'Tb,' on the other hand, are sentences in their own right, so 'Ta • Tb' uses the '•' appropriately.

In general, as already mentioned, the sentence operators we have been using in SL remain on board in PL, and we will be interpreting them in the same way. Using the above translation key, for example, we can generate the following translations in PL:

The English sentence . . .	. . . is translated into PL as . . .
Both Bob and Alice are tall.	Ta • Tb
Either Alice or Bob is tall.	Ta ∨ Tb
Alice is not tall.	~Ta
If Alice is tall, then Bob is tall.	Ta ⊃ Tb
Alice is tall if and only if Bob is tall.	Ta ≡ Tb

In each case here, the operator symbol operates on sentences and not on parts of sentences.

Here, then, is a method we can follow when translating sentences of English into sentences of PL:

Translating an English Sentence into PL

Step 1: Write out a symbolization key for the sentence. At this point, this involves two steps:
  (a) Select some upper-case letters to symbolize each predicate of the sentence.
  (b) Select some lower-case letters to symbolize any proper name that appears in the sentence. These are the individual constant letters.

Step 2: Identify any sentence operator words or phrases. If there are no sentence operator words or phrases, then the sentence is translated as a singular sentence of PL. Combine the predicate letter and the individual constant letter you have selected in **Step 1** to form this sentence. You will not need to proceed to **Step 3**.

Step 3: Symbolize the sentences on which the operators you identified in **Step 2** operate. This will involve combining predicate letters with individual constant letters more than once.

Step 4: Use the appropriate operator symbols to translate the rest of the sentence.

Let's work through an example. Consider the following sentence of English:

Jason is happy, but Meredith is not happy.

Step 1 asks us to draw up a symbolization key. There are two proper names here—Jason and Meredith. There is just one predicate—being happy. Here is the key:

Hx: x is happy.
j: Jason
m: Meredith

Step 2 requires that we identify any operator words in the sentence. There are two operator words: "but," and "not." Clearly, then, this is not a singular sentence, but will be a truth-functional compound sentence. So, we move on to **Step 3**, which gives us the following semi-translation:

Hj, but not-Hm.

With **Step 4**, then, we end up with the following sentence of PL:

Hj • ~Hm

As usual, with some practice, you will probably end up doing some of these steps in your head. Also, in some cases, a symbolization key will already be provided, which means you can skip **Step 1**.

Exercise Set 7.1

Q1. Translate the following sentences of English into the language of Predicate Logic (PL). The symbolization key is provided for you in each case. Write your answers in the space provided. The first one is done for you.

1. Carol is grumpy.

Symbolization Key:	**Gx:** x is grumpy.
	c: Carol
Translation:	Gc

2. Jennifer is tall and fast.

Symbolization Key:	**Fx:** x is fast.
	Tx: x is tall.
	j: Jennifer
Translation:	

3. Alice will go to the movie only if she gets done work early.

Symbolization Key:	**Mx:** x will go to the movie.
	Dx: x will get work done early.
	a: Alice
Translation:	

4. Tara will win the game if, and only if, she scores more points than her opponent.

Symbolization Key:	**Wx:** x will win the game.
	Sx: x scores the most points.
	t: Tara
Translation:	

5. Syracuse is not the capital of the United States, but Washington DC is.

Symbolization Key:	**Cx:** x is the capital of the United States.
	s: Syracuse
	w: Washington DC
Translation:	

6. Bob has either blue eyes or green eyes.

> **Symbolization Key:**   **Bx:** x has blue eyes.
>   **Gx:** x has green eyes.
>   **b:** Bob
>
> **Translation:**

7. Both Samir and Tanya live in Boston.

> **Symbolization Key:**   **Bx:** x lives in Boston.
>   **s:** Samir
>   **t:** Tanya
>
> **Translation:**

8. Mark is rich and Nathan is rich, but Olga is not rich.

> **Symbolization Key:**   **Rx:** x is rich.
>   **m:** Mark
>   **n:** Nathan
>   **o:** Olga
>
> **Translation:**

9. If either James or Kenneth goes to the party, then Meredith will go too.

> **Symbolization Key:**   **Px:** x goes to the party.
>   **j:** James
>   **k:** Kenneth
>   **m:** Meredith
>
> **Translation:**

10. Rover and Shep are not both sheepdogs, but they are both good boys.

> **Symbolization Key:**   **Gx:** x is a good boy.
>   **Sx:** x is a sheepdog.
>   **r:** Rover
>   **s:** Shep
>
> **Translation:**

Q2. Using the symbolization key, translate the following sentences into the language of PL.

Symbolization Key:
    Px: *x* is president.
    Cx: *x* is charismatic.
    Vx: *x* is on vacation.
    b: Bush
    o: Obama
    t: Trump

1. Trump is president.
2. Obama is not president.
3. Either Bush or Obama is president, but Trump is on vacation.
4. Obama is president and he is charismatic.
5. Neither Bush nor Trump is charismatic.
6. If Obama is president, then neither Bush nor Trump is president.
7. It's not the case that Obama is both president and charismatic.
8. If Trump is president and Obama isn't, then Bush is on vacation.
9. Obama is on vacation only if Trump is president.
10. Either Obama or Trump is president, but not both of them are presidents.

Q3. Translate the following sentences of English into the language of PL. Make sure to provide a symbolization key in each case.

1. Alex will go to the game, but Barney will not.
2. Either Paul or Quentin committed the crime.
3. Chris will go on vacation only if he can afford the trip.
4. I don't like *Star Trek* and I don't like *Star Wars* either.
5. The first *Godfather* movie is excellent, and *The Godfather Part II* is excellent, but *The Godfather III* is not.
6. It is not the case that if Olivia graduates then she will go to college.
7. If I eat candy, then I will get cavities, unless I brush my teeth.
8. Lily, Siri, and Molly are all awesome dogs.
9. If Pluto is a planet but Ceres is not a planet, then I don't want to be an astronomer.
10. I will help move the bookshelves if and only if Megan and Kevin help as well.
11. The *Titanic* ship was unsinkable, and the *Titanic* movie was unwatchable.
12. If Darwin was not a scientist, then neither was Einstein.
13. I will not go to the mall unless I finish my work early and go to the bank.
14. Russell Wilson is a quarterback who plays for the Seattle Seahawks.
15. Timmy and Sinead are both farmers, but they are not both wealthy.

7.2 Quantifiers

Consider the following symbolization key:

Fx: x is fluffy.
b: Betty

As already emphasized, the predicate expression 'Fx' is not a sentence and therefore does not have a truth-value. Such an expression is called an ***open sentence***. And we have seen that by inserting an individual constant letter into the 'x' position, we can transform this predicate expression into a complete sentence:

Fb

However, in PL we will also have to deal with sentences that do not involve any specific named individual, i.e. sentences that do not have any individual constant letters. Here is one such sentence:

Everything is fluffy.

Note, first, that this *is* a sentence, i.e. it is an assertion about the world that has a truth-value. Clearly, translating this sentence into PL will involve using the predicate expression 'Fx,' as defined in the above symbolization key. But how do we capture the claim that *everything* is fluffy? Well, perhaps we could assign an individual constant letter to every individual entity in the universe and then write out a huge conjunction:

Fa • Fb • Fc • Fd • . . .

To name everything in the universe and then state that each and every one of these named things is fluffy would, indeed, capture the claim that *everything* is fluffy—but such an approach is wildly impractical! Instead, to capture the form of the above sentence in PL, we use what is called a ***universal quantifier***. Rephrasing the sentence a few times will help us to better understand how this goes. Here is a first paraphrase:

Everything is such that it is fluffy.

Using the individual variable letter 'x,' we can also understand this sentence as saying the following:

Every x such that it (i.e. x) is fluffy.

Using the predicate expression 'Fx,' this becomes the following:

Every x is such that Fx.

We now have to symbolize the "every x is such that" clause of this sentence. To do this, we introduce the expression '∀x,' and we end up with the following sentence of PL[3]:

∀xFx

This can be read in a number of different ways:

- For all x, Fx.
- For any x, Fx.

---

[3] The universal quantifier is sometimes symbolized using just parentheses. For example, the sentence '∀xFx' is written as '(x)Fx.'

- Every x is such that it is F.
- Every x is an F.

Each of these locutions amounts to the same assertion: everything is fluffy. The sentence '$\forall x Fx$' is a **universally quantified sentence**: it makes an assertion about everything. Notice that there is no mention of a specific, named entity in this sentence; that is, the sentence has no individual constant letter. We called the expression 'Fx' an open sentence, and in a sense the universal quantifier "closes" it. We will speak of the variable 'x' as being **bound** by the universal quantifier at the front of the expression 'Fx.' In other words, the 'x' here is a **bound variable**, as opposed to the *free variable* 'x' in the expression 'Fx.'

In PL, we also have **existentially quantified sentences**, which make assertions about *some* things, instead of *all* things. Sticking with the same predicate, consider the following English sentence:

Some things are fluffy.

Interpreting the word "some things" to mean "there is at least one thing," we can rephrase this as follows:

There is at least one thing that is fluffy.

Making use of the variable letter 'x,' this becomes the following:

There is at least one thing x such that it (i.e. x) is fluffy.

Using our predicate expression 'Fx,' this then becomes:

There is at least one thing x such that Fx.

We now have to symbolize "there is at least one thing x such that." We introduce the expression '$\exists x$' to do this, and we end up with the following sentence of PL:

$\exists x Fx$

This can be read in a number of different ways:

- For some x, Fx.
- There is at least one thing x such that x is F.
- Some x's are F's.
- At least one thing is an F.

Each of these locutions captures the same assertion: some things are fluffy. Again, notice that there is no mention of a specific, named entity; that is, the sentence has no individual constant letter. The sentence is committed to there being at least one thing that is fluffy, but it does not say anything about *which* things are fluffy. In this case, the variable 'x' is bound by the existential quantifier at the front of the expression 'Fx.' This is another way to "close" an open sentence like 'Fx.'

The universal and existential quantifiers, together with the truth-functional sentence operators, turn PL into a very powerful language, and we can now assert all kinds of things. Let's work through some examples. Here is a new symbolization key to work from:

Bx: x is blue.
Fx: x is fluffy.
a: Alice

First, we will look at how the quantifiers work with the negation symbol, '~.' Examine the following table of translations closely:

The sentence . . .	. . . is translated into PL as . . .
Everything is blue.	∀xBx
Not everything is blue.	~∀xBx
Everything is not blue.	∀x~Bx
Some things are blue.	∃xBx
Nothing is blue.	~∃xBx
Some things are not blue.	∃x~Bx

Notice that the location of the '~' matters a lot, so, be very careful! Also, did you see that in some of these examples we are repeating ourselves? To say that not everything is blue, for example, is to say that some things are not blue. That is, the following two sentences of PL are equivalent:

Likewise, to say that everything is not blue is to say that nothing is blue. This means that the following two sentences are equivalent:

$$\forall x\text{~}Bx \quad \Longleftrightarrow \quad \text{~}\exists xBx$$

In fact, it turns out that a sentence that is translated using the universal quantifier, i.e. '∀,' will always have an equivalent translation that uses the existential quantifier, i.e. '∃.' In other words, the quantifiers are *interdefinable*:

$$\forall xPx \quad \Longleftrightarrow \quad \text{~}\exists x\text{~}\boldsymbol{P}x$$

$$\exists xPx \quad \Longleftrightarrow \quad \text{~}\forall x\text{~}\boldsymbol{P}x$$

To convince yourself of this interdefinability, consider the English versions of these sentences of PL:

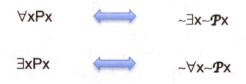

Again, make sure you take the time to recognize that the sentences in each pair really do mean the same thing.

Now, let us take some first steps in understanding how the quantifiers work with the '•' and the '∨.' Consider the following sentence:

Some things are blue and some things are fluffy.

There are two quantifier terms here: two instances of the word "some." The "and" in the middle pulls everything together. So, in PL, this is a conjunction of two existentially quantified sentences:

∃xBx • ∃xFx

To check that this correctly captures the sentence, we can always translate this sentence back into English. The result is the following:

There is at least one thing x such that it is blue, and there is at least one thing x such that it is fluffy.

And yes, this is an accurate paraphrase of the original sentence. Note, however, that there are some superficially similar translations that do not work. Consider this one, for example:

$$\exists x Bx \cdot Fx \quad \longleftarrow \quad \textbf{INCORRECT!}$$

Here, the 'x' in the 'Bx' is bound by the existential quantifier; however, the 'x' in the 'Fx' is *not* bound by it, i.e. it is a free variable. What is after the '•' here, then, is only a predicate expression, and cannot really be a conjunct at all. Consequently, we don't have a complete sentence here; in English, this candidate translation would say something like the following:

Some things are blue, and fluffiness.

Obviously, this is not a sentence in the logical sense: it does not have a truth-value.
Here is another candidate translation you might be thinking of:

$$\exists x(Bx \cdot Fx) \quad \longleftarrow \quad \textbf{INCORRECT!}$$

Unlike the previous candidate, this *is* a sentence, i.e. it has a truth-value. The difference is that what comes after the existential quantifier is grouped in such a way that everything is bound by the one existential quantifier. Here is what this sentence says in English:

There is at least one thing x such that it (i.e. x) is both blue and fluffy.

This is not the same sentence that we started with, however. The original sentence asserts that some things are blue and some things are fluffy; there is no commitment to there being anything *both* blue *and* fluffy. It was important, therefore, to notice that the original sentence had two English quantifier terms—two "some things"—which meant that there had to be two quantifier symbols in the translation.

Here is another example:

Everything is either fluffy or not fluffy.

As indicated just now, it is important to keep track of the number of quantifier words or phrases in the sentence we are translating. In this case, there is just one quantifier word: "everything." This will be translated with the '∀.' We also need to make sure that there are no open sentences in our translation. We end up with the following sentence of PL:

$$\forall x(Fx \vee {\sim}Fx)$$

Going from this sentence of PL back into English, we get the following:

For all x, it is either the case that it (i.e. x) is fluffy or it (i.e. x) is not fluffy.

This is a good paraphrase of the original sentence. Notice, though, how this translation is different from the following:

$$\forall x Fx \vee \forall x {\sim}Fx$$

This is a legitimate sentence of PL, but if we translate this back into English, we get this:

Everything is fluffy or everything is not fluffy.

But there are *two* quantifier terms here, while the original sentence had just one. In addition, the original sentence is true—everything *is* either fluffy or not fluffy, but this most recent sentence is false: both disjuncts are false. Consequently, this cannot be an adequate translation.

With the quantifiers on board, we need to expand on our translation method:

Translating an English Sentence into PL

Step 1:   Write out a symbolization key for the sentence. At this point, this involves two steps:
  (a)   Select some upper-case letters to symbolize each predicate of the sentence.
  (b)   Select some lower-case letters to symbolize any proper name that appears in the sentence. These are the individual constant letters.
Step 2:   Identify any quantifier terms (e.g., "all," "every," "some," etc.)
Step 3:   Identify any sentence operator words or phrases.
  If there are no quantifier terms and no sentence operator words or phrases, then the sentence is translated as a singular sentence of PL. Combine the predicate letter and individual constant letter you have selected in **Step 1** to form this sentence. You will not need to proceed to **Step 4**.
Step 4:   Using the appropriate quantifier symbols and operator symbols that you identified in **Steps 2** and **3** write out the sentence of PL that captures the logical form of the English sentence. The details here will differ in each case, but here are some general guidelines:
  • Pay close attention to whether the sentence will be a quantified sentence (i.e., a sentence in which everything is within the scope of a quantifier), or a truth-functional sentence (i.e., a sentence in which one of the five sentence operators is the main operator and does not fall inside the scope of a quantifier).
  • Make sure that your translation has no free variables: every variable in a sentence of PL must be bound by a quantifier.
  • Translate the PL sentence you end up with back into English to make sure that it really does capture the form of the original sentence.

Let's work through an example. Consider the following sentence of English:

Some things are small but Mount Fujiyama is not.

Step 1 asks us to write out a symbolization key. The sentence has just one predicate—"being small," and just one constant—"Mount Fujiyama." So, we can generate the following symbolization key:

Sx: x is tall.
f: Mount Fujiyama

Step 2 asks us to identify any quantifier terms. In this sentence, there is just one: the word "some." **Step 3** requires that we pick out the sentence operator words. Here, there are two: "but" and "not." **Step 4** asks for a sentence of PL. Reading the sentence again, the word "but" pulls everything together, so this will be a truth-functional sentence with the '•' as the main operator. Everything to the left of the "but" will fall inside the scope of an existential quantifier, while everything to the right of the "but" will not be a quantified sentence. All of these considerations give us the following sentence of PL:

∃xBx • ~Ba

There are no free variables here, as required. And, as suggested, let's translate this sentence of PL back into English to see if we have captured the meaning of the original sentence:

There is at least one thing x such that it (i.e. x) is small, and it is not that case that Mount Fujiyama is small.

A moment's reflection will convince us that this does indeed capture the form of the original sentence.

Before moving on, we need to consider what we will call the *existential commitments* of quantified sentences. Existentially quantified sentences, like '∃xFx,' are committed to the existence of some things—in this case, some things that are 'F.' Any sentence in which it is clear that some things exists can be translated as an existentially quantified sentence. In fact, any sentence that *explicitly* claims that such-and-such a thing exists doesn't even take the word "exists" to be a predicate; instead, the existence claim is just taken to be included in the '∃x.' Take the following sentence for example:

Wombats exist.

At first glance, you might think that two predicate letters are required in order to translate this sentence into PL: a predicate letter for "being a wombat" and a predicate letter for "existing." We would then end up with the following sentence of PL (using the obvious predicate letters):

∃x(Wx • Ex)

However, translating this back into English results in the following:

There is a least one thing x such that it (i.e. x) is a wombat and it (i.e. x) exists.

This sentence is a bit odd! There are now *two* existence claims: "there is an x," and "it exists." To prevent this kind of situation, the convention is that we do not treat existence as a predicate in PL. Any claims about what does or does not exist are "packed into" the existential quantifier, so to speak. For the above sentence, then, we need just one predicate letter—a 'W'—and we generate the following translation:

∃xWx

In English, this says the following:

There is at least one thing x such that it (i.e. x) is a wombat.

And this does enough to capture the original claim: wombats exist.

What about the existential commitments of a universally quantified sentence? Consider one of our earlier sentences, for example:

Everything is fluffy.

We translate this as follows:

∀xFx

Does this commit us to the existence of fluffy things? Generally speaking, yes—but let's be careful here. What is included in the word "everything"? Perhaps we are talking about everything in the entire universe, in which case to say that everything is fluffy does commit us to the existence of fluffy things. When we intend for the word "everything" to cover the whole universe like this, we say that the quantifier **ranges over** everything, or that we are quantifying over the **universal domain**. In other words, what we will call our **Universe of Discourse** (**UD**) is "everything." In most contexts, however, we do *not* intend for the word "everything" to cover the entire universe; with the above sentence, for example, we might be talking about "everything in this box on the table," or "everything in Anna's room." In these cases, we have narrowed the UD significantly—though the sentence still commits us to the existence of fluffy things.

When translating sentences from English into PL, it can be a good idea to include a specification of the UD in the symbolization key. For example, a symbolization key for the above sentence might look like this:

UD: everything in the box on the table
Fx: x is fluffy

Once our UD is defined, then it is understood that any quantifier that is used in a sentence will range over *just those things in that* UD. So, for example, the sentence '∀xFx' is understood to be saying the following:

For all x in the box on the table, x is fluffy.

Specifying a UD is especially useful when we are quantifying over people. Consider the following sentence, for example:

Everyone is happy.

This sentence is clearly talking about just those things in the universe that happen to be persons; that is, something is being asserted of every*one*, i.e. every *person*, and not every *thing*. So, the following symbolization key suffices:

UD: all persons
Hx: x is happy.

We do not need a separate predicate to cover "being a person," because our UD tells us that we are talking only about persons. Given this symbolization key, our translation is very simple:

∀xHx

That is:

For all x that is a person, he/she (i.e. this x) is happy.

And this captures the form of the original sentence.

How small can our UD be? Answer: as small as the context requires. In some unusual cases, this might mean a UD with just one thing—though we won't encounter any such contexts in this book. Is there such a thing as an *empty* UD? That is, can we quantify over absolutely nothing? Such a possibility is conceivable, though it brings with it some complications, which we will not consider here. Let us just insist on our UD having at least one member. This, then, will ensure that any universally quantified sentence will involve existential commitments. In terms of the above sentence, then: in a non-empty UD, if everything is fluffy, we are guaranteed that there is at least one thing that is fluffy.

Do we have to specify a UD for *every* sentence that we translate? Well, yes—though moving forward, we will usually be operating within the universal domain, i.e. with a UD of "everything." That is, in most cases, our translation task is not greatly simplified by trying to narrow things down.[4] However, sometimes, articulating a narrower UD can help us out, and in those cases we will pay due attention to getting the UD right.

---

[4]As it happens, quantifying over absolutely everything raises its own philosophical problems, but these need not concern us here.

Exercise Set 7.2

Using the symbolization key, translate the following sentences into the language of Predicate Logic (PL). Write your answers in the spaces provided. The first one is done for you.

Symbolization Key:
   UD: Everything
   Bx: *x* is blue.
   Fx: *x* is fast.
   Rx: *x* is red.
   Tx: x is tall.
   b: Batman
   e: Mount Everest
   k: Mount Kilimanjaro
   s: Spiderman

1. Spiderman is red and blue.

Translation:	Rs • Bs

2. Everything is blue.

Translation:

3. Some things are red but some things are not red.

Translation:

4. Some things are blue and Batman is one of those things.

Translation:

5. Nothing is red.

Translation:

6. Not everything is blue, but some things are red.

> **Translation:**

7. Not everything is fast.

> **Translation:**

8. Everything is not fast, and everything is not blue.

> **Translation:**

9. Either Spiderman is blue or everything is red.

> **Translation:**

10. If everything is red, then nothing is blue

> **Translation:**

11. Everything is either fast or not fast.

> **Translation:**

12. Mount Everest is tall or nothing is tall.

> **Translation:**

13. Mount Everest is tall only if Mount Kilimanjaro is tall.

> **Translation:**

14. If everything is tall, then nothing is not tall

> **Translation:**

15. Both Batman and Spiderman are fast, but Mount Everest isn't.

> **Translation:**

16. At least one thing is fast, and if this is true, then Batman is blue.

> **Translation:**

17. If everything is blue, so is Batman, and if everything is red, so is Spiderman.

> **Translation:**

18. Spiderman is tall and fast if and only if Batman is tall and fast.

> **Translation:**

19. It is not the case that if some things are tall then some things are fast.

> **Translation:**

20. Everything is either blue or red.

> **Translation:**

Q2. Translate each of the following sentences into the language of PL. I have listed the obvious predicate letters, and constant letters, to use in your translation. In each case, assume the universal domain. Write your answers on a separate sheet of paper.

1. Goblins exists (G).
2. Unicorns do not exist (U).
3. Nothing is sacred (S).
4. There are no leopards (L).
5. Everything sucks (S).
6. If everything is blue, then everything has a color (B, C).
7. Either there is a god or Donald Trump is president (G, P, t).
8. If ghosts do not exist, then neither do hobgoblins and orcs (G, H, O).
9. If the Moon is made of cheese, then there is at least one thing made of cheese (m, C).
10. If some things are heavy, then not all things are light (H, L).

7.3 Some Common Sentence Types

Some types of sentences in PL deserve special attention. Consider, for example, the following sentence from the argument at the beginning of this chapter:

All dogs are mammals.

How shall we translate this into PL? The word "all" tells us that we will be using the quantifier symbol '∀.' Clearly, however, the sentence is not saying that everything is a dog, and it is also not saying that everything is a mammal. Let's paraphrase and see if we can capture what it *is* saying:

Everything that is a dog is a mammal.

This can also be put as follows:

For all x, if x is a dog, then it (i.e. x) is a mammal.

There is just one quantifier term here, and it looks like the entirety of the conditional sentence that comes after it should be inside the scope of this quantifier. Using the obvious predicate letters, then, we end up with the following:

∀x(Dx ⊃ Mx)

And this does, indeed, capture the form of the original sentence. The parentheses are crucial here in that they bind the variables within them to the quantifier at the front of the parentheses. Without the parentheses, we would have the following open sentence:

∀xDx ⊃ Mx ⟵ **INCORRECT!**

This is not a universally quantified sentence. Instead, it is a conditional sentence, but with a free variable—the 'x' in the consequent 'Mx.'

Any sentence like this one that can be paraphrased as "***All A's are B's***," is called a ***Universal Affirmative***. Such a sentence makes a universal claim about all members of one category, i.e. the ***A***'s—namely that they all belong in another category, i.e. the ***B***'s.[5] All sentences of this kind should be translated as above. Notice that the main operator inside the parentheses that follow the universal quantifier is a '⊃.' It is worth taking a look at how the other operators would fare if they were used in an attempt to translate the sentence:

∀x(Dx • Mx)	For all x, x is both a dog and a mammal.	This is false. It is not the case the everything is both a dog and a mammal!
∀x(Dx ∨ Mx)	For all x, x is either a dog or a mammal.	This is false. There are many things that are neither dogs nor mammals!
∀x(Dx ≡ Mx)	For all x, x is a dog if and only if x is a mammal.	This is false. Recall that an 'if and only if' sentence includes two conditionals. In this case, then, we would have the claim "for all x, if x is a dog, then x is a mammal, and if x is a mammal, then x is a dog. As discussed, the first conditional does capture the sentence, but the second conditional goes too far—many mammals are *not* dogs.

---

[5]This way of understanding such sentences, as well as the label *Universal Affirmative*, comes from the system of ***Categorical Logic*** that was developed by the ancient Greek philosopher, Aristotle (384-322BCE). (The label for each different kind of sentence in this section are also taken from Categorical Logic). Aristotle's system of logic has been hugely influential in the history of philosophy in the West.

In general, in a universally quantified sentence the main operator will usually be the '⊃.' That is, if there is a '∀' "on the outside," then the main operator "on the inside" (i.e., within the parentheses) will be the '⊃.' This will not *always* be the case, but it is a good rule of thumb to have on board.

We can also translate universal affirmatives using the existential quantifier. We can convince ourselves of this in two ways. First, we can simply paraphrase the original English sentence we are working with. To say that all dogs are mammals is to say the following:

No dogs are non-mammals.

Or, in other words:

There do not exist any dogs that are not mammals.

One more paraphrase provides us with the following:

It is not the case that there is an x such that it (i.e. x) is a dog and not a mammal.

There is one quantifier phrase here, i.e. "there is an x." There are two negations—one at the front that will operate on the entire sentence and one that will operate on just the "mammal" part. There is also an "and," which means there will be a conjunction. Here is the full translation:

~∃x(Dx • ~Mx)

So this also captures the form of the original sentence. Here are the two equivalent sentences side by side:

$$\forall x(Dx \supset Mx) \quad \Longleftrightarrow \quad \sim\exists x(Dx \bullet \sim Mx)$$

Transforming one sentence into the other here involves four easy steps:

1. Add a negation to the front of the sentence; remove any resultant double negations.
2. Change the quantifier.
3. Change the main operator within the parentheses from a '⊃' to a '•,' or vice versa.
4. Add a negation to what comes after the main operator; remove any resultant double negations.

Make sure to take the time to see that these four steps transform the sentence on the left into the sentence on the right, and that they also transform the sentence on the right into the sentence on the left.

To further appreciate how it is that these two sentences are logically equivalent, we can make use of some of our rules of inference from the last chapter:

∀x(Dx ⊃ Mx)	The first version of the translation of the universal affirmative.
~∃x~(Dx ⊃ Mx)	Recall from earlier in this chapter that the quantifier symbols are inter-definable.
~∃x~(~Dx ∨ Mx)	This follows via an application of the **MC** rule to everything inside the parentheses.
~∃x(~~Dx • ~Mx)	This follows via an application of the **DeM** rule to everything after the '~∃x'.
~∃x(Dx • ~Mx)	This follows via an application of the **DN** rule to the first conjunct inside the parentheses.

We won't be encountering PL proofs until the next chapter, so we are getting ahead of ourselves a little bit here. Nevertheless, such considerations are useful when trying to appreciate the inter-definability of the two quantifiers.

Notice that this sentence does not commit us to the existence of either dogs or mammals. All it says is that, for all things in our UD—and remember, our default UD here is "everything"—if something is a dog, then that something is a mammal. The sentence does not insist that there *is* something that is a dog, nor does it is insist that there *is* something that is a mammal. It is helpful here to recall that a conditional sentence is true when its antecedent is false: even if there are no dogs, it is still true to say that if something is a dog, then it is a mammal. To further emphasize this point, consider the following sentence:

All unicorns have one horn.

Using the obvious predicate letters, this is translated as follows:

$\forall x(Ux \supset Hx)$

We can stick to a UD of "everything" here—there are no unicorns in this universe, right? Yet, we can still consider this sentence to be true: *if* something is a unicorn, then that something has one horn.

Here is another sentence for us to consider:

Some cats are playful.

This type of sentence, and all sentences that can be paraphrased as "***Some A's are B's***," is called an ***Existential Affirmative***. It asserts that at least some of the members of one category, i.e. the *A*'s, also belong to another category of things, i.e. the *B*'s. In this case, some things that are in the category of cats are also in the category of playful things. Let's see how we can capture the form of this sentence in PL. We can start with a paraphrase:

There is at least one thing such that it is a cat and it is playful.

This then becomes the following:

There is at least one thing x such that it (i.e. x) is a cat and it (i.e. x) is playful.

This obviously calls for the existential quantifier symbol, and we end up with the following (using the obvious predicate letters):

$\exists x(Cx \bullet Px)$

There are two important things to note here. First of all, the parentheses play a vital role: everything within the parentheses lies within the scope of the existential quantifier out at the front. So, the following would *not* capture the form of the sentence:

$$\exists xCx \bullet Px \qquad \longleftarrow \text{ INCORRECT!}$$

This is an open sentence. It would read as something like "there are some cats and playfulness"—this is not a sentence in the logical sense at all. The second thing to note is that the main operator within the parentheses is the '•.' This is appropriate: the sentence says that some cats are playful, i.e. there is at least one thing that is *both* a cat *and* playful. The sentence is committed to the existence of at least one playful cat! The rule of thumb this time is that whenever we have an existential quantifier on the "outside," then the main operator on the "inside" of the parentheses after the quantifier will be a '•.' Again, there will be some exceptions to this rule of thumb, but the vast majority of cases end up like this.

It is worth summarizing why the other operators do not work for this kind of sentence:

∃x(Cx ⊃ Px)	There is at least one thing x such that if it is a cat, then it is playful.	This may be true, but note that it can be true in the absence of any cats at all! The original sentence is committed to the existence of playful cats, as is the correct translation above.
∃x(Cx ∨ Px)	There is at least one thing x such that it is either a cat or playful.	Again, this may be true—but it is again not committed to the existence of cats that are playful. A disjunction is true whenever at least one of its disjuncts is true. Consequently, this translation is true in a world that has playful things but no cats.
∃x(Cx ≡ Px)	There is at least one thing x such that it is a cat if and only if it is playful.	This is an incorrect translation for the same reason that having a conditional sentence inside the parentheses is an incorrect translation: the sentence can be true in the absence of cats.

We can also translate existential affirmatives using the universal quantifier. And, as before, we can convince ourselves of this in two ways. First, we can paraphrase the original English sentence we're working with: to say that some cats are playful is to say the following:

Not all cats are not playful.

That is:

It is not the case that everything that is a cat is not playful.

This sentence can be re-stated as follows:

It is not the case that for all x, if x is a cat, then x is not playful.

And this generates the following sentence of PL:

~∀x(Cx ⊃ ~Px)

So, this also captures the original sentence. Here are the two equivalent sentences side by side:

$$∃x(Cx • Px) \qquad \Longleftarrow \qquad ~∀x(Cx ⊃ ~Px)$$

Transforming one sentence into the other is simply a matter of following the same four steps outlined earlier. And to further appreciate that these two sentences of PL are logically equivalent, we can once more make use of some of our rules of inference from the last chapter:

∃x(Cx • Px)	The first version of the translation of the existential affirmative
~∀x~(Cx • Px)	Recall from earlier in this chapter that the quantifier symbols are inter-definable.
~∀x(~Cx ∨ ~Px)	This follows via an application of the **DeM** rule to everything after the '~∀x'.
~∃x(Cx ⊃ ~Px)	This follows via an application of the **MC** rule to the formula inside the parentheses.

Once more, this line of reasoning pertains to PL proofs, which we haven't yet considered. Nevertheless, I hope it helps you see how everything fits together.

Let us next consider the following sentence:

No dogs are reptiles.

This type of sentence, and all sentences that can be paraphrased as *"No A's are B's,"* is called a *Universal Negative*. To see why this is an appropriate description, note that the sentence can be rephrased as follows:

All dogs are not reptiles.

That is, the sentence is making a universal claim: all things that belong to the category of dogs do not belong to the category of reptiles. This can be translated very similarly to a universal affirmative sentence: we simply need an appropriately placed negation:

$\forall x(Dx \supset {\sim}Rx)$

Note that on the "outside" we have a universal quantifier, which means that on the "inside" the main operator is a '$\supset$.' And, as before, this can also be translated using an existential quantifier. Using the steps described earlier, the sentence becomes the following:

${\sim}\exists x(Dx \bullet Rx)$

In English, this can be read as follows:

There is no thing x such that it (i.e. x) is both a dog and a reptile.

And this can obviously be turned into our original sentence:

No dogs are reptiles.

Which of these sentences of PL should we offer as the translation? Answer: that's up to you! For some people, the most natural translation is the one that uses the universal quantifier; for others, it's the translation with the existential quantifier. Both translations adequately capture the form of the original sentence.

One final kind of sentence to cover here is called an *Existential Negative*. Here is an example of this:

Some trees are not evergreens.

This kind of sentence can be paraphrased as *"some A's are not B's"*; it asserts that some things in one category do not belong to some other category. The translation here is similar to that for an existential affirmative, but with an appropriately placed negation, as follows:

$\exists x(Tx \bullet {\sim}Ex)$

That is, there is at least one thing that is both a tree and not an evergreen. Using the steps outlined earlier, we can also write out a translation that has the universal quantifier:

${\sim}\forall x(Tx \supset Ex)$

Stating this in English, we get the following:

Not all trees are evergreens.

In other words, some trees are not evergreens—which is the sentence we started out with. Here, then, is a summary of what we covered in this section:

Sentences of this form . . .	. . . are translated into PL as follows:
Universal Affirmative All A's are B's *which is equivalent to* No A's are not B's	$\forall x(Ax \supset Bx)$ *which is equivalent to* $\sim\exists x(Ax \bullet \sim Bx)$
Existential Affirmative Some A's are B's *which is equivalent to* Not all A's are not B's	$\exists x(Ax \bullet Bx)$ *which is equivalent to* $\sim\forall x(Ax \supset \sim Bx)$
Universal Negative All A's are not B's *which is equivalent to* No A's are B's	$\forall x(Ax \supset \sim Bx)$ *which is equivalent to* $\sim\exists x(Ax \bullet Bx)$
Existential Negative Some A's are not B's *which is equivalent to* Not all A's are B's	$\exists x(Ax \bullet \sim Bx)$ *which is equivalent to* $\sim\forall x(Ax \supset Bx)$

Exercise Set 7.3

Q1. Translate each of the following sentences into the language of Predicate Logic (PL). In each case, provide *two* correct translations, one that uses the universal quantifier and one that uses the existential quantifier. I have listed the obvious predicate letters to use in your translation. Assume the universal domain. Write your answers in the spaces provided. The first one is done for you.

1. All nurses have degrees (N, D).

Translation with '∀':	**Translation with '∃':**
∀x(Nx ⊃ Dx	~∃x(Nx • ~Dx)

2. Some trees are old (O, T).

Translation with '∀':	**Translation with '∃':**

3. Not all video games are fun (V, F).

Translation with '∀':	**Translation with '∃':**

4. No vegetables contain seeds (V, S).

Translation with '∀':	**Translation with '∃':**

5. Some snails are not fast (S, F).

Translation with '∀':	**Translation with '∃':**

6. No tooth is not made of enamel (T, E).

Translation with '∀':	**Translation with '∃':**

7. Not all footballs are not round (F, R).

> **Translation with '∀':**   **Translation with '∃':**

8. All non-persons have no rights (P, R).

> **Translation with '∀':**   **Translation with '∃':**

9. Every dooble is a pooble (D, P).

> **Translation with '∀':**   **Translation with '∃':**

10. None of my potato plants have grown (P, G).

> **Translation with '∀':**   **Translation with '∃':**

Q2. Translate each of the following sentences into the language of PL. In this case, just one correct translation, using either quantifier, is sufficient. I have listed the obvious predicate letters to use in your translation. Assume the universal domain. Write your answers in the space provided. The first one is done for you.

1. All giraffes are vegetarians (G, V).

> **Translation:**   ∀x(Gx ⊃ Vx)

2. No primates have tails (P, T).

> **Translation:**

3. All Klingons are not Vulcans (K, V).

> **Translation:**

4. Some criminals are not evil (C, E).

> **Translation:**

5. Some maps are three-dimensional (M, T).

> **Translation:**

6. Not all jellyfish are poisonous, but some are (J, P).

> **Translation:**

7. Some TVs are digital, and some are not digital (T, D).

> **Translation:**

8. Some cats are nice, but none of them are derpy (C, N, D).

> **Translation:**

9. Whales are mammals, but sharks are not (W, M, S).

> **Translation:**

10. If no iPhones are cheap, then all iPhones must be awesome (I, C, A).

> **Translation:**

11. Every atom has a nucleus, and all of them have protons; however, some atoms do not have neutrons (A, N_1, P, N_2).

> **Translation:**

12. Some, but not all, chimpanzees know sign language (C, K).

> **Translation:**

13. If every dog is a fish and if all fish are mammals, then all dogs are mammals (D, F, M).

Translation:

14. Platypuses are mammals, even though they lay eggs (P, M, E).

Translation:

15. Some cats can swim, some cats can't swim, but all of them do not like water (C, S, W).

Translation:

7.4 More Complex Sentences

Some sentences will have more than just two predicates to deal with. In such cases, however, we can usually rephrase and make use of our insights in the previous section. Consider the following sentence, for example:

All pet lizards are sleepy.

Here is a symbolization key that we can use to translate this sentence:

UD: everything
Px: x is a pet.
Lx: x is a lizard.
Sx: x is sleepy.

Even though there are more than two categories involved here, we can still analyze the sentence as a universal affirmative:

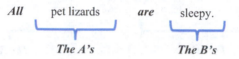

Everything between the words "All" and "are" here falls into the **A** category. In this case, this includes all those things that are both pets and lizards. Everything after the word "are" falls into the **B** category. In this case, these are the things that are sleepy. We translate as follows:

∀x[(Px • Lx) ⊃ Sx] .

We have to be careful here to include everything within the scope of the quantifier. Also, remember our rule of thumb: there is a universal quantifier on the "outside," so the main operator on the "inside" is a '⊃.' Here is another example:

Some expensive houses are neither old nor big.

Here is a symbolization key that we can use to translate this sentence:

UD: everything
Bx: x is big.
Ex: x is expensive.
Ox: x is old.

Even though there are more than two categories involved here, we can analyze the sentence as an existential affirmative:

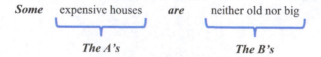

Everything between the words "Some" and "are" falls into the **A** category. In this case, this includes all those things that are expensive and are also houses. Everything after the word "are" falls into the **B** category. In this case, this includes those things that are neither old nor big. Remembering how to translate "neither" sentences, we translate as follows:

∃x[(Ex • Hx) • ~(Ox ∨ Bx)]

Again, we were careful to include everything within the scope of the quantifier. Also, notice that the main connective "inside" is the '•'—this corresponds to our rule of thumb for cases where there is an existential quantifier on the "outside."

Here is one more example in the same vein:

Not all computers or smartphones use either Microsoft or Apple software.

Here is a symbolization key:

UD: Everything
Cx: x is a computer.
Sx: x is a smartphone.
Mx: x uses Microsoft software.
Ax: x uses Apple software.

Looking closely at this sentence, we can analyze it as follows:

Not all   computers or smartphones   *use*   Microsoft or Apple software.

The A's   *The B's*

We can interpret the phrase "use Microsoft or Apple software" as "are such that they use Microsoft or Apple software," and understand the sentence as taking the form "***Not all A's are B's***." We end up with the following translation:

$\sim\forall x[(Cx \vee Sx) \supset (Mx \vee Ax)]$

Or, equivalently:

$\exists x[(Cx \vee Sx) \bullet \sim(Mx \vee Ax)]$

"Only" Sentences

Just like in SL, in PL we have to be careful with "only" sentences. Consider the following, for example:

Only lawyers are rich.

Note right away that this does *not* assert that all lawyers are rich. Instead, it is asserting the following:

For all x, x is rich only if x is a lawyer.

From SL, recall that the "only if"-clause of a sentence is the consequent of a conditional. This means that the following sentence of PL captures the above-mentioned sentence (using the obvious predicate letters):

$\forall x(Rx \supset Lx)$

In general, if a sentence can be rephrased as "***Only A's are B's***," it is translated as the following:

$\forall x(Bx \supset Ax)$

Here is another example:

The only mammal that lays eggs is the platypus.

This is a tricky sentence. Not only do we have three predicates or categories to worry about, the English sentence is constructed in such a way that the "only" *category* is located in the sentence away from the *word* "only." As usual, paraphrasing can make the sentence more manageable:

Only platypuses are egg-laying mammals.

That is:

For all x, x is a mammal and lays eggs only if x is a platypus.

Using the obvious predicate letters, we end up with:

$\forall x[(Mx \bullet Ex) \supset Px]$

"And" Complications

Here is another sentence that has the potential to trip us up:

Dogs and cats are mammals.

At first glance, we might offer the following translation (using the obvious predicate letters):

$$\forall x[(Dx \bullet Cx) \supset Mx] \longleftarrow \text{ INCORRECT!}$$

This however, would be a mistake! Changing this sentence of PL back into English, we would end up with the following:

For all x, if x is both a dog and a cat, then x is a mammal.

However, the original English sentence is surely *not* asserting that anything that is both a dog and a cat—a dog-cat or cat-dog?—is a mammal! Rather, looking more closely at the original sentence, we can see that it is asserting the following:

All dogs are mammals and all cats are mammals.

What we have, then, is a conjunction of two universally quantified sentences. This can be translated easily enough:

$\forall x(Dx \supset Mx) \bullet \forall x(Cx \supset Mx)$

Alternatively, we can interpret the original sentence as asserting the following:

Anything that is either a dog or a cat is a mammal.

This gives us the translation:

$\forall x[(Dx \vee Cx) \supset Mx]$

Both of these translations are correct. In general, sentences that can be rephrased as "*A's and B's are C's*" are translated as follows:

$\forall x(Ax \supset Cx) \bullet \forall x(Bx \supset Cx)$

or as follows:

$\forall x[(Ax \lor Bx) \supset Cx]$

Let us examine one more potential complication in the same vein. Here is the sentence for us to consider:

Some doctors and nurses drink coffee.

We know we should be careful here! Let's paraphrase:

Some doctors drink coffee and some nurses drink coffee.

This results in the following translation (using the obvious predicate letters):

$\exists x(Dx \bullet Cx) \bullet \exists x(Nx \bullet Cx)$

And, like in the earlier example, there is an equivalent translation:

$\exists x[(Dx \lor Nx) \bullet Cx]$

In English, this latter can be read as follows:

There is at least one thing that is either a doctor or a nurse and drinks coffee.

Let us us summarize from this section:

Sentences of this form . . .	. . . are translated into PL as follows:
Only A's are B's.	$\forall x(Bx \supset Ax)$
A's and B's are C's.	$\forall x(Ax \supset Cx) \bullet \forall x(Bx \supset Cx)$ *which is equivalent to* $\forall x[(Ax \lor Bx) \supset Cx]$
Some A's and some B's are C's.	$\exists x(Ax \bullet Cx) \bullet \exists x(Bx \bullet Cx)$ *which is equivalent to* $\exists x[(Ax \lor Bx) \bullet Cx]$

Exercise Set 7.4

Q1. Translate each of the following sentences into the language of Predicate Logic (PL). In each case, I have listed the obvious predicate letters to use in your translation. Assume the universal domain. Write your answers in the space provided. The first one is done for you.

1. Some movies are big and loud (M, B, L).

Translation:	∃x(Mx • Bx • Lx)

2. All loud movies are exciting (L, M, E).

   Translation:

3. Only the good die young (G, D).

   Translation:

4. Not all gray elephants are from Africa (G, E, A).

   Translation:

5. All burgers that are well done are too dry (B, W, T).

   Translation:

6. There are no small people in the NBA (S, P, N).

   Translation:

7. Broccoli is the only super-vegetable (B, S).

   Translation:

8. All people are either happy or sad (P, H, S).

> **Translation:**

9. Both snakes and lizards are reptiles (S, L, R).

> **Translation:**

10. Some friendly politicians should not be trusted (F, P, T).

> **Translation:**

11. A few lions are nice and cuddly (L, N, C).

> **Translation:**

12. All well-crafted musical instruments play beautifully (W, M, P).

> **Translation:**

13. All kids are well-behaved unless they are hungry (K, W, H).

> **Translation:**

14. Only well-trained dogs don't bite (W, D, B).

> **Translation:**

15. Hammers and saws are not toys (H, S, T).

> **Translation:**

16. Some liquids and gases are poisonous and should be avoided (L, G, P, A).

> **Translation:**

17. Not all cars and motorcycles are legal (C, M, L).

> **Translation:**

18. All emojis are neither fun nor interesting (E, F, I).

> **Translation:**

19. All dogs wag their tail and shed hair (D, W, S).

> **Translation:**

20. A robot won the marathon (R, W).

> **Translation:**

21. A robot is an artificial human (R, A).

> **Translation:**

22. Anything that makes me laugh is either funny or absurd (M, F, A).

> **Translation:**

23. Not every pumpkin is huge and orange (P, H, O).

> **Translation:**

24. Labrador Retrievers are either black or yellow or chocolate (L, B, G, C).

> **Translation:**

25. No Labrador Retrievers are blue unless they have been painted (L, B, P).

> **Translation:**

Q2. Using the symbolization key given, translate each sentence into the language of PL.

UD: Everything
Dx: x is a dinosaur.
Fx: x has feathers.
Bx: x is a bird.
Cx: x is cute.
Lx: x can fly.
d: Daffy
t: Tweety

1. Tweety is a cute bird, but Daffy is not.
2. All birds are feathered dinosaurs.
3. Not all dinosaurs are feathered birds.
4. Only birds have feathers.
5. Both Tweety and Daffy are feathered dinosaurs.
6. Some birds are dinosaurs and some are not dinosaurs.
7. Daffy is a cute feathered dinosaur.
8. Tweety is a bird and only birds can fly.
9. Feathered dinosaurs and birds can fly.
10. All and only cute birds can fly.
11. If Tweety is a bird and also a feathered dinosaur, then everything that is a bird is a feathered dinosaur.
12. If only birds are feathered dinosaurs, then Tweety is a feathered dinosaur.

Q3. Translate each of the following sentences into the language of PL. I have listed the obvious predicate letters, and constant letters, to use in your translation. Assume the universal domain.

1. If everyone has an immortal soul, then Abigail has one (P, I, a).
2. Either every elephant has floppy ears or no elephant has floppy ears (E, F).
3. Some doctors have medical degrees, but none have PhDs (D, M, P).
4. Some people like tea, while others like coffee (P, T, C).
5. Some itches can be scratched, but some are impossible to reach (I, S, R).
6. Not all exercise will help, but only exercise will help (E, H).
7. Melanie is a cheerleader, and Naomi is a cheerleader, but not everyone enrolled in University College is a cheerleader (m, n, U, P, E).
8. All pianists have ten fingers, but a few have eleven fingers (P, T, E).
9. Anything that is either sweet or salty is yummy (S_1, S_2, T).
10. Lions, tigers, and ocelots are all cats (L, T, O, C).
11. Either Stephen Curry or LeBron James are basketball players, or no one is (s, l, B, P).
12. All books are worth reading if they are fictional (B, W, F).

7.5 Relational Predicates

All the predicates we have looked at so far have been one-place, or monadic, predicates. Not all predicates are like this, however. Consider the following sentence, for example:

Jorge is faster than Herbert.

Taking the names out of this sentence, with a view to using individual constant letters to symbolize them, we are left with something like the following symbolization key, which includes a predicate with *two* "gaps" (notice that we are using a narrower UD as well):

UD: All persons
F__ __: __ is faster than __
h: Herbert
j: Jorge

We can dip into our box of variable letters to describe the predicate here as follows:

Fxy: x is faster than y.

'F' here is a ***two-place***, or ***dyadic***, or ***relational***, predicate. Once more, the predicate expression is not a sentence all by itself: 'Fxy' is describing a *relation* "is faster than" that can exist between two entities. In this relation, whatever is in the 'x' position is faster than whatever is in the 'y' position. To transform this into a sentence, we insert an individual constant letter into each variable position:

Fjh

This correctly captures the claim that Jorge is faster than Herbert. Note that it is crucial that we position each individual constant letter appropriately. The following PL sentence is importantly different, for example:

Fhj

In this case, the claim is that Herbert is faster than Jorge. We can also describe predicates with more than two "gaps." Consider this sentence:

Mary is closer to Niamh than Olivia.

Here is a symbolization key for the sentence, which includes a ***three-place*** predicate:

UD: All persons
Cxyz: x is closer to y than z.
m: Mary
n: Niamh
o: Olivia

The sentence can then be translated as follows:

Cmno

Again, the order in which the individual constant letters are "inserted into" the predicate is crucial here. It is possible to describe predicates with even more "gaps." Three-place predicates, and predicates with more than three "gaps," are called *many-valued*, or *polyadic,* predicates. With the exception of just a few straightforward three-place predicates, we will not be concerned with such predicates in this book.

Combining Quantifiers and Relational Predicates

To work through some examples here, let's use the following symbolization key:

UD: All persons
Lxy: x loves y.
j: John
m: Mary

Here is an easy sentence to start with:

John loves Mary.

This is translated as follows:

Ljm

Here is another one:

Someone loves John.

The "some" here tells us that using the existential quantifier will be the most natural way to translate the sentence. Remember, also, that the UD includes only persons here, so there is no need for our translation to insist that the entity that is loving John is a person. Consequently, the sentence can be rephrased as follows:

There is at least one person x such that he/she (i.e. this x) loves John.

We end up with the following sentence of PL:

∃xLxj

One of the "gaps" in the relational predicate expression 'Lxy' is filled with a constant, while the other one remains a variable; this variable is bound by the existential quantifier. Here is another sentence:

Mary loves somebody.

We can paraphrase this as follows:

There is at least one person x such that Mary loves him/her (i.e. this x).

And this is captured in PL as follows:

∃xLmx

You might be wondering why this translation uses the variable letter 'x' instead of the variable letter 'y.' After all, the predicate as defined in the symbolization key has 'x' in the first position—the "loving" position, so to speak; and it has 'y' in the second position—the "being loved" position. So, shouldn't the translation be the following:

∃yLmy

Well, as it turns out, these two translations amount to the same thing. Remember, a variable is basically just a placeholder for some constant or other to come along. All of our translations so far that have used the variable letter 'x' could have been written using the variable letter 'y.' We could also have used the letter 'z.' However, we have followed the convention that when there is one variable letter required, we use 'x.' If more than one is required, then we move on to using 'y' and 'z.'

Let's try another sentence:

Everyone who loves John also loves Mary.

We can paraphrase this sentence as follows:

For all persons x, if he/she (i.e. this x) loves John, then he/she (i.e. this x) also loves Mary.

And this can be captured in PL like this:

$\forall x(Lxj \supset Lxm)$

Things can get even more complicated. Consider the following sentence, for example:

Everybody loves everybody.

There are two instances of the word "everybody" here, so our translation should have two universal quantifier symbols. Also, note that no person is named in this sentence, so there will be no constant letters in the translation. Let's try to paraphrase:

All persons x love all persons y.

With the appearance of the second quantifier term, we use a second variable letter 'y.' Here is another paraphrase that will guide us toward an adequate translation:

For all persons x and for all persons y, x loves y.

This sentence is translated into PL as follows:

$\forall x \forall y Lxy$

What we have here is a sentence with *multiple* quantifiers, or *nested* quantifiers, i.e. sentences in which one quantifier is contained within the scope of another quantifier. Here is another sentence that will involve multiple quantifiers:

Everyone loves someone.

Paraphrasing this sentence, we get the following:

For all persons x there is at least one person y such that x loves y.

In PL, this ends up as:

$\forall x \exists y Lxy$

Unsurprisingly, the order in which these nested quantifiers appear can change the meaning of a sentence. Consider this sentence of PL, for example:

$\exists x \forall y Lxy$

In English, this says something like the following:

There is at least one person x such that for all persons y, x loves y.

Or, somewhat less awkwardly:

Someone loves everyone.

Sentences with multiple quantifiers can be tricky, so make sure to take the time to understand how they work. Let's do one more example. Consider this sentence:

No one at this party has ever met before.

We describe two new predicates and add them to the above symbolization key:

Px: x is at this party.
Mxy: x has met y before.

Here is a way of paraphrasing the sentence:

All persons x at this party are such that there is no person y at this party that x has met before.

Or, alternatively:

For all persons x, if x is at this party, then there is no person y such that y is at this party and x has met this y.

In PL, this becomes following:

$\forall x [Px \supset {\sim}\exists y (Py \bullet Mxy)]$

This is arguably the most complicated sentence of PL we have encountered so far. Take all the time you need to convince yourself that it captures the original English sentence. And make sure to work your way through Exercise Set 7.5!

Exercise Set 7.5

Q1. Translate each of the following sentences into the language of Predicate Logic (PL). In each case, a symbolization key is provided. Unless otherwise stated, assume the universal domain. Write your answers in the spaces provided. The first one is done for you.

1. Cuba will engage in diplomatic ties with the United States if the United States will engage in diplomatic ties with Cuba.

Symbolization Key:	**Dxy:** x will engage in diplomatic ties with y.
	c: Cuba
	u: The United States
Translation:	Duc ⊃ Dcu

2. Superman is faster than Batman, but Batman is cooler than Superman.

Symbolization Key:	**Fxy:** x is faster than y.
	Cxy: x is cooler than y.
	b: Batman
	s: Superman
Translation:	

3. If France goes to war with Germany, then France will also go to war with Italy.

Symbolization Key:	**Wxy:** x goes to war with y.
	f: France
	g: Germany
	i: Italy
Translation:	

4. No one is taller than Delia *[In this case, the **UD** is "all persons"]*

Symbolization Key:	**Txy:** x is taller than y.
	d: Delia
Translation:	

5. Malcolm does not visit Nigel, and vice versa.

Symbolization Key:	**Vxy:** x visits y.
	m: Malcolm
	n: Nigel
Translation:	

6. If Middle Earth goes to war with Narnia, and Narnia goes to war with The Upside Down, then Middle Earth goes to war with The Upside Down.

Symbolization Key:　　　　　　**Wxy:** x goes to war with y.
　　　　　　　　　　　　　　　　　　　　　m: Middle Earth
　　　　　　　　　　　　　　　　　　　　　n: Narnia
　　　　　　　　　　　　　　　　　　　　　u: The Upside Down

Translation:

---

7. Jeremiah has at least one cousin. *[In this case, the **UD** is "all persons."]*

Symbolization Key:　　　　　　**Cxy:** x is y's cousin.
　　　　　　　　　　　　　　　　　　　　　j: Jeremiah

Translation:

---

8. Everybody has at least one cousin. *[In this case, the **UD** is "all persons."]*

Symbolization Key:　　　　　　**Cxy:** x is y's cousin.

Translation:

---

9. No planet is bigger than Jupiter.

Symbolization Key:　　　　　　**Bxy:** x is bigger than y.
　　　　　　　　　　　　　　　　　　　　　j: Jupiter

Translation:

---

10. Every movie directed by James Cameron has a lot of action sequences.

Symbolization Key:　　　　　　**Ax:** x has lots of action sequences.
　　　　　　　　　　　　　　　　　　　　　Mx: x is a movie.
　　　　　　　　　　　　　　　　　　　　　Dxy: x is directed by y.
　　　　　　　　　　　　　　　　　　　　　j: James Cameron

Translation:

---

11. Sarah died of a tropical disease.

> **Symbolization Key:**   **Dx:** x is a disease.
> **Tx:** x is tropical.
> **Dxy:** x died of y.
> **s:** Sarah
>
> **Translation:**

12. Everything has a gravitational attraction to something.

> **Symbolization Key:**   **Gxy:** x has a gravitational attraction to y.
>
> **Translation:**

13. Timmy is a pacifist, but if Vernon hits him, then Timmy will hit Vernon back.

> **Symbolization Key:**   **Px:** x is a pacifist.
> **Hxy:** x hits y.
> **t:** Timmy
> **v:** Vernon
>
> **Translation:**

14. If Eileen is more closely related to Fred than Greg is, then Damien is more closely related to Eileen than Harry is.

> **Symbolization Key:**   **Cxyz:** x is more closely related to y than z is.
> **d:** Damien
> **e:** Eileen
> **f:** Fred
> **g:** Greg
> **h:** Harry
>
> **Translation:**

15. Every scientist who discovers something is either a genius or a hard worker.

> **Symbolization Key:**   **Sx:** x is a scientist.
> **Gx:** x is a genius.
> **Hx:** x is a hard worker.
> **Dxy:** x discovers y.
>
> **Translation:**

16. Jason failed every quiz that Maura passed.

Symbolization Key:	**Qx:** x is a quiz.
	Fxy: x failed y.
	Pxy: x passed y.
	j: Jason
	m: Maura
Translation:	

Q2. Using the symbolization key given, translate each sentence into the language of Predicate Logic (PL).

UD: All persons
Ax: x is American.
Cx: x is a CEO.
Px: is a professional athlete.
Ex: x is European.
Rxy: x is richer than y
Vxy: x has visited y.
p: The pope
q: The queen

1. The pope has visited the queen, and the queen has visited the pope.
2. No one has visited the pope.
3. Every American has visited the queen.
4. Every professional athlete who is a CEO has visited the queen.
5. Everyone has visited the pope, but no one has visited the queen.
6. No CEO has visited both the queen and the pope.
7. Some CEOs are professional athletes, some professional athletes are European, but no CEOs are European.
8. All American professional athletes are richer than the pope.
9. Everyone has visited someone.
10. The pope is European, and all Europeans have visited the queen.
11. The queen has visited everyone the pope has visited.
12. All Europeans have visited someone who is a CEO.

7.6 Identity

Consider the following sentence:

Stefani Germanotta is Lady Gaga.

(This sentence is true: the person we know as "Lady Gaga" grew up in New York under the name "Stefani Germanotta"). How should we translate this sentence into PL? Removing the proper names with a view to translating those with individual constant letters, we are left with the following:

_____ is _____

What should we do with the word "is"? Sometimes when we use the word "is," we are ascribing a property to someone or something. For example, "Lady Gaga is talented." However, this is not what is going on in the above sentence. At other times when we use the word "is," we are simply asserting that someone or something exists. For example, "Stefani Germanotta is." Again, this is not what is going on in our example. Rather, what we have in the sentence is an assertion that the entity referred to by the name "Stefani Germanotta" is *related* in some way to the entity referred to by the name "Lady Gaga." More specifically, these two entities are *identical*, i.e. they are one and the same entity. We could capture this relation as follows:

Ixy: x is identical to y.

Logicians call this ***the "is" of identity***. It is a relation that holds between an entity and itself. It is such an important relational predicate, however, and can help us capture the form of so many different kinds of sentences, that it is conventional to use a special symbol to refer to it. This symbol is one we are all familiar with: '=.' It is not usually included in a symbolization key. Using the obvious individual constant letters, then, we can now translate the above sentence as follows:

$s = l$

This seems nice and straightforward! And all simple identity statements are treated like this. We will also use the symbol '$\neq$' sign to indicate that this relation does not apply between two entities. For example, using the obvious individual constant letters, the sentence

Vladimir Putin is not Donald Trump

is translated as

$p \neq t$

Let us put the identity symbol to work in more complicated examples. We will use the following symbolization key:

UD: everything
Px: x is a planet.
Rx: x is red.
Sx: x is a star.
Bxy: x is bigger than y.
m: Mars
j: Jupiter

"... at least ..."

We have been using the existential quantifier to capture sentences like the following:

There is at least one planet.

Here is the sentence's translation into PL:

∃xPx

How about a sentence like this?

There are at least two planets.

It looks like we should use two existential quantifiers here: Maybe '∃xPx • ∃yPy.' Or perhaps '∃x∃y(Px • Py).' However, there is nothing in either of these translations to indicate that the variables 'x' and 'y' pick out two *different* planets. The original sentence is asserting that there are at least two *non-identical* planets. We can use the identity symbol to capture this aspect of the sentence:

∃x∃y(Px • Py • x ≠ y)

This can be read as follows:

There is at least one thing x and at least one thing y such that x is a planet, and y is a planet, and x is not identical to y.

As far as this sentence is concerned, two non-identical things are planets—as required. To symbolize the assertion that there are at least three planets, we would need to use the individual variable letter 'z':

∃x∃y∃z(Px • Py • Pz • x ≠ y • x ≠ z • y ≠ z)

Similar, and ever-longer, sentences of PL can capture sentences that assert the existence of at least four planets, at least five planets, and so on.

"... at most ..."

Here is the example we will use here:

There is at most one star.

In this case, we need to insist that any time it looks like we have identified two things that are stars, these two things are, in fact, one and the same thing. Here, then, is a paraphrase:

For all x and for all y, if both x and y are stars, then x is identical to y.

In PL, this becomes the following:

∀x∀y[(Sx • Sy) ⊃ x = y]

Note that this does not commit us to the existence of any stars. Instead, it says that *if* there are any stars, there is at most one of them. Let's try another sentence:

There are at most two stars.

Here is a paraphrase, similar to the one we outlined for the previous sentence:

For all x, for all y, and for all z, if x, y, and z are all stars, then two of them must be identical.

And this can be captured in PL as follows:

$\forall x \forall y \forall z [(Sx \bullet Sy \bullet Sz) \supset (x = y \lor x = z \lor y = z)]$

Again, this sentence does not commit us to the existence of any stars.

". . . exactly one thing . . ."

Here is our example:

There is exactly one star.

Unlike the previous sentences, this sentence *is* committed to the existence of a star. However, we have to rule out the existence of any *other* star. Here is a paraphrase that will help us on our way:

There is at least one thing x such that x is a star and, for all things y, if y is a star, then x is identical to y.

Here, we rule out the existence of any other star by insisting that any star we come across is identical to the star that we asserted exists. In PL, this becomes:

$\exists x [Sx \bullet \forall y (Sy \supset x = y)]$

We can also capture the assertion that there are exactly two stars. Here is a paraphrase of that claim:

There is at least one thing x and at least one thing y such that x is a star, y is a star, x is not identical to y, and for all things z, if z is a star, then x is identical to z, or y is identical to z.

In other words, there are two non-identical things that are stars, and anything that is a star must be identical to one of these two stars. In PL, this is written as follows:

$\exists x \exists y \{Sx \bullet Sy \bullet x \neq y \bullet \forall z [Sz \supset (x = z \lor y = z)]\}$

This is obviously not the most easily-parsed sentence, but take some time to work through it.

". . . The only . . ."

Here is another sentence for us to consider:

Mars is the only planet.

In this case, we need to state that Mars is a planet, but we also need to rule out the possibility that anything else is a planet. Here is a paraphrase that will help us get to a translation in PL:

Mars is a planet, and for all things x, if x is a planet, then x is identical to Mars.

Or, alternatively:

Mars is a planet, and all planets are identical to Mars.

And here is the sentence in PL:

$Pm \bullet \forall x(Px \supset x = m)$

Let's try another, slightly more complicated, example:

Mars is the only red planet.

Here is the same sentence paraphrased:

Mars is a planet and Mars is red, and anything x that is a red planet is identical to Mars.

Here is this sentence in PL:

$Pm \bullet Rm \bullet \forall x[(Px \bullet Rx) \supset x = m]$

Superlatives

Let's try to translate the following sentence:

Jupiter is the biggest planet.

Here, we need to assert that Jupiter is a planet, but also that no planet is bigger than Jupiter. Here is a paraphrase:

Jupiter is a planet, and if anything is a planet and not identical to Jupiter, then Jupiter is bigger than it.

This can also be stated as follows:

Jupiter is a planet, and for all things x, if x is a planet and not identical to Jupiter, then Jupiter is bigger than it (i.e. x).

In PL, this becomes:

$Pj \bullet \forall x[(Px \bullet x \neq j) \supset Bjx]$

Definite Descriptions

Recall that, in English, a proper name is a singular term that picks out just one individual entity. In PL, we use individual constant letters to translate proper names. A **definite description** is another type of singular term in that it also picks out one specific entity—by *describing* it instead of *naming* it. Here are a few sentences that use definite descriptions:

- The tallest man in the room has red hair
- The author of the Harry Potter book series is from Scotland
- The man in the high castle is a Nazi

In each of these sentences, the first phrase (selected) picks out just one entity; the second part of the sentence attributes some property or other to that entity. Translating proper names was easy, but working with definite descriptions is somewhat more complex. Let's work through an example, using the same symbolization key as given earlier. Here is the sentence:

The planet is red.

The key to understanding definite descriptions is to see how they successfully "zoom in" on one, and only one, entity. In this case, we have to capture the claim that something is a planet and that, in the current context at least, *nothing else* is a planet. Then, of course, we have to articulate that this entity is red. We can paraphrase, as follows:

There is at least one thing x such that:

- x is a planet.
- For all things y, if y is a planet, then x = y.
- x is red.

This results in the following sentence of PL:

$\exists x[Px \bullet \forall y(Py \supset y = x) \bullet Rx]$

All definite descriptions can be treated in a similar way.

Exercise Set 7.6

Q1. Using the symbolization key given, translate each sentence into the language of Predicate Logic. Write your answers in the space provided. The first one is done for you.

UD: all people
Px: x is president of the United States.
Txy: x is taller than y.
o: Barack Obama
t: Donald Trump

1. Donald Trump and Barack Obama are not the same person.

Translation:	$t \neq o$

2. Donald Trump is US president and Barack Obama is not.

Translation:

3. There is more than one president of the United States.

Translation:

4. There is exactly one president of the United States.

Translation:

5. There is no president of the United States.

Translation:

6. The president of the United States is Donald Trump.

Translation:

7. Nobody is president of the United States except Donald Trump.

Translation:

8. Barack Obama is the tallest president of the United States.

> **Translation:**

9. Barack Obama is taller than Donald Trump, and no one is taller than Barack Obama.

> **Translation:**

10. Barack Obama is not the president of the United States.

> **Translation:**

Q2. Translate each of the following sentences into the language of PL. In each case, there is a symbolization key provided. Assume a UD of "all persons."

1. Abraham Lincoln is not George Washington (**l:** Abraham Lincoln; **w:** George Washington).
2. There is only one person coming to the party. (**Px:** x is coming to the party.)
3. There are at least two Duke fans at the game. (**Dx:** x is a Duke fan; **Gx:** x is at the game.)
4. There is at most one leader of each political party. (**Px:** x is a leader of a political party.)
5. The Swedish Chef lives in New York (**Sx:** x is Swedish; **Cx:** x is a chef; **Lx:** x lives in New York; **n:** New York).
6. Only the best people get hired. (**Hx:** x gets hired; **Bxy:** x is better than y.)
7. There are exactly two Germans living in Russia (**Gx:** x is German; **Lxy:** x lives in y; **r:** Russia).
8. Sean Combs is P Diddy, and he is also Puff Daddy (**s:** Sean Combs; **p:** P Diddy; **u:** Puff Daddy).
9. There is exactly one queen of England (**Qxy:** x is queen of y; **e:** England).
10. Bob owns at least two mirrors (**Mx:** x is a mirror; **Oxy:** x owns y; **b:** Bob).
11. There is only one Joe Biden (**b:** Joe Biden).
12. If anyone can save the United States, then Captain America can (**Sxy:** x can save y; **a:** Captain America; **u:** the United States).
13. The new guy is tall, dark, and handsome. (**Dx:** x is dark; **Hx:** x is handsome; **Nx:** x is a new guy; **Tx:** x is tall.)
14. There are at least two people waiting for the bathroom. (**Bx:** x is a bathroom; **Wxy:** x is waiting for y.)
15. Mary is the only person who brought lunch (**Lx:** x brought lunch; **m:** Mary).
16. The boy in the bubble has a baboon heart. (**B$_1$x:** x is a boy; **B$_2$x:** x is in a bubble; **B$_3$x:** x has a baboon heart.)
17. Only Shakespeare and James Joyce wrote masterpieces (**Mx:** x wrote masterpieces; **j:** James Joyce; **s:** Shakespeare).
18. There are no boys at the party except Roderick and Ultan (**Bx:** x is a boy; **Px:** x is at the party; **r:** Roderick; **u:** Ultan).
19. Bob is the only living boy in New York (**Bx:** x is a boy; **Lx:** x is living; **Ixy:** x is in y; **n:** New York).
20. Tommy loves Billy, and also himself, but he does not love anyone else (**Lxy:** x loves y; **b:** Billy; **t:** Tommy).

Q3. Translate each of the following sentences into the language of PL. In each case, there is a symbolization key provided. Assume the universal domain.

1. There is only one elephant in the room. (**Ex:** x is an elephant; **Rx:** x is in the room.)
2. There is at most one space station. (**Sx:** x is a space station.)
3. There are at least two beers on tap. (**Bx:** x is a beer; **Tx:** x is on tap.)
4. There are no more than two spiral galaxies. (**Sx:** x is a spiral galaxy.)
5. There is no mountain taller than Mount Everest (**Mx:** x is a mountain; **Hxy:** x is higher than y; **e:** Mount Everest).
6. Cleveland and Cincinnati are in Ohio, and there are no more big cities in that state (**Bx:** x is big; **Cx:** x is a city; **Ixy:** x is in y; **c:** Cleveland; **n:** Cincinnati; **o:** Ohio).
7. No one owns more than two cellphones. (**Cx:** x is a cellphone; **Oxy:** x owns y.)
8. Germany has at least one pop singer, but no more than two (**Px:** x is a pop singer; **Fxy:** x is from y; **g:** Germany).
9. There are at most two lions at the zoo. (**Lx:** x is a lion; **Zx:** x is at the zoo.)
10. The president of Uganda is the only president with a green tie (**Gx:** x has a green tie; **Px:** x is a president; **Pxy:** x is president of y; **u:** Uganda).
11. Los Angeles is the biggest city in America, but it is not the biggest city in the World. (**Cx:** x is a city; **Bxy:** x is bigger than y; **a:** America; **w:** the World).
12. No country in Europe except Spain has a king (**Cx:** x is a country; **Ex:** x is in Europe; **Kx:** x has a king; **s:** Spain).
13. The king of Mordor is evil (**Kxy:** x is a king of y; **Ex:** x is evil; **m:** Mordor).
14. Jupiter and Saturn are gas giants, and there are at least two other gas giants in the Solar System (**Gx:** x is a gas giant; **Ixy:** x is in y; **j:** Jupiter; **s:** Saturn; **y:** The Solar System).
15. All countries have exactly one national anthem. (**Cx:** x is a country; **Nxy:** x is a national anthem of y.)
16. My neighbor's dog is hairy and kind. (**Dx:** x is a dog; **Hx:** x is hairy; **Kx:** x is kind; **Nx:** x belongs to my neighbor.)
17. Portugal is not the only team from Europe that has won both the European Championship and the World Cup (**Txy:** x is a team from y; **Wxy:** x has won y; **e:** The European Championship; **p:** Portugal; **w:** The World Cup).
18. Turkey has at least two rugby teams, but the United States has only one (**Rx:** x has a rugby team; **t:** Turkey; **u:** the United States).
19. Alaska is the biggest state in the United States (**Sx:** x is a state; **Bxy:** x is bigger than y; **a:** Alaska; **u:** the United States).
20. Either the cat with a hat or the mouse with a house will win (Cx: x is a cat; Hx: x is with a hat; Mx: x is a mouse; Hx: x is with a house; Wx: x will win)

Chapter 8

Predicate Logic: Arguments—Proofs and Counterexamples

In the previous chapter, we learned how to capture the logical form of individual sentences by translating them into the language of Predicate Logic (PL). So, we should now be able to capture the logical form of *arguments* in PL. This is the focus of the first section of this chapter. Once we articulate an argument in the language of PL, we will then have to develop ways of evaluating it for validity. Accordingly, we will have to extend the proof system we developed in Chapters 5 and 6. Later in the chapter, we will also briefly look at a method for showing that a PL argument is invalid.

8.1 Arguments in Predicate Logic

Here is the argument we discussed at the beginning of Chapter 7:

All dogs are mammals. Ollie is a dog. Therefore, Ollie is a mammal.

Let us translate this into the language of PL. First, as we know from our experience of translating arguments into Sentential Logic (SL), every translation of an argument will need a symbolization key. Here is one for this argument:

UD: everything
Dx: x is a dog.
Mx: x is a mammal.
o: Ollie

As you can see, we are using the universal domain here. We might have limited it to all living things, or perhaps all things on earth, or something like that. However, unless narrowing the universe of discourse will obviously simplify the translation process, we will stick to using the universal domain. The argument certainly requires predicate letters for something's being a dog and something's being a mammal. The only named individual is Ollie, so we need just one individual constant letter. Here is the translation:

$$\forall x(Dx \supset Mx)$$
$$Do$$
$$\overline{}$$
$$\therefore Mo$$

And that's it! As with translating arguments into SL, other than getting the translation of the individual sentences right, the main issue is organizational: the premises and the conclusion must be clearly identified. So, let's modify the method we used in Chapter 2 for capturing the logical form of an argument in SL:

Translating an Argument from English into Predicate Logic

Step 1: Read through the argument and decide on an appropriate universe of discourse.

Step 2: Read through the argument again, and decide on *(a)* the predicate letters you will need and *(b)* the individual constant letters you will need.

Step 3: Write out the symbolization key. Make sure to include the universe of discourse, the predicate letters, and the individual constant letters.

Step 4: Identify the conclusion of the argument; the other sentences will be the argument's premises.

Step 5: Write out the logical form of the argument in PL.

With some practice, **Steps 1**, **2**, and **4** here may end up being performed at the same time, and ultimately inside your head. This is fine, as long as you end up with a neatly articulated symbolization key and the logical form of the argument.

Let's look at a more complicated example. Here is the argument:

> All schoolteachers have degrees. And only schoolteachers have the summer months off. The vice-president's wife is a schoolteacher. So, she must have a degree and have the summer months off.

Step 1 asks us to decide on a universe of discourse (UD). This argument is concerned with schoolteachers and wives, so a UD of "all people" is appropriate, and will simplify the translation process. **Step 2** is all about identifying the predicate letters and individual constant letters we will need. It looks like we will need to have predicate letters for all of the following: being a schoolteacher, having a degree, having the summer months off, and being a vice-president's wife. There is no person mentioned by name in the argument, so we will not need any individual constant letters. There is a definite description, though, i.e. "the vice-president's wife," so we will need to watch out for that! Here's our symbolization key:

> **UD:** All persons
> **Sx:** x is a schoolteacher.
> **Dx:** x has a degree.
> **Mx:** x has the summer months off.
> **Wx:** x is a vice-president's wife.

And that is **Step 3** done. **Step 4** asks us to identify the argument's conclusion. This is straightforward here: the conclusion is the last sentence of the argument. Finally, **Step 5** asks us to write out the logical form of the argument in PL. Here it is:

$$\forall x(Sx \supset Dx)$$
$$\forall x(Mx \supset Sx)$$
$$\exists x[Wx \bullet \forall y(Wy \supset y = x) \bullet Sx]$$
$$\overline{}$$
$$\therefore \exists x[Wx \bullet \forall y(Wy \supset y = x) \bullet Dx \bullet Mx]$$

You should look at each sentence here and convince yourself that it correctly translates the corresponding sentence of the argument. At this point, we will not concern ourselves with whether the argument is valid.

Exercise Set 8.1

Q1. Translate the following arguments into the language of Predicate Logic (PL). Make sure to provide a symbolization key, including a UD, in each case. Write your answers in the space provided. Ignore the issue of whether the argument is valid. The first one is done for you.

1. All elephants are mammals. All mammals have hair. Dumbo doesn't have hair. Therefore, Dumbo is not an elephant.

Symbolization Key:

UD: Everything
Ex: x is an elephant.
Mx: x is a mammal.
Hx: x has hair.
d: Dumbo.

Translation:

$\forall x(Ex \supset Mx)$
$\forall x(Mx \supset Hx)$
~Hd

_____

∴ ~Ed

---

2. If everyone goes to school, then at least some people will be educated. And if some people end up educated, then all of us will be better off. Consequently, if everyone goes to school, then all of us will be better off.

Symbolization Key:

Translation:

---

3. Tom works for Evelyn. Aubrey also works for Evelyn. We can conclude that at least two people work for Evelyn.

Symbolization Key:

Translation:

4. Everyone who has food poisoning was either at Martha's party or ate at the local restaurant. Fred was at Martha's party, so Fred must have food poisoning.

Symbolization Key:

Translation:

5. The president of the United Kingdom was born in Ghana. Anyone born in Ghana is highly intelligent. Therefore, the president of the United Kingdom is highly intelligent.

Symbolization Key:

Translation:

6. Some trees are carnivores and some trees are herbivores. However, no trees are omnivores. We can conclude, then, that Zelda is not a tree, seeing as she is not an omnivore.

Symbolization Key:

Translation:

7. iPhones and Android phones are both smartphones. I own a Google phone, so I must not own a smartphone.

Symbolization Key:

Translation:

8. Dogs are cute. Dogs are cuddly. Therefore, dogs are cute and cuddly.

Symbolization Key:

Translation:

9. All tall people who have taken a logic course are super-cool. Penelope is tall, but she has not taken a logic course. We have to conclude that Penelope is not super-cool.

Symbolization Key:

Translation:

10. If everybody is sad, then nobody is happy. However, Pharrell Williams is happy. Therefore, it must not be the case that everybody is sad.

Symbolization Key:

Translation:

11. Only rich people can run for president. Furthermore, only rich people can run for Congress. Consequently, Melissa cannot run for president or congress, since she isn't rich.

> **Symbolization Key:**
>
> **Translation:**

12. Some college students work hard. Furthermore, anybody who works hard will do well in life. Consequently, if college students work hard, they will do well in life.

> **Symbolization Key:**
>
> **Translation:**

8.2 Predicate Logic Proofs I: Universal Elimination and Existential Introduction

In PL, we will understand proofs in the same way as we understood SL proofs. That is, each line of a proof will either be a premise of the argument at hand, or derived from an earlier line of the proof via a valid inference rule. Furthermore, we will keep on board all the rules of inference we used when constructing proofs in SL: the basic inference rules, the derived inference rules, and the substitution rules. However, we will need some new rules to deal with the two quantifiers. We will focus on proving arguments that involve monadic predicates only. Proofs involving relational predicates are beyond the scope of this book.

We will be introducing a total of five new inference rules to our proof system. Here is a quick summary of each one:

Universal Elimination ($\forall$E)	This rule will enable us to validly remove the '$\forall$' from a universally quantified sentence.
Universal Introduction ($\forall$I)	This rule will enable us to validly create a universally quantified sentence.
Existential Elimination ($\exists$E)	This rule will enable us to validly remove the '$\exists$' from an existentially quantified sentence.
Existential Introduction ($\exists$I)	This rule will enable us to validly create an existentially quantified sentence.
Quantifier Exchange (QE)	This rule appeals to the fact that the '$\forall$' and the '$\exists$' are inter-definable. This is the sole Substitution Rule we will add.

As you can see, we are sticking with the Introduction/Elimination approach that we used in the SL natural deduction system. Let's work through each of these new inference rules.

Universal Elimination ($\forall$E)

A universally quantified sentence makes an assertion about *all* things; consequently, if the sentence is true, I can validly infer that what it says about all things is true of one *particular* thing. To use a familiar example: if it truly is the case that everything is fluffy, then, no matter what entity I encounter, I am guaranteed that it will be fluffy. That is, given that all things are fluffy, I can infer that Adam, or Bob, or any particular thing, is fluffy. In general, I can remove the universal quantifier and validly make an assertion about a specific case. All of the following, then, are valid inferences:

From . . .	. . . I can validly infer . . .
$\forall$xFx	Fa (for any constant a)
$\forall$x(Fx $\supset$ Gx)	Fs $\supset$ Gs (for any constant s)
$\forall$x[Px $\vee$ (Qx • Rx)]	Pb $\vee$ (Qb • Rb) (for any constant b)
$\forall$x~(Wx $\equiv$ Vx)	~(Wg $\equiv$ Vg) (for any constant g)

Each sentence in the left column is a universally quantified sentence. Each sentence in the right column is a *substitution instance* of the corresponding sentence in the left column: it results from removing the universal quantifier, and replacing each occurrence of the variable 'x' with an individual constant letter. This type of valid inference forms the basis of our first new inference rule, *Universal Elimination* ($\forall$E):

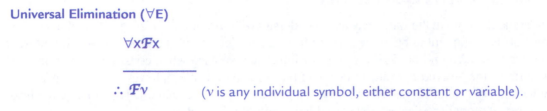

$$\forall x \mathcal{F}x$$
$$\overline{\qquad\qquad}$$
$$\therefore \mathcal{F}v \qquad\qquad (v \text{ is any individual symbol, either constant or variable}).$$

There are some important things to note about how this rule is articulated. First of all, the formula '$\forall x \mathcal{F}x$' represents *any* universally quantified sentence; that is, the '$\mathcal{F}x$' represents *any* formula involving a variable that lies inside the scope of the universal quantifier. Secondly, notice that in all of the above examples, I replaced a universally quantified sentence with a substitution instance involving an individual constant letter. However, the rule states that in '$\mathcal{F}v$,' the 'v' represents *any* individual symbol, either a constant *or a variable*. So, for example, from the sentence '$\forall x Px$' I can validly infer 'Px.' This might look a little weird—'Px' isn't even a sentence!—but it does make sense. However, let us postpone discussion of this until a little later. For the time being, anytime we apply the $\forall$**E** rule, we will use individual constant letters.

We can view this rule as a machine for removing universal quantifiers. If a universal quantifier is in the way, so to speak, then insert the universally quantified sentence into this rule, and out pops a non-quantified sentence that we can more easily work with:

A word of warning before moving on. The $\forall$**E** rule can be used whenever an *entire* line of a proof consists of a universally quantified sentence. So, remember: a universally quantified sentence is a sentence in which *everything* in the sentence lies within the scope of the universal quantifier. Not *all* sentences that have the universal quantifier in them are automatically universally quantified sentences. Here are some examples where the $\forall$**E** rule is *mis*applied:

From . . .	. . . I CANNOT use the $\forall$**E** rule to get . . .
~$\forall$x(Fx $\supset$ Gx)	~(Fa $\supset$ Ga)
$\forall$xPx $\lor$ $\forall$xQx	Pb $\lor$ Qb
Ge $\bullet$ $\forall$xTx	Ge $\bullet$ Te

All of the sentences in the left-hand column include a universal quantifier, but *none* of them is a universally quantified sentence—so the $\forall$**E** rule *cannot* be applied to them. In the third example, the inference from the sentence in the left-hand column to the sentence in the right-hand column is valid, but we would have to use the $\bullet$**E** and $\bullet$**I** inference rules to get from one to the other. Remember, we record *every* valid inference when we are constructing a proof!

It is time for some examples. Let's try to prove the following argument:

$\forall$x(Dx $\supset$ Mx), Do $\therefore$ Mo

We begin in the usual manner:

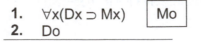

And, as usual, we pause and see if we can figure out how to trace a valid path from the premises to the conclusion. At first glance, lines 1 and 2 together look like they present an opportunity to use the ⊃E rule, which would result in the conclusion right away. However, the sentence on line 1 is not a conditional sentence—it is a universally quantified sentence; consequently, no application of the ⊃E rule is possible. But notice that the ∀**E** rule allows us to write out the conditional sentence we need:

1. ∀x(Dx ⊃ Mx)   ☐ Mo
2. Do
───────────────────────
3. Do ⊃ Mo   ∀E 1

When applying the ∀**E** rule to the sentence on line 1, we can replace the variable letter 'x' with any individual constant letter we want; we chose 'o' because it is being used in line 2, and will enable us to apply the ⊃**E** rule, as follows:

1. ∀x(Dx ⊃ Mx)   ☐ Mo
2. Do
───────────────────────
3. Do ⊃ Mo   ∀E 1
4. Mo   ⊃E 1, 2

And this is the complete proof! "Getting rid" of the quantifier on line 1 allowed us to make use of the familiar rules from the SL proof system. This kind of thing happens a lot when we are constructing proofs in PL. Here is the start of another PL proof:

1. ∀x(Px ⊃ Qx)   ☐ ~Pa
2. ∀x(Qx ⊃ Sx)
3. ~Sa
───────────────────────

It looks like there might be an opportunity to use the Hypothetical Syllogism (**HS**) inference rule here, and also the Modus Tollens (**MT**) rule. However, as things stand, the universal quantifiers on lines 1 and 2 are getting in the way. So, let's get rid of them (validly, of course!):

1. ∀x(Px ⊃ Qx)   ☐ ~Pa
2. ∀x(Qx ⊃ Sx)
3. ~Sa
───────────────────────
4. Pa ⊃ Qa   ∀E 1
5. Qa ⊃ Sa   ∀E 2

Again, when applying the ∀**E** rule to lines 1 and 2 we could have chosen to replace the 'x' with any individual constant letter; we chose 'a' because this allows us to use line 3. Here is the completed proof:

1. ∀x(Px ⊃ Qx)   ☐ ~Pa
2. ∀x(Qx ⊃ Sx)
3. ~Sa
───────────────────────
4. Pa ⊃ Qa   ∀E 1
5. Qa ⊃ Sa   ∀E 2
6. Pa ⊃ Sa   HS 4, 5
7. ~Pa   MT 3, 6

Once more, eliminating the universal quantifiers allowed us to make use of our "old" inference rules.

Existential Introduction (∃I)

Imagine a scenario in which my friend, Julio, is sick. From this fact about Julio, I can straightforwardly infer that there is at least one thing that is sick. That is, from an assertion about a particular entity, I can validly infer another assertion that does not refer to this particular entity in any way. In terms of the language of PL, if I know that some particular individual has a particular property, then I can validly infer that there is at least one thing that has that property—that is, I can introduce the existential quantifier and make a more general assertion. All of the following, then, are valid inferences:

From . . .	. . . I can validly infer . . .
Sj	∃xSx
Fa ⊃ Ga	∃x(Fx ⊃ Gx)
Ps ∨ Qs	∃x(Px ∨ Qx)
~Wb ≡ Vb	∃x(~Wx ≡ Vx)

This type of valid inference forms the basis of the ***Existential Introduction*** (∃**I**) rule of inference:

Existential Introduction (∃I)

𝓕ν   (ν is any individual symbol, either constant or variable).

∴ ∃x**𝓕**x

Similar to the formulation of the ∀**E** rule, the formula '∃x**𝓕**x' represents *any* existentially quantified sentence; that is, '**𝓕**x' represents *any* formula involving a variable that lies inside the scope of the existential quantifier. Note, also, that the 'ν' represents *any* individual symbol, either a constant *or a variable*. Again, this might strike you as odd: the rule allows us to validly go from 'Px' to '∃xPx,' for example. Once more, however, we can postpone dealing with this aspect of the rule. For the time being, we will be applying the ∃**I** rule to sentences of PL that contain an individual constant letter.

We can view the ∃**I** inference rule as a machine for creating existentially quantified sentences. In a proof, if we need an existentially quantified sentence, then line up your non-quantified sentence in the right way, insert it into the ∃**I** rule . . . and out pops the existentially quantified sentence you need:

We have to be careful not to misapply the ∃**I** rule. First of all, as we just saw, we can apply the ∃**I** rule to formulas involving either a constant or a variable. And this individual symbol must be the *only* individual symbol that appears in that formula (as long as we are sticking to monadic predicates). Here is an example that illustrates why this has to be the case. Let's say that Julio is sick and Barbara is happy. Can I infer that there is at least one entity that is both sick and happy? Well, no! Maybe Julio is not happy. And maybe Barbara is not sick. It is clearly possible that there is no one thing in the universe that is in *both* the sick camp *and* the happy camp. Representing all this in PL, the move from 'Sj • Hb' to '∃x(Sx • Hx)' is invalid. Here are some more examples of *mis*applying the ∃**I** rule in this kind of way:

From . . .	. . . I CANNOT use the ∃I rule to get . . .
~Fa ∨ ~Gb	∃x(~Fx ∨ ~Gx)
Pr ⊃ Sx	∃x(Px ⊃ Sx)

The ∃**I** inference rule is also applied only to full lines. When using the rule, *everything* in a line ends up within the scope of an existential quantifier. Applying the rule to a part of a line is illegitimate. Here are some examples of the ∃**I** rule being *mis*applied in this kind of way:

From . . .	. . . I CANNOT use the ∃I rule to get . . .
Fa • ~Da	∃xFx • ~Da
∀xPx ∨ Mr	∀xPx ∨ ∃xMx

Let's work through a couple of examples. Here is the start of a proof:

> 1. ∀x(Tx ⊃ Sx)   ∃xSx
> 2. Ta

The conclusion here is an existentially quantified sentence. Our new rule, ∃**I**, enables us to create these kinds of sentences. In this case, to validly infer '∃xSx' all we need is an instance in which the predicate 'Sx' is true of some individual. Line 2 involves the individual constant letter 'a,' so let's try to derive 'Sa'; if we can do this, then we will be able to derive the conclusion. Lines 1 and 2 *almost* provide us with the resources to get 'Sa'; however, the universal quantifier on line 1 is in the way. Consequently, our first step will be to get rid of that pesky universal quantifier—via an application of the ∀**E** rule—so that our more familiar rules can get going. Here is the complete proof:

> 1. ∀x(Tx ⊃ Sx)   ∃xSx
> 2. Ta
> 3. Ta ⊃ Sa   ∀E 1
> 4. Sa   ⊃E 2, 3
> 5. ∃xSx   ∃I 4

When using the ∀**E** rule on line 3, we could have chosen any individual symbol we wanted, but the individual constant letter 'a' was the obvious choice, given that it was involved in line 2. Line 4 is a straightforward application of the ⊃**E** rule. And because line 4 says that 'Sa' is true, we can validly infer, via the ∃**I** rule, that '∃xSx' is true. And notice that we replaced the constant letter 'a' with the variable letter 'x' when we used the ∃**I** rule.

Here is the start of another PL proof for us to complete:

> 1. Pb   ∃x(Px • Qx)
> 2. Qb

Once more, our conclusion is an existentially quantified sentence. All of our premises involve the constant letter 'b,' so, let's aim for 'Pb • Qb.' If we can derive this sentence, then one more step, via the ∃I rule, will get us to the conclusion. Here is the complete proof:

1.	Pb	∃x(Px • Qx)
2.	Qb	
3.	Pb • Qb	•I 1, 2
4.	∃x(Px • Qx)	∃I 3

In this case, we used a familiar inference rule to line things up, so that a straightforward application of the ∃I rule would get us what we wanted.

Exercise Set 8.2

Q1. Fill in the gaps in each of the following proofs. Except for assumption lines, each line of a proof should have three elements: the line number, a sentence of PL that is validly derived from earlier sentences in the proof, and a record of the inference rule that is being used to derive that sentence together with the line numbers of the proof to which the inference rule is being applied.

1.
1. ∀x(Ax ⊃ Bx)   Ba
2. Aa
3.   ∀E 1
4. Ba

2.
1. ∀x(Gx ⊃ Hx)   Mb
2. ∀x(Hx ⊃ Mx)
3. Gb
4.   ∀E 1
5.   ∀E 2
6. Mb

3.
1. Ld   ∃x(Lx • Sx)
2. Sd
3.   •I 1, 2
4. ∃x(Lx • Sx)

4.
1. ∀x(Mx ⊃ ~Nx)   ∃x~Mx
2. Nd
3.   ∀E 1
4. ~~Nd
5.   MT 4, 5
6. ∃x~Mx

5.
1. ∀x[Fx ⊃ ~(Bx ∨ Cx)]   ∃x~Bx
2. Fm
3.   ∀E 1
4.   ⊃E 3, 2
5. ~Bm • ~Cm
6.   •E 5
7. ∃x~Bx

Q2. On a separate sheet of paper, construct a proof for each of the following valid arguments.

1. ∀x[Gx ⊃ (Hx ∨ Fx)], ∀x(Gx ⊃ ~Fx), Gg   ∴ Hg

2. ∀xBx, Cg   ∴ Cg • Bg

3. ∀x(Ex ⊃ Sx), Ea • Eb   ∴ Sa • Sb

4. ∀x(Dx ⊃ Ex), ∀x(Fx ⊃ Gx), Da ∨ Fa   ∴ Ea ∨ Ga

5. ∃xPx ⊃ ∀xGx, ∃xPx • ∃xQx   ∴ Gb

6. ∀x(Rx ⊃ Dx), ∀x(Dx ⊃ Ex), Fs ⊃ ~Es, Fs   ∴ ∃x~Rx

7. ∀x(Tx ⊃ Ux), ~Uc • ~Vc   ∴ ∃x~(Tx ∨ Vx)

8. ∀x[Ax ⊃ (Bx ⊃ ~Cx)], Aa   ∴ ∃x~(Bx • Cc)

9. ∃xBx ⊃ ∀x[Hx ⊃ (Gx ⊃ Fx)], (Bb • Hb) • Gb   ∴ Fb

10. ∀x(Gx ≡ Hx), ~Ha   ∴ ∃x~Gx

8.3 Predicate Logic Proofs II: Existential Elimination

Consider the following inference:

> The general public will not be happy if this tax bill is passed. Therefore, John Smith will not be happy if this tax bill is passed.

This is an invalid inference. The fact that the general public will not be happy if this tax bill is passed does not guarantee that anyone named "John Smith" will not be happy if it is passed. Maybe some (or all) of the John Smiths will be deliriously happy if the tax bill is passed! Now consider this inference:

> The general public will not be happy if this tax bill is passed. Therefore, John Q. Public will not be happy if this tax bill is passed.

This inference has the same form as the previous one, but it appears to be valid. What is the difference? Well, both "John Smith" and "John Q. Public" are names; however, while there are real, flesh-and-blood individuals called "John Smith," there is no one *really* called "John Q. Public." The second sentence of the argument merely uses a proper name to assert what must be the case, given the first sentence: *some* individual or other will not be happy if this tax bill is passed. We are not committing ourselves to anything other than the claim that there is at least one such individual—and this follows from the first sentence.[1]

This latter way of using a proper name in English can help us to understand our next inference rule, **Existential Elimination** (∃E). In PL, individual constant letters function as names, so we can use a constant in the same way that we use the name "John Q. Public." However, we have to be careful: if we are to use an individual constant letter in the way we used "John Q. Public" above, we will have to ensure that this constant is not *already* being used to refer to an individual. So, for example, the inference from '∃xFx' to 'Fa' will be valid in a proof—as long as I have not already used the individual constant letter 'a' in the proof up to that point. With this same restriction, the following inferences are also valid:

From . . .	. . . I can validly infer . . .
∃x(Fx • Gx)	Fa • Ga
∃x[Px • (Qx ⊃ Rx)]	Pb • (Qb ⊃ Rb)
∃x~(Wx ≡ Vx)	~(Wg ≡ Vg)

Here is a formal statement of the rule:

Existential Elimination (∃E)

> ∃x𝓕x
>
> ──────────
>
> ∴ 𝓕ν   (ν is any individual constant that has not previously been used in the proof).

Like the ∀E rule, the ∃E rule is a machine for removing quantifiers. If an existential quantifier is in the way, simply insert the quantified sentence into the ∃E rule . . . and out pops an unquantified sentence that you hopefully can work with in the proof:

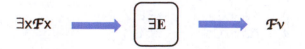

$$\exists x\mathcal{F}x \quad \longrightarrow \quad \exists E \quad \longrightarrow \quad \mathcal{F}\nu$$

───────────

[1]There are a number of variants to "John Q. Public" you might be familiar with: "Jane Q. Public," "Joe Blow," "Joe Six-pack." In the United Kingdom and Ireland, people use the name "Joe Bloggs" in a similar fashion.

One consequence of the above restriction, which makes sure that when using the ∃E rule in a proof we use an individual constant letter that has not been previously used in the proof, deserves special mention. In many proofs, we will be required to apply both the ∀E rule and the ∃E rule in the same proof; in these cases, we should always apply the ∃E rule first. Let's again look at an example in English to understand why this has to be the case. Consider the following two sentences:

Everything is tall [*in PL, this would be a universally quantified sentence*].

Some things are blue [*in PL, this would be an existentially quantified sentence*].

Are there any sentences involving proper names that we can infer from these two quantified sentences? Well, if everything is tall, then it must be the case that Bob, for example, is tall. That is, we can use the reasoning behind the ∀E rule to derive the following sentence:

Bob is tall.

Can we *also* infer that Bob is blue? No! There is no guarantee that Bob is one of the things that is blue. However, if we *first* work with the existentially quantified sentence to generate a sentence involving a proper name, *then* we can appeal to the universally quantified sentence to generate a claim involving that same name. Of course, we have to use a proper name that has not been used before—let's use "Schmob" for this purpose. So, from the fact that some things are blue, we can derive the following:

Schmob is blue.

And now, seeing as everything is tall, we can now work with the first sentence to also generate the following claim:

Schmob is tall.

In this way, we can derive two sentences that use the same proper name.
Let's now work through a proof that will need us to apply both the ∀E and ∃E rules.

1. ∀x(Ax ⊃ Cx) | ∃x(Gx • Cx) |
2. ∃x(Ax • Gx)

The first thing to notice here is that all of the premises are quantified sentences, and the conclusion is an existentially quantified sentence. This suggests that to validly go from the former to the latter, we will need to get rid of the quantifiers in the premises and then use our "old" inference rules to line things up, so that we can use the ∃I rule on the next-to-last line. Let's begin this process:

1. ∀x(Ax ⊃ Cx) | ∃x(Gx • Cx) |
2. ∃x(Ax • Gx)
3. Aa • Ga   ∃E 2
4. Aa ⊃ Ca   ∀E 1

As you can see, we made sure to apply the ∃E rule to line 2 first, using the individual constant letter 'a.' Then, because the requirement that we use a constant that has not been used already in the proof does not apply to the ∀E rule, we used line 1 to generate a sentence that also refers to 'a.' Once we reach this stage, then it is a matter of getting the conjunction 'Ga • Ca' on a line, so that we can apply the ∃I rule to get the conclusion. Here is the complete proof:

1.	∀x(Ax ⊃ Cx)	∃x(Gx • Cx)
2.	∃x(Ax • Gx)	
3.	Aa • Ga	∃E 2
4.	Aa ⊃ Ca	∀E 1
5.	Aa	•E 2
6.	Ga	•E 2
7.	Ca	⊃E 4, 5
8.	Ga • Ca	•I 6, 7
9.	∃x(Gx • Cx)	∃I 8

Similar to the ∀E rule, the ∃E rule can only be used whenever an *entire* line of a proof consists of an existentially quantified sentence. So, remember: an existentially quantified sentence is a sentence in which *everything* in the sentence is within the scope of the universal quantifier. That is, not *all* sentences that have the existential quantifier in them are automatically existentially quantified sentences. Here are some examples where the ∃E rule is *mis*applied:

From . . .	. . . I CANNOT use the ∃E rule to get . . .
~∃x(Fx • Gx)	~(Fa • Ga)
∃xPx ∨ ∃xQx	Pb ∨ Qb
Ge • ∃xTx	Ge • Te

All of the sentences in the left-hand column include an existential quantifier, but *none* of them is an existentially quantified sentence—so the ∃E rule *cannot* be applied to them.

Let's do another example. Here is the start of a proof:

1.	∃x(Mx • Gx)	∃xPx
2.	∃xMx ⊃ ∀xPx	

Two things should jump out at us here. First of all, unlike in the previous example, not all of the premises are quantified sentences. The second sentence is a conditional sentence: the antecedent is the existentially quantified sentence '∃xMx'; the consequent is the universally quantified sentence '∀xPx.' So, yes, we will need to do something with the quantifiers as they appear in the premises, but we will need to proceed very carefully! Secondly, the conclusion is an existentially quantified sentence. Chances are that we will need to derive 'Pa' or something similar in order to apply the ∃I rule on the last line. How can we derive a sentence like 'Pa'? There is a 'Px' in the consequent of the second line, so let's try to get this consequent by itself. We could do this if we had the antecedent of this conditional by itself—then we would be able to apply the ⊃E rule. The antecedent is '∃xMx,' so let's make that our target. There is an

'Mx' in the first line, but we first need to remove the existential quantifier from this line before we can get anything going:

1.	∃x(Mx • Gx)	∃xPx
2.	∃xMx ⊃ ∀xPx	
3.	Ma • Ga	∃E 1

There are no constants in the proof up to this point, so we just choose the individual constant letter 'a' when applying the ∃**E** rule. How do we get '∃xMx' from this? Answer: get 'Ma' by itself and apply the ∃**I** rule. Once we do this, we can use ⊃**E** to derive the consequent of the conditional in line 2:

1.	∃x(Mx • Gx)	∃xPx
2.	∃xMx ⊃ ∀xPx	
3.	Ma • Ga	∃E 1
4.	Ma	•E 3
5.	∃xMx	∃I 4
6.	∀xPx	⊃E 2, 5

Now, we have to validly go from '∀xPx' to '∃xPx.' The fact that everything is a 'P' obviously entails the fact that at least one thing is a 'P,' but, as always, we will not depend on what's obvious. Instead, we use the resources available to us: we write out a substitution instance of '∀xPx' and then use the ∃**I** rule. Here is the completed proof:

1.	∃x(Mx • Gx)	∃xPx
2.	∃xMx ⊃ ∀xPx	
3.	Ma • Ga	∃E 1
4.	Ma	•E 3
5.	∃xMx	∃I 4
6.	∀xPx	⊃E 2, 5
7.	Pa	∀E 6
8.	∃xPx	∃I 7

I again used the constant letter 'a' on line 7, even though it had been used already in the proof. This is fine, given that, when applying the ∀**E** rule, there is no requirement that I use a constant that has not been used in the proof. In this case, though, any substitution instance of the sentence on line 6, using any individual constant letter, would have enabled me to use the ∃**I** rule to derive the conclusion.

Exercise Set 8.3

Q1. Fill in the gaps in each of the following proofs.

1.
    1. ∃x(Fx • Gx) | ∃xGx |
    2.   ∃E 1
    3. Ga
    4. ∃xGx

2.
    1. ∃xHx ⊃ ∃xNx | Nb |
    2. Ha
    3.   ∃I 2
    4.   ⊃E 1, 3
    5. Nb

3.
    1. ∀x(Ax ⊃ Bx) | ∃xBx |
    2. ∃xAx
    3.   ∃E 2
    4. Aa ⊃ Ba
    5.   ⊃E 3, 4
    6. ∃xBx

4.
    1. ∃xAx ⊃ ∀xFx | ∃x(Fx • Gx) |
    2. Aa
    3. ∃xGx
    4.   ∃I 2
    5.   ⊃E 1, 4
    6. Fb
    7.   ∃E 3
    8.   •I 6, 7
    9. ∃x(Fx • Gx)

5.
    1. ∀x[Hx ⊃ (Mx • Sx)] | ∃x~Hx |
    2. ∃x~Sx
    3.   ∃E 2
    4.   ∀E 1
    5. ~Ma ∨ ~Sa
    6.   DeM 5
    7. ~Ha
    8. ∃x~Hx

Q2. Construct a proof for each of the following valid arguments.

1. $\forall x(Px \supset Qx), \exists xPx \quad \therefore \exists xQx$

2. $\exists xJx \supset \forall x(Hx \lor Sx), \forall xJx \quad \therefore Hb \lor Sb$

3. $\exists x(Tx \bullet \sim Nx), \forall x(Tx \supset Lx) \quad \therefore \exists x(Lx \bullet \sim Nx)$

4. $\forall x(Qx \bullet Sx), \exists xQx \supset \exists x(Gx \bullet Mx) \quad \therefore \exists xSx \bullet \exists x(Gx \bullet Mx)$

5. $\forall x(Dx \supset Wx), \exists x(Dx \bullet Gx) \quad \therefore \exists x(Wx \bullet Gx)$

6. $\exists x(Ax \bullet Hx), \exists xAx \supset \exists x(Qx \bullet Hx), \forall x(Qx \supset Vx) \quad \therefore \exists x(Vx \bullet Hx)$

7. $\exists x(Zx \bullet Rx), \exists x(Cx \bullet Sx), \exists xZx \supset \forall x[Cx \supset (Sx \supset Ex)] \quad \therefore \exists x(Cx \bullet Ex)$

8. $\exists x(\sim Lx \bullet \sim Nx), \forall x(Tx \supset Lx) \quad \therefore \exists x \sim (Tx \lor Nx)$

9. $\exists x(Tx \bullet Gx), \sim \exists x(Qx \bullet Gx) \supset \sim \exists xTx, \forall x(Qx \supset Vx) \quad \therefore \exists x(Vx \bullet Gx)$

10. $\forall x(Mx \supset \sim Px), \exists x(Sx \bullet Mx) \quad \therefore \exists x(\sim Px \bullet Mx)$

8.4 Predicate Logic Proofs III: Universal Introduction (∀I)

A universal introduction inference rule would allow us to write out a universally quantified sentence in a proof. But what kind of sentence could we apply such a rule to? That is, what would have to be the case in order for us to be justified in saying that something is true of *everything*? From the fact that Alice is tall, for example, we cannot infer that everyone or everything is tall! Or, as stated in the language of PL, from the sentence 'Ta,' we cannot validly infer that the sentence '∀xTx' is true. It just doesn't seem possible ever to go from a claim about one specific thing to a claim about all things. Yet there *is* a Universal Introduction rule! To more fully appreciate how there can be such a rule, let's revisit an aspect of the ∀E rule that we have put off until now. Recall that the ∀E rule says that, from a sentence of the form '∀x𝓕x,' we can derive '𝓕v,' where 'v' represents any individual symbol, either a constant or a variable. Up to this point, we have been using constants when applying this rule. Let us now see how and when we can use variables.

Let's look again at the example we used when introducing the ∀E inference rule. From the fact that all things are fluffy, I can infer that Adam, or Bob, or *any particular thing*, is fluffy. There are two ways of capturing this valid inference:

(A) I can give a *name* to this particular thing—Adam, Bob, etc.—and so end up with sentences like "Adam is fluffy," "Bob is fluffy," and so on. In the language of PL, from the sentence '∀xFx,' I can validly derive the sentences 'Fa,' 'Fb,' and so on. In each of these derived sentences, something is asserted of *a particular named entity*—individual constant letters are the proper names of PL.

(B) I can simply keep in mind that if I were to "zoom in" on *any* arbitrarily chosen individual thing, then that thing would be fluffy. However, I can choose *not* to name any particular entity. In the language of PL, I can represent this by removing the quantifier from the sentence, but holding onto the variable letter and not replacing it with a constant letter. Consequently, I can understand the sentence '∀xFx' as entailing 'Fx.'

The ∀E inference rule says that from any universally quantified sentence I can validly infer any substitution instance of this sentence. And both of these options adequately represent this valid inference. Of course, option **(B)** may strike you as being a little weird: 'Fx' is not a sentence of PL, after all. However, option **(B)** does describe a viable form of reasoning. An example from mathematics, where this way of proceeding is common, may help remove any lingering doubts you might have. Say, for example, that I am trying to prove Pythagoras' Theorem. This theorem says that in any right-angled triangle, the square of the hypotenuse is equal to the sum of the squares of the other two sides. To help me construct the proof, I might draw a triangle like this one:

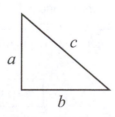

Based on this representation, the theorem states the following: '$a^2 + b^2 = c^2$.' Note, though, that if I successfully prove the theorem, I have not merely shown that '$a^2 + b^2 = c^2$' is true of *this particular* triangle. The triangle I have drawn represents *any* right-angled triangle. That is, this triangle is not my focus in the proof—it just helps me work through the proof. There is nothing about this triangle that makes it special—it doesn't matter if I draw this one, or some other right-angled triangle. Something similar goes on when we choose option **(B)** above. If '∀xFx' is true, then *everything* is an 'F,' i.e. 'Fa' is true, 'Fb' is true, 'Fc' is true, and so on. We could choose any one of these substitution instances of '∀xFx' at random. Instead of writing down any one of these, though, we can use 'Fx' to represent the fact that *any* of these substitution instances of '∀xFx' would be true.

Here, then, is a formal description of the ∀I inference rule:

$\mathcal{F}y$ (y is a variable that represents any arbitrarily chosen individual).

_____

∴ ∀x$\mathcal{F}$x

We can view this rule as a machine for creating universally quantified sentences. In a proof, if you need a universally quantified sentence, then line everything up in the way you need—making sure that you are not using any individual constant letters—and insert it into the ∀I rule . . . and out pops the universally quantified sentence you need:

We should also remember that the ∃I rule comes into play here. The ∃E rule says that from '$\mathcal{F}$v' we can derive the sentence '∃x$\mathcal{F}$x,' where the 'v' represents _any_ individual symbol, either a constant or a variable. So, for example, the ∃I rule allows us to validly go from 'Px' to '∃xPx' in a proof. This should now make sense: we use the formula 'Px' to represent the fact that any arbitrarily chosen individual is a 'P,' and it clearly follows from this that there is at least one thing that is a 'P.'

You might be asking: If I need to use the ∀I rule, when do I use a constant letter and when do I use a variable letter? To figure this out, let's work through an example. Here is the start of a proof:

1.	∀xHx	∀x(Hx • Jx)
2.	∀xJx	

This is clearly a valid argument: if everything that is a 'H' and everything is a 'J,' then it follows that everything is both a 'H' and a 'J.' However, we will need to use our new inference rule, ∀I, to construct a proof. How should we proceed? Both premises are universally quantified sentences, so we will need to apply the ∀E rule to each of these before we can put them to work for us. When applying this rule, should we go with option (**A**) or option (**B**) above? To help us choose, we look at where we need to end up in the proof, i.e. the conclusion, which is also a universally quantified sentence. If we remove the quantifiers in lines 1 and 2, then arriving at a universally quantified sentence will require us to reintroduce the universal quantifier, via an application the ∀I rule. The ∀I rule cannot be used to replace an individual constant letter with a variable letter, so we ought to choose option (**B**). Here is the complete proof:

1.	∀xHx	∀x(Hx • Jx)
2.	∀xJx	
3.	Hx	∀E 1
4.	Jx	∀E 2
5.	Hx • Jx	•I
6.	∀x(Hx • Jx)	∀I 5

Once more, removing the quantifiers from our premise lines allowed us to apply one of the "old" rules. We then reintroduced the quantifier we needed on the last line.

We can use this proof to further appreciate what is going on when we use a variable letter instead of an individual constant letter when applying the ∀E rule. The above proof can be articulated in English, as follows:

1.	For all x, x is a 'H.'	
2.	For all x, x is a 'J.'	
3.	Anything I choose will be a 'H.'	∀E 1
4.	Anything I choose will be a 'J.'	∀E 2
5.	Anything I choose will be both a 'H' and a 'J.'	HS 3, 4
6.	For all x, x is both a 'H' and a 'J.'	∀I 5

Clearly, the move from line 5 to line 6 is valid: if *anything* I choose will be both a 'H' and a 'J,' then it follows that *everything* is both a 'H' and a 'J.'

Here is another proof for us to consider:

1.	∀x(Px ⊃ Dx)	∀x(Px ⊃ Gx)
2.	∀x(Dx ⊃ Gx)	

Keeping an eye on the conclusion, we can see that we will have to apply the ∀I rule in this proof. Consequently, when applying the ∀E rule to the premises, we will use option **(B)** above and use a variable. Here is the complete proof:

1.	∀x(Px ⊃ Dx)	∀x(Px ⊃ Gx)
2.	∀x(Dx ⊃ Gx)	
3.	Px ⊃ Dx	∀E 1
4.	Dx ⊃ Gx	∀E 2
5.	Px ⊃ Gx	HS 3, 4
6.	∀x(Dx ⊃ Gx)	∀I 5

As with the other quantifier rules we have introduced, the ∀I rule is applied to whole lines and never to parts of lines. That is, when using the rule, *everything* in a line ends up within the scope of a universal quantifier. Applying the rule to a part of a line is illegitimate. Here are some examples of the ∀I rule being *mis*applied:

From . . .	**. . . I CANNOT use the ∀I rule to get . . .**
Fx • ~Dx	∀xFx • ~Dx
∃xPx ∨ Mx	∃xPx ∨ ∀xMx
Gx ⊃ Hx	∀xGx ⊃ Hx

The ∀I rule is arguably the least straightforward quantifier inference rule, so this is why I covered it last. Before moving on, make sure to convince yourself that it is a plausible way of reasoning!

Exercise Set 8.4

Q1. Fill in the gaps in each of the following proofs.

1.
1.	∀x(Vx ⊃ Wx)
2.	∀x(Wx ⊃ Yx)
3.	Vx ⊃ Wx
4.	
5.	
6.	~Vx ∨ Yx
7.	∀x(~Vx ∨ Yx)

$\boxed{∀x(\sim Vx ∨ Yx)}$

4. ∀E 2
5. HS 3, 4

2.
1.	∀x(Sx ⊃ Tx)
2.	∀xSx
3.	Sx ⊃ Tx
4.	
5.	
6.	∀xTx

$\boxed{∀xTx}$

4. ∀E 2
5. ⊃E 3, 4

3.
1.	∀x(Px ⊃ Qx)
2.	∀x(~Sx ⊃ ~Qx)
3.	Px ⊃ Qx
4.	
5.	Sx ∨ ~Qx
6.	
7.	
8.	Px ⊃ Sx
9.	∀x(Px ⊃ Sx)

$\boxed{∀x(Px ⊃ Sx)}$

4. ∀E 2
6. Comm 5
7. MC 6

4.
1.	∀x(Gx ≡ Hx)
2.	∀xHx
3.	Gx ≡ Hx
4.	
5.	∀xGx

$\boxed{∀xGx}$

4. ≡E 2, 3

5.
1.	∀xUx ⊃ ∃x(Vx • Zx)
2.	∀x(Ux • Wx)
3.	
4.	Ux
5.	∀xUx
6.	
7.	
8.	Za
9.	∃xZx

$\boxed{∃xZx}$

3. ∀E 2
6. ⊃E 1, 5
7. ∃E 6

Q2. Construct a proof for each of the following valid arguments.

1. $\forall x(Mx \supset Nx)$, $\forall x(Nx \supset Mx)$ $\therefore$ $\forall x(Mx \equiv Nx)$

2. $\exists xSx \supset \forall x(Tx \supset Ux)$, $\forall x(\sim Ux \lor Jx)$, Sd $\therefore$ $\forall x(\sim Tx \lor Jx)$

3. $\forall x[Ax \supset (Bx \lor Cx)]$, $\forall xAx$, $\forall x\sim Cx$ $\therefore$ $\forall xBx$

4. $\forall x[(Jx \bullet Kx) \supset Lx]$, $\exists x(Kx \bullet \sim Lx)$ $\therefore$ $\forall x\sim Jx$

5. $\forall x(Mx \supset Nx)$, $\forall x(Nx \supset Ox)$, $\forall x(Ox \supset \sim Px)$ $\therefore$ $\forall x(Mx \supset \sim Px)$

6. $\exists xFx \supset \forall xSx$, $\exists xFx \supset \forall xGx$, Fa $\therefore$ $\forall x(Sx \bullet Gx)$

7. $\forall x[Mx \supset (Ix \bullet Sx)]$, $\forall x[(Ix \bullet Sx) \supset Rx]$, $\forall xMx$ $\therefore$ $\forall xRx$

8. $\forall x[(Wx \lor Cx) \supset (Yx \lor Zx)]$, $\forall xWx$, $\forall x\sim Zx$ $\therefore$ $\forall xYx$

9. $\exists x\sim Fx \lor \forall x(Gx \supset Hx)$, $\forall xGx$, $\sim Fb$ $\therefore$ $\forall xHx$

10. $\sim Ra \supset \sim \exists xRx$, $\sim \forall xSx \supset \exists xRx$, $\forall xSx \supset \forall x(Sx \supset Px)$, $\sim Ra$ $\therefore$ $\forall xPx$

8.4 Predicate Logic Proofs IV: Quantifier Exchange (QE)

We will introduce just one new Substitution Rule to our proof system. This rule grows out of something that we outlined in the previous chapter: the quantifier symbols are inter-definable. Recall that every instance of '∀' can be replaced by '~∃~' and every instance of '∃' can be replaced by '~∀~.' The motivation for introducing such a rule is clear: we cannot apply the quantifier elimination rules to negations, but if we can change a negated universally quantified sentence into an existentially quantified sentence, and a negated existentially quantified sentence into a universally quantified sentence, then we *will* be able to use one of these elimination rules. It will also sometimes be the case that we will need to change a quantified sentence into a negated quantified sentence, so a rule that allows us to do this is a good idea.

The rule can be stated as a list of four pairs of equivalent sentences, as follows:

Quantifier Exchange (QE)

$$\forall x \mathcal{F}x \Leftrightarrow \sim\exists x \sim \mathcal{F}x \quad | \quad \exists x \mathcal{F}x \Leftrightarrow \sim\forall x \sim \mathcal{F}x$$

$$\sim\forall x \mathcal{F}x \Leftrightarrow \exists x \sim \mathcal{F}x \quad | \quad \sim\exists x \mathcal{F}x \Leftrightarrow \forall x \sim \mathcal{F}x$$

Again, the fact that the sentences here are logically equivalent should not come as a surprise. Of course, knowing *when* to use the **QE** rule in a proof can take some practice! Here are some instances of the **QE** rule. Remember that, as a substitution rule, the **QE** rule can be applied to parts of lines.

∀xPx	⟷	~∃x~Px
∃x(Mx • Nx)	⟷	~∀x~(Mx • Nx)
~∀x(Wx ⊃ Zx)	⟷	∃x~(Wx ⊃ Zx)
∀x~(~Sx ∨ ~Tx)	⟷	~∃x(~Sx ∨ ~Tx)
Da • ~∃xRx	⟷	Da • ∀x~Rx

Make sure to convince yourself that the sentences above *are* logically equivalent, based on the **QE** rule. Let's look at an example. Here is the start of a proof:

1.	∀xDx ⊃ ∀xGx	∃x~Dx
2.	~Gs	

Notice that the conclusion has negated "D stuff." And the antecedent of the conditional in line 1 has "D stuff." This suggests that there will be an application of the **MT** rule somewhere in the proof. Can we get the negation of the consequent of the conditional? Well, yes—let's use the ∃I rule on line 2 and then use the **QE** rule to change the resultant sentence into the negation of the consequent. Here is the completed proof:

1.	∀xDx ⊃ ∀xGx	∃x~Dx
2.	~Gs	
3.	∃x~Gx	∃I 2
4.	~∀xGx	QE 3
5.	~∀xDx	MT 1, 4
6.	∃x~Dx	QE 5

As with all substitution rules, the **QE** rule allows us to substitute one line, or part of a line, with something that is logically equivalent; this then helps move the proof forward. How can we tell if the **QE** rule will help? Answer: practice! The more you get used to using the rule, the more you will be able to see when it can help you out in a proof.

Predicate Logic Proofs with Sub-proofs

When constructing proofs in PL, all of the inference rules in the SL natural deductive system remain available to us. Strictly speaking, then, when we construct a proof in PL that uses sub-proofs, we will not be doing anything new. Nevertheless, it will be worth our while going over a few proofs. Consider the following, for example:

1.	∀xAx ⊃ ~(Ba ∨ ~Bb)	∀xAx ⊃ ∃xBx

The conclusion here is a conditional sentence. Let's assume its antecedent and try to derive its consequent. Here is the completed proof:

1.	∀xAx ⊃ ~(Ba ∨ ~Bb)	∀xAx ⊃ ∃xBx
2.	∀xAx want ∃xBx	
3.	~(Ba ∨ ~Bb)	⊃E 1, 2
4.	~Ba • ~~Bb	DeM 3
5.	~~Bb	•E 4
6.	Bb	DN 5
7.	∃xBx	∃I 6
8.	∃xBx	⊃I 2–7

Let us also construct a proof that uses a reductio sub-proof. Here is the start of one:

1.	∀xBx ∨ ∃xFx	∃Fx
2.	∀x(Bx ⊃ Fx)	

Note that the sentence on line 1 here is not a quantified sentence; it is a disjunction of two quantified sentences. Consequently, I cannot use either quantifier elimination rule on line 1. I could use the ∀E rule on line 2, but that won't get me anywhere. So, let's just assume the negation of the conclusion *for reductio*. This assumption immediately brings line 1 into play:

1.	∀xBx ∨ ∃xFx	∃Fx
2.	∀x(Bx ⊃ Fx)	
3.	~∃xFx for reduction	
4.	∀xBx	∨E 1, 3

But where do we go from here? Somehow, we need to derive a contradiction. We have a ready-made negation in our provisional assumption on line 3—maybe we can derive the non-negated version of this, i.e. '∃xFx'? To do this, we will have to get the 'F' part by itself, and it *looks* like we should be able to use the ⊃E rule on lines 2 and 4 to do so—as long as we eliminate the quantifiers on those lines. Let's see what happens:

1.	∀xBx ∨ ∃xFx	∃xFx
2.	∀x(Bx ⊃ Fx)	

3.	~∃xFx for reduction	
4.	∀xBx	∨E 1, 3
5.	Bx	∀E 4
6.	Bx ⊃ Fx	∀E 2
7.	Fx	⊃E 5, 6
8.	∃xFx	∃I 7
9.	~∃xFx	R 3
10.	∃xFx	~E 3-9

You may have had to brush off some negation-rule rustiness to fully grasp what is going on in this proof, but take the time to convince yourself that everything here is valid; I assure you that there is nothing new going on as far as the *reductio* proofs are concerned. Note that we could have used individual constant letters on lines 5 and 6 when using the ∀E rule, given that we ended up using the ∃I rule, and not the ∀I rule, later in the proof. However, the use of variables serves to illustrate that we can use the ∃I rule on lines that don't involve any constant letters, as the statement of this rule allows.

And that concludes our look at PL proofs. I hope you enjoy the exercises that follow!

Exercise Set 8.5

Q1. Fill in the gaps in each of the following proofs.

1.
1.	∀xBx ⊃ ∃xAx	∃x~Bx
2.	∀x~Ax	
3.		QE 2
4.		MT 1, 3
5.	∃x~Bx	

2.
1.	~∀xSx	∃x~(Sx • Px)
2.		QE 1
3.	~Sa	
4.	~Sa ∨ ~Pa	DeM 4
5.		
6.	∃x~(Sx • Px)	

3.
1.	~∀x(Sx ⊃ ~Tx)	∃x(Sx • Tx)
2.		QE 1
3.	~(Sa ⊃ ~Ta)	
4.	~(~Sa ∨ ~Ta)	
5.		DeM 4
6.	Sa • Ta	
7.	∃x(Sx • Tx)	

4.
1.	∀x[(Bx ∨ Px) ⊃ Lx]	∀x(Gx ⊃ ~Bx)
2.	∀x(Gx ⊃ ~Lx)	
3.	Gx want ~Bx	
4.	Gx ⊃ ~Lx	
5.		⊃E 3, 4
6.	(Bx ∨ Px) ⊃ Lx	
7.	~(Bx ∨ Px)	DeM 7
8.		
9.	~Bx	
10.		⊃I 3–9
11.	∀x(Gx ⊃ ~Bx)	

5.
1.	~∃xSx	∀x(Sx ⊃ Bx)
2.	∀x~Sx	
3.	~Sx	
4.		∨I 5
5.	Sx ⊃ Bx	
6.	∀x(Sx ⊃ Bx)	

Q2. Construct a proof for each of the following valid arguments.

1. ~∀xOx ∨ ∃xFx, ∀x~Fx   ∴ ∃x~Ox

2. ∀x[(Ax ∨ Px) ⊃ Gx]   ∴ ∀x(Ax ⊃ Gx)

3. ∃xKx ⊃ ∀xMx, ∀xMx ⊃ ∀xLx   ∴ Ka ⊃ La

4. ∀x(Fx ⊃ Gx), ∀x(Fx ⊃ Hx)   ∴ ∀x[Fx ⊃ (Gx • Hx)]

5. ~∀x(~Ex ∨ Nx), ∀x(Ex ⊃ Zx)   ∴ ∃x(Zx • ~Nx)

6. ∀xGx ⊃ ∃xHx, ∀x(~Hx • ~Jx)   ∴ ∃x~Gx

7. ~∃x(Mx • Px), ∃x(Sx • Mx)   ∴ ∃x(Sx • ~Px)

8. ∀xLx ⊃ ∃xMx, ∃x~Lx   ∴ ∃xMx

9. ∃xGx ⊃ ∀xFx, ~Fa   ∴ ~Ga

10. ∀xTx ≡ ∃x(Fx • Cx), ∀x(Cx ⊃ Fx)   ∴ ∀xTx ≡ ∃xCx

8.6 Showing Invalidity: Counterexamples

Recall that the natural deduction system we developed for SL is *sound*; that is, correct application of all the inference rules enables us to prove only valid arguments. It turns out that, taking PL to be an extension of SL, and then adding the five rules we covered in this chapter, also results in a sound natural deduction system. Furthermore, every valid argument in PL is provable using these inference rules. That is, the PL natural deduction system is *complete*.[2] Using proofs, then, is a good way to show that a PL argument is valid. However, how can it be shown that a PL argument is invalid? We will cover this issue briefly in this section.

Recall the counterexample method of checking an SL argument for validity: when presented with an argument in English, if we can construct a counterexample to the argument, i.e. a scenario in which the premises are true and the conclusion is false, then the argument is invalid. We can do something similar to show that a PL argument is invalid, though we need to take into account the fact that we have since defined validity in terms of an argument's *form*. If an argument has a valid argument form, then that argument is valid, and if an argument has an invalid argument form, then that argument is invalid. This means that we can show that an argument stated in PL is invalid as long as we can come up with an argument—in English—that matches this logical form, but which is clearly invalid. In other words, an argument in PL is invalid if we can generate at least one *substitution instance* of this form—in English—that has all true premises and a false conclusion. Here is an example for us to consider:

∀x(Fx ⊃ Gx)
~Fa
_____

∴ ~Ga

This is an argument form stated in the language of PL. Let's try to construct an obviously invalid substitution instance of this argument form. We can think of this task in terms of reverse translation: we must translate this argument into English, so that what we end up with is indisputably an invalid argument. It is a good idea to consider this reverse translation to be a two-step process. First, articulate the argument form in a semi-translated format, as follows:

All F's are G's.
a is not an F.
_____

∴ a is not a G.

Laying out the argument form like this makes it easier to generate the invalid substitution instance. We are looking for a case in which it is actually true that all F's are G's, and in which some particular thing is not an F, but in which it is false to assert that this same particular thing is not a G. A little imagination results in the following:

All dogs are mammals.
Barack Obama is not a dog.
_____

Therefore, Barack Obama is not a mammal.

Clearly, this is an argument with all true premises and a false conclusion—*and* it matches the PL argument form articulated above. That is, this argument is an invalid substitution instance of, i.e. a counterexample to, the above PL argument. The fact that such a thing is possible means that the PL argument form is invalid.

_____

[2] Logicians have proved that the PL natural deduction system is both sound and complete; however, these proofs are beyond the scope of this book.

We can articulate the foregoing as a method for showing that a PL argument is invalid:

Counterexample Method for showing that a PL argument is INVALID

Step 1:   Write out the argument in a semi-translated format.

Step 2:   Based on this semi-translated form, write out an argument, in English, that has *actually* true premises and an *actually* false conclusion. This argument is an invalid substitution instance, or counterexample, to the PL argument.

Let's work through another example. We are asked to show that the following PL argument is invalid:

∃xFx
∃xGx

_____

∴ ∃x(Fx • Gx)

Step 1 asks us to articulate the argument in a semi-translated state:

There is at least one thing that is an F.
There is at least one thing that is a G.

_____

∴ There is at least one thing that is both an F and a G.

Step 2 challenges us to do the following: write out an argument in English that matches this form and has actually true premises and an actually false conclusion? Well, yes! Here is one:

There is at least one thing that is a dog.
There is at least one thing that is a cat.

_____

Therefore, there is at least one thing that is both a dog and a cat.

Note that each counterexample should have premises that are, as far as possible, indisputably true. It should also have a conclusion that is, as far as possible, indisputably false. In this sense, the sentences' content comes back into the picture in this method of showing invalidity. This is fine, at least for present purposes: we are still successfully showing that the *form* of an argument is invalid. Nevertheless, this does mean that, as with the counterexample method in SL, the counterexample method in PL is somewhat limited by our imagination. With practice, however, it is possible to get pretty good at coming up with counterexamples that show an argument to be invalid. In fact, you might even enjoy the challenge!

There is another way of checking a PL argument for invalidity, one that isn't so dependent on our imagination. It involves constructing what is called a *model* or *interpretation* of an argument in which the premises are true and the conclusion is false. We will not discuss this method in this book, however.

Exercise Set 8.6

Q1. Use the *Counterexample Method* to show that the following arguments are invalid. Write your answers in the space provided. The first one is done for you.

1.	$\forall x(Fx \supset Gx)$ Ga _____ $\therefore Fa$ *Counterexample*: All cats are mammals. *[This is true]* Lily is a mammal. *[This is true: Lily is my dog]* _____ Therefore, Lily is a cat. *[This is false]*
2.	$\exists x(Fx \bullet Gx)$ _____ $\therefore \forall x(Fx \supset Gx)$ *Counterexample*:
3.	$\forall x(Fx \supset Gx)$ $\forall x(Gx \supset Hx)$ $\sim Fa$ _____ $\therefore \sim Ha$ *Counterexample*:

4.

$\exists x(Hx \bullet \sim Gx)$

$\forall x(Fx \supset Gx)$

_____

∴ $\exists x(Fx \bullet \sim Hx)$

Counterexample:

5.

$\forall x(Fx \supset Gx)$

_____

∴ $\exists x Fx$

Counterexample:

6.

$\forall x(Fx \vee Gx)$

$\sim Ga$

_____

∴ $\forall x Fx$

Counterexample:

7.

$\exists x Fx \vee \exists x Gx$

Fa

_____

∴ $\sim Ga$

Counterexample:

8.

$\forall x(Fx \supset Gx)$

$\overline{\quad\quad\quad\quad\quad\quad}$

$\therefore \forall xFx \lor \forall xGx$

Counterexample:

9.

$\forall x(Fx \supset Gx)$
$\forall x(Hx \supset Gx)$

$\overline{\quad\quad\quad\quad\quad\quad}$

$\therefore \forall x(Fx \supset Hx)$

Counterexample:

10.

$\forall x(Fx \supset Gx)$
$\exists x(Gx \bullet Hx)$

$\overline{\quad\quad\quad\quad\quad\quad}$

$\therefore \exists x(Fx \bullet Hx)$

Counterexample:

8.7 Concluding Remarks

At this point, you are well on your way to understanding the basics of formal logic. If you end up pursuing logic at a higher level, then the material covered in this book will serve you well. There is so much more to explore in the discipline of logic! If you end up not pursuing logic beyond the confines of what is covered in this book, then you at least have some idea of what the discipline of logic does, and what it can do for you. Remember, if you are someone who reasons (and you are—we all reason all the time), and if you want to reason *well* (which, presumably, you do), then logic has the toolbox for you!

Appendix A
Quick Reference

The Sentential Operators of Sentential Logic (SL)

Operator symbol	Operator name	Used to translate	Type of sentence
•	Dot	. . . and . . .	Conjunction
∨	Wedge	Either . . . or . . .	Disjunction
~	Tilde	Not . . .	Negation
⊃	Horseshoe	If . . . then . . .	Conditional
≡	Triple bar	. . . If and only if . . .	Biconditional

Common Translation Forms in SL

Sentences like this . . .	. . . are translated as . . .
P and Q P but Q P, also Q P, however Q	P • Q
Either P or Q P, otherwise Q	P ∨ Q
Not-P It is not the case that P	~ P
If P, then Q Q if P Q, provided that P P only if Q P is a sufficient condition for Q Q is a necessary condition for P	P ⊃ Q

Sentences like this . . .	. . . are translated as . . .
P if and only if Q P iff Q P is a necessary and sufficient condition for Q	P ≡ Q
P unless Q	P ∨ Q *OR* ~Q ⊃ P
Neither P nor Q	~ (P ∨ Q) *OR* ~P • ~Q
Both not-P and not-Q	~P • ~Q *OR* ~ (P ∨ Q)
Not both P and Q	~ (P • Q) *OR* ~P ∨ ~Q

Truth Tables for each Sentence Operator in SL ('𝒫' and '𝒬' are Sentence Variables)

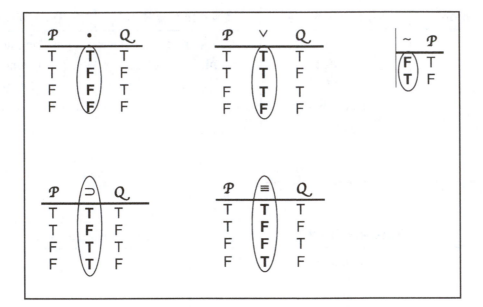

Truth Table Rules in English

A **CONJUNCTION** is true when both conjuncts are true; it is false otherwise.
A **DISJUNCTION** is false when both disjuncts are false; it is true otherwise.
A **NEGATION** is false when the sentence being negated is true; a negation is true when the sentence being negated is false.
A **CONDITIONAL** is false when the antecedent is true and the consequent is false; a conditional is true otherwise.
A **BICONDITIONAL** is true when the left-hand side and the right-hand side have identical truth-values.

Common Translation Forms in Predicate Logic (PL)

Sentences like this . . .	. . . are translated as . . .
Universal Affirmative All A's are B's *which is equivalent to* No A's are not B's	$\forall x(Ax \supset Bx)$ *which is equivalent to* $\sim\exists x(Ax \cdot \sim Bx)$
Existential Affirmative Some A's are B's *which is equivalent to* Not all A's are not B's	$\exists x(Ax \cdot Bx)$ *which is equivalent to* $\sim\forall x(Ax \supset \sim Bx)$
Universal Negative All A's are not B's *which is equivalent to* No A's are B's	$\forall x(Ax \supset \sim Bx)$ *which is equivalent to* $\sim\exists x(Ax \cdot Bx)$
Existential Negative Some A's are not B's *which is equivalent to* Not all A's are B's	$\exists x(Ax \cdot \sim Bx)$ *which is equivalent to* $\sim\forall x(Ax \supset Bx)$
Only A's are B's	$\forall x(Bx \supset Ax)$
A's and B's are C's	$\forall x(Ax \supset Cx) \cdot \forall x(Bx \supset Cx)$ *which is equivalent to* $\forall x[(Ax \vee Bx) \supset Cx]$
Some A's and some B's are C's	$\exists x(Ax \cdot Cx) \cdot \exists x(Bx \cdot Cx)$ *which is equivalent to* $\exists x[(Ax \vee Bx) \cdot Cx]$
There are at least two F's	$\exists x\exists y(Fx \cdot Fy \cdot x \neq y)$

Sentences like this . . .	. . . are translated as . . .
There is at most one F	$\forall x \forall y[(Fx \cdot Fy) \supset x = y]$
There are at most two F's	$\forall x \forall y \forall z[(Fx \cdot Fy \cdot Fz) \supset (x = y \lor x = z \lor y = z)]$
There is exactly one F	$\exists x[Fx \cdot \forall y(Fy \supset x = y)]$
There are exactly two F's	$\exists x \exists y\{Fx \cdot Fy \cdot x \neq y \cdot \forall z[Fz \supset (x = z \lor y = z)]\}$
a is the only F	$Fa \cdot \forall x(Fx \supset x = a)$
Superlatives a is the biggest F	$Fa \cdot \forall x[(Fx \cdot x \neq j) \supset Bjx]$
Definite Descriptions the F is a G.	$\exists x[Fx \cdot \forall y(Fy \supset y = x) \cdot Gx]$

Basic Inference Rules

Conjunction Introduction (•I)

$$\mathcal{P}$$
$$\mathcal{Q}$$
$$\therefore \mathcal{P} \bullet \mathcal{Q}$$

Conjunction Elimination (•E)

$$\underline{\mathcal{P} \bullet \mathcal{Q}} \qquad \underline{\mathcal{P} \bullet \mathcal{Q}}$$
$$\therefore \mathcal{P} \qquad \qquad \therefore \mathcal{Q}$$

Disjunction Introduction (∨I)

$$\underline{\mathcal{P}} \qquad \qquad \underline{\mathcal{P}}$$
$$\therefore \mathcal{P} \vee \mathcal{Q} \qquad \therefore \mathcal{Q} \vee \mathcal{P}$$

Disjunction Elimination (∨E)

$$\mathcal{P} \vee \mathcal{Q} \qquad \mathcal{P} \vee \mathcal{Q}$$
$$\underline{\sim\mathcal{P}} \qquad \quad \underline{\sim\mathcal{Q}}$$
$$\therefore \mathcal{Q} \qquad \qquad \therefore \mathcal{P}$$

Conditional Introduction (⊃I)

$$\begin{array}{|l} \mathcal{P} \quad\quad \textit{want } \mathcal{Q} \\ \hline \mathcal{Q} \end{array}$$
$$\therefore \mathcal{P} \supset \mathcal{Q}$$

Conditional Elimination (⊃E)

$$\mathcal{P} \supset \mathcal{Q}$$
$$\underline{\mathcal{P}}$$
$$\therefore \mathcal{Q}$$

Biconditional Introduction (≡I)

$$\mathcal{P} \supset \mathcal{Q}$$
$$\underline{\mathcal{Q} \supset \mathcal{P}}$$
$$\therefore \mathcal{P} \equiv \mathcal{Q}$$

Biconditional Elimination (≡E)

$$\mathcal{P} \equiv \mathcal{Q} \qquad \mathcal{P} \equiv \mathcal{Q}$$
$$\underline{\mathcal{P}} \qquad \qquad \underline{\mathcal{Q}}$$
$$\therefore \mathcal{Q} \qquad \qquad \therefore \mathcal{P}$$

Negation Introduction (~I)

$$\begin{array}{|l} \mathcal{P} \quad \textit{for reductio} \\ \hline \mathcal{Q} \\ \sim\mathcal{Q} \end{array}$$
$$\therefore \sim\mathcal{P}$$

Negation Elimination (~E)

$$\begin{array}{|l} \sim\mathcal{P} \quad \textit{for reductio} \\ \hline \mathcal{Q} \\ \sim\mathcal{Q} \end{array}$$
$$\therefore \mathcal{P}$$

Reiteration (R)

$$\underline{\mathcal{P}}$$
$$\therefore \mathcal{P}$$

Derived Inference Rules

Modus Tollens (MT)

$$\mathcal{P} \supset \mathcal{Q}$$
$$\underline{\sim \mathcal{Q}}$$
$$\therefore \sim \mathcal{P}$$

Constructive Dilemma (CD)

$$\mathcal{P} \vee \mathcal{Q}$$
$$\mathcal{P} \supset \mathcal{R}$$
$$\underline{\mathcal{Q} \supset S}$$
$$\therefore \mathcal{R} \vee S$$

Hypothetical Syllogism (HS)

$$\mathcal{P} \supset \mathcal{Q}$$
$$\underline{\mathcal{Q} \supset \mathcal{R}}$$
$$\therefore \mathcal{P} \supset \mathcal{R}$$

Substitution Rules

Commutivity (Comm)
$$(\mathcal{P} \bullet \mathcal{Q}) \Leftrightarrow (\mathcal{Q} \bullet \mathcal{P})$$
$$(\mathcal{P} \vee \mathcal{Q}) \Leftrightarrow (\mathcal{Q} \vee \mathcal{P})$$
$$(\mathcal{P} \equiv \mathcal{Q}) \Leftrightarrow (\mathcal{Q} \equiv \mathcal{P})$$

Double Negation (DN)
$$\mathcal{P} \Leftrightarrow \sim\sim\mathcal{P}$$

De Morgan's (DeM)
$$\sim(\mathcal{P} \bullet \mathcal{Q}) \Leftrightarrow (\sim\mathcal{P} \vee \sim\mathcal{Q})$$
$$\sim(\mathcal{P} \vee \mathcal{Q}) \Leftrightarrow (\sim\mathcal{P} \bullet \sim\mathcal{Q})$$

Material Conditional (MC)
$$(\mathcal{P} \supset \mathcal{Q}) \Leftrightarrow (\sim\mathcal{P} \vee \mathcal{Q})$$
$$(\mathcal{P} \vee \mathcal{Q}) \Leftrightarrow (\sim\mathcal{P} \supset \mathcal{Q})$$

Material Equivalence (Equiv)
$$(\mathcal{P} \equiv \mathcal{Q}) \Leftrightarrow [(\mathcal{P} \supset \mathcal{Q}) \bullet (\mathcal{Q} \supset \mathcal{P})]$$

Quantifier Exchange (QE)
$$\forall x \mathcal{F}x \Leftrightarrow \sim\exists x \sim\mathcal{F}x \qquad \exists x \mathcal{F}x \Leftrightarrow \sim\forall x \sim\mathcal{F}x$$
$$\sim\forall x \mathcal{F}x \Leftrightarrow \exists x \sim\mathcal{F}x \qquad \sim\exists x \mathcal{F}x \Leftrightarrow \forall x \sim\mathcal{F}x$$

Quantifier Rules

Universal Introduction ($\forall$I)

$$\underline{\mathcal{F}y}$$

$$\therefore \exists x \underline{\mathcal{F}}x$$

(y is a variable that represents any arbitrarily chosen individual).

Universal Elimination ($\forall$E)

$$\underline{\forall x \mathcal{F}x}$$

$$\therefore \mathcal{F}v$$

(v is any individual symbol, either constant or variable).

Existential Introduction ($\exists$I)

$$\underline{\mathcal{F}v}$$

$$\therefore \exists x \underline{\mathcal{F}}x$$

(v is any individual symbol, either constant or variable).

Existential Elimination ($\exists$E)

$$\underline{\exists x \underline{\mathcal{F}}x}$$

$$\therefore \mathcal{F}v$$

(v is any individual constant that has not previously been used in the proof).

Bibliography

Baronett, S. 2016. *Logic*. New York, NY: Oxford University Press

Herrick, P. 2013. *Introduction to Logic*. New York, NY: Oxford University Press

Hurley, P. J. 2015. *A Concise Introduction to Logic* (12th ed.). Stamford, CN: Cengage

Magnus, P. D. 2009. *For all x*. Offered under a Creative Commons License (Attribution-ShareAlike 3.0). Retrieved from https://www.fecundity.com/logic/

Pospesel, H. 2000. *Introduction to Logic: Propositional Logic* (Revised 3rd ed.). Upper Saddle River, NJ: Prentice Hall